Hot Water

The Life Repair Manual

Hot Water

And Your Perceived Identity

How to Overcome
Difficult People
Confusion
Unhappiness
Depression
Arrogance
Jealousy
Fear
Doubt
Lies

R Lindemann

Aleph Publications
Wisconsin, USA

Aleph Publications
Manitowoc, WI

Paperback Edition
ISBN-13: 978-1-956814-14-9

32 31 30 29 28 27 26 25 24 23   1 2 3 4 5

Dedication

This book is dedicated to all of the people in this world, whether man or woman, and regardless of race, creed, color, or political conviction. Everyone who still has a heartbeat deserves the right to hear this message and choose, for themselves, the direction they want to take in life. Choosing the proper direction in life will bring eternal order into your life with which to better see the true light of success, joy, and happiness that we all want in our own lives.

Thank you, everyone, for just *being*, and never let anyone hold you back from being *your* best. Your best is *your* best, and no one else's best can ever be better for you than *your* best. Always remember this and share it with everyone you know. Place this message into the hands of as many people as you can so that our world is a safer and more loving place to live.

It is our combined effort to share with the world this message that will change the world into the kind and loving way that it is meant to be.

Disclaimer

All information, views, thoughts, and opinions expressed herein are those of the author(s) and are being presented only for your consideration and should not be interpreted as advice to take any action. Any action you take with regard to implementing or not implementing the information, views, thoughts, and opinions contained within this published work is your own responsibility. Under no circumstances are distributor(s) and/or publisher(s) and/or author(s) of this work liable for any of your actions.

Anyone, especially those who have been victim of misdirected explanation and understanding, may be best served seeking wise counsel before deciding to implement any information, views, thoughts, opinions, or anything else that is offered for your consideration in this work. All information, views, thoughts, and opinions in this work are not advice, directive, recommendation, counsel, or any other indication for anyone to take any action. All information, views, thoughts, and opinions offered herein are offered only as suggestions for your personal consideration, which is done of your own free will. Your life is your own responsibility; use it wisely.

Any use of trade names or mention of commercial sources is for informational purposes only and does not imply endorsement or affiliation.

Contents

Acknowledgements

In the process of writing this book I have had the opportunity to meet and work with many good people. The replies I received from those who have reviewed and edited this book were overwhelming, and I am grateful for having had such a wonderful supporting group of people behind me in this effort. The people who helped have lives beyond editing and reviewing and did all the work in their spare time—many did it free or for the experience. Anyone who has ever done a full edit or review understands how much effort it takes to do it well.

There are many people in the process of preparing a book to thank all by name and it would take an entire book just to do so. So, thank you all for your, love, support, input, reviews, edit work, patience, and resistance when things needed to be stated better in the book. You all have been wonderfully supportive! Special thanks to Amy Brocker and to Lisa A Miller; our discussions, together with your effort, have been insightful and revealing.

All the people involved in the process of the editing, publishing, printing, and distribution of *Hot Water* have brought this book to a level far beyond my initial goals. I could not have asked for a better group of people to work with.

Thank you all for your input, support, and prompt response. It was truly a wonderful experience to work with all of you!

Introduction

Everywhere I look I see people living in confusion and trying to find meaning in all of the goings-on in our world. Young children are trying to be what they are not; young adults are trying to prove themselves to the world; and adults are trying to survive and raise their families in, what appears to be, an often confused and cruel world.

Human interaction is the most important function that we have in our lives, and it is tainted by our past. Too many of us are living today on a foundation based upon yesterday's failures while still trying to achieve a better life for tomorrow. Much of the interaction in our lives is with doctors, teachers, co-workers, friends, family, and even advertising. All of these have had many effects on our culture, both for good and for bad. It is each our own responsibility to properly separate the good from the bad in life. It is our ability to properly separate good and bad that makes the difference in our interaction with our world. Depending upon our ability to separate good and bad, our world can range from robust and wonderful, all the way down to enslaved and torturous. Understanding *why* we seem trapped in our often difficult lives is the most important investment we will ever be able to make for ourselves and for those who are in our daily lives.

Repair manuals offer instructions and suggestions as to how things are put together and how and why they work as they do. This helps the person using the manual to better understand how and why something broke to begin with, and how to quickly repair it to its original state. This manual is does something similar, but it is for personal changes. The end goal of this book is to get everyone to understand their own true nature and essence so that we can all live more satisfying and full lives. Following the basic principle laid out in this book will do that for you. Only the truth will solve our problems for us, and unless we start with ourselves we will never be able to change the world! This book will become a comfortable reference for you as you progress in life. You will likely refer to it on occasion to remind yourself of what to keep your life clear of from now on. You will also learn why "religion", government, money, people, and the things that you have, cannot make you truly happy. By the time you complete this book, you should fully understand the true source of most all of the problems that you encounter in your life. You can also have a handle on your life like you have never dreamed of!

Chapter 1

Why We are Not Satisfied with Ourselves

Getting rid of the troubles and the pain that we feel in life is one of the most frustrating and difficult tasks for any of us to conquer. Many of us seek the help of counselors, for years, with no apparent success, often ending in years of dissatisfaction with ourselves and others—dissatisfaction that is sometimes equal to or greater than before the counseling began.

There are solutions to our troubles, but the problem is that few people know or are willing to tell us the truth about the solutions. There's a reason for this. It's because most people either do not know, or cannot explain it well enough for it to make any sense to us. Here you will read many new views, thoughts, and opinions for your own consideration. What you do after considering these views, thoughts, and opinions is your own responsibility, and your choices will determine your future, so choose wisely regarding what you will consider. Since only you know your full life story, only you can decide what is best for you. But with the proper information to consider, while deciding your new direction in life, you can make choices that will better guide the life you truly want to live.

In order to have the later parts of this book make sense and be effective in explaining the simple correction procedures for eliminating all of our problems, I have dedicated the critical first few chapters to drawing comparisons and setting up examples for you to relate to in order to grasp just how easily and how often all of this affects our lives and actions. Almost all of us overlook these simple corrective actions because we do not understand how they relate to us personally, *if* we were even aware of those corrective procedures at all. As you read through these first few chapters, relate the examples to similar situations that have occurred in your own life. The subsequent chapters then explain how it all came to this point and *what to do* **to make it go away.** We all have to make our own decisions, but to do so we must be aware of how *others* affect us. This book is not about being critical of others; rather, it is about our own awareness of their effects on us. I have never witnessed anyone who has not greatly improved their life from living by the fundamental principle discussed within these pages.

Conquer Your Troubles

In *Hot Water* we are going to dive deep into why we are the way we are, so that you are able to conquer and defeat the bad things that try to drag you down as they come your way. Few of us have been trained for this kind of battle, instead we have wrongly been taught to just accept things as they are.

Here you will learn how to identify these troublesome areas in your life as we explore the abyss of your *Hot Water*. Not enough people are as courageous and willing to dive into their *Hot Water* and look into these difficult areas of life as you are. Only those who truly want a joyous life are courageous enough to understand these mysteries through understanding this information.

Many books paint a bright and cheery picture in order to lift the spirits of the reader and make them feel better. These books are helpful and often provide a great service to the readers. *Hot Water* is different; the purpose of *Hot Water* is *not* to make you feel uplifted while reading by painting rosy pictures; but rather, the purpose of *Hot Water* is to show you where your problems are, and then to teach you to effectively remove those problems. With this skill you can, in turn, teach this to those around you, especially to your children if or when you have them. When you remove a problem and you understand the principle detailed in this book, then true joy will fill the void that is left from removing the problems.

Before we can find *true* and *lasting* joy we must find and exterminate the "weeds" that grow inside each one of us. Until we are able to detect the contaminations within ourselves, we will be trapped in the abyss of darkness, and our troubles *will* remain with us and bar us from moving forward and finding true joy.

Hot Water takes you through the unpleasant areas of life in order to help you clearly identify the troubled spots that so many of us share. Once you have become aware of how the roots of pain in your life came to be, then you will quickly and effectively be able to conquer those roots.

As we travel through the depths of where these unpleasant things stem from, keep the following in the forefront of your mind: ***You cannot truly fix a problem if you do not know its cause or source.*** This is perhaps the most important lesson a human being can ever learn, and yet, too few people know this.

People Feel "Off"

A great number of us feel that the world is spiraling out of control. There's much cynicism in many of us—and for good reason! Too many of us live in doubt and fear, never able to feel certain about anything. We no longer feel that we can trust anyone, and we can't quite seem to change things in our own lives.

We often see people who work at their jobs just going through the motions. Every day they go to work and "put in their time." Some do it with joy, some with a smile, some unhappily, and some angrily. Many people struggle just to make ends meet, having barely enough to make-do, while others fall behind. Then there are professionals who have attended college; many of whom have well-paying jobs that supply all of their needs while affording them beautiful cars, homes, and vacations whenever they please.

Whether financially very well-off, or barely getting by, the story is the same; people feel "off." We all know people who try to escape this "off" feeling. In fact, many of us feel this way ourselves. How did we get this way? And when and how did this happen to us?

If you feel depressed or unhappy, it's likely that you are also feeling a bit jealous of others who seem to have the world at their command. Arrogant-jealousy can also be a difficult problem to deal with when we try to solve our own problems. Often, from our own perspective, everyone else seems to be moving ahead in life, while we sit dissatisfied with our own situation.

There are some of us who may have been exposed to severe abuse in our early years; and for those people, experiencing confusion and trouble in life is understandable. However, most of us have *not* experienced that type of emotion and/or physical abuse, and yet we still have this feeling of being *off*. And even though others may have more, *or* less, than we have in life, we often envy their happiness.

Let's wind back the clock a bit. When we were children, we were innocent and happy to just *be*. We didn't know race, creed, color, political affiliation, or any other dividing factor; and we would play with anyone who wanted to be a part of our game. We wanted to be included by others and we wanted to include others. In our pure beautiful innocence, we wanted to give and receive love.

From birth to about seven years old, children have a very innocent nature and are accepting of most other people. And they themselves generally feel and assume that *they* will be accepted by others. Of course, there are varying degrees of this because each child had his or her own set of circumstances while growing up. At around age seven, give or take a couple years, children begin to feel the pressures of life and of their local culture. Before this age we are generally unaware and in a state of childlike bliss; but, as you will see as you read through this book, this is not always the case. Children have the *innocence* trait, but their hearts are often tainted by their surroundings.

I'm referring to "innocence" specifically in the sense of *not* being tainted by society. This should be thought of differently than a young child who is guilty for knowingly doing wrong. When innocence is lost through experience, rather than being lost through guilt of actions, we typically refer to the resulting view of life as "cynical" or "distrusting." When a child becomes distrusting, the distrust brings many life changes with it. A child's thoughts, words, and actions will be affected by their distrust of others and by their distrust of the world. Some of this distrust is warranted and some is not.

These sources of distrust can happen at any time during life. Often, they occur throughout the duration of our entire life depending upon who surrounds us in terms of acquaintances, friends, and family. These feelings of distrust will deepen in the mind of the innocent person as their years progress, often causing the innocent person to behave cynically back towards others.

Where does all this cynicism come from? When does it start? And more importantly, how do we stop it in our own lives? We will answer these questions and get deep into the core of this problem as we explore this topic throughout this book.

In order to understand it all, we must first dissect *why* people feel *off*, and more importantly, why many of us feel *off* **and don't even realize it.** The reason we do not completely realize that we feel off, is because we have lived this way since our infancy—since before we can remember. A question or statement that people often have is, "If I don't know why I feel off, then who cares, because I am happy?", which is often stated in a questioning tone, with "happy" being the key word.

We humans are a fickle bunch, one minute you can look at almost any one of us and see a scowl, and then when you ask, "What's the matter?" we often say, "Oh, nothing." and then smile it away.

If you try to explain to a person who is troubled, and who does not know exactly why they're troubled—that they don't seem happy deep down—a common reply from them will be, "What do you mean?, I'm happy!" Too many of us are more often troubled than we are happy. If this is what true happiness is, then I'll have no part of it.

There are many reasons why people may be unhappy, and in this book you will learn how to conquer those reasons. Some of our unhappiness is of our own doing, and some is caused by the people who are involved in our day-to-day lives.

If you desire to permanently conquer sadness and strife in your life, and if you desire to develop an unshakable foundation made of solid rock, you can start by taking some time right now to think. Be honest when thinking about this—this is for *you!* Simply think about the way you see yourself: what you like and don't like and why, and what you want and don't want and why. Think about how you see yourself and why you feel that way about yourself. Thinking about this as you read through this information will prove to be one of the most important things you will ever have done for yourself in your entire life. If you truly desire to improve your life and the lives of those around you, then write all the information about yourself on paper. Fill a couple pages, or more if you'd like. Write both the good and the bad things that you feel about yourself and why you feel that way. It doesn't need to be pretty or perfect in any way because it's for your eyes only.

The benefits of writing about yourself will unfold as you read through this book and discover why you feel the way you do. In the process you will become much more aware of the source of any turmoil or dissatisfaction in your life, giving you the ability to quickly make it better. When you're done writing, fold the paper in half and tuck it in between the pages of this book. Later you'll come to realize why this process is so valuable in getting to the root of your own dissatisfaction.

Why am I Unsatisfied?

Our lack of joy has its roots in dissatisfaction, and most of us live our lives in a relative state of dissatisfaction. From early childhood on we try and try, but often fall short of our mini-missions—those tasks that we do each day. These tasks may be things like getting around to cleaning the windows, or even as simple as trying to smile at someone, or to think happy thoughts during the day, or maybe it's just to finish your day's work. We try and try and repeatedly fall short. When we try something long enough we will usually catch on and succeed over time. This is often referred to as *practice*, as in "practice makes perfect."

With knowing that "practice makes perfect," we could assume that if we keep trying until we succeed, then we will have satisfaction and be happy, but this is not the case. Yes, when we work at something and succeed, the success often brings with it a brief euphoric feeling of accomplishment; but this feeling is often fleeting. We thrive on the accomplishment of doing things over and over, that we are not proficient at, until we get them right. And we usually succeed in the long term, but the feeling of victory often does not last and we feel dissatisfied shortly after our successes. This dissatisfied or unfulfilled feeling has a reason.

As we live our lives we have pressures all around us. This is especially true as we age and enter the workforce. When we go to work we want to please our boss, and so we commit to things that we don't have time for. In order to please them, we often feel obligated to demonstrate to them that we can do the requested task for them. In doing this, we believe we prove to ourselves, and to them, that we can do it. This is not a bad thing in itself, but it can be. This isn't exclusive to the workplace; our feeling of obligation to please is also seen in our own home lives. Working moms are commonly the victims of this, especially in our modern obsessive world. And in addition, with each new technological advance, there's an even greater pressure for us to do more and more. Voicemail, cell phones, email, and other electronic communications have compounded this problem.

If you're an email user, you're probably guilty of dumping *your* work junk or responsibilities onto others. We all want to please, so when someone sends us a task we feel obligated to do it. Sometimes it's simply a forwarded email to read, sometimes it's a long letter or a message dumped on our voicemail. We often have difficulty asking people to do things when we are face-to-face, but when we leave voicemail, text, or email, then it's easy to just say it or send it, which ends up giving the people we sent it to more to do than they want or deserve. Add all of this together, and you have people stealing many minutes and even hours from your day. This is true even if we actually like and want the information that they send us. In our human nature we want to please people. Through this false sense of obligation, we have a tendency to set about reading or completing the presented tasks that consume much of our precious time. Coupled with everything else in life, this leaves us with little time for ourselves. The tasks that others throw at us are distractions, and these distractions are *not* what *we* want. If these distractions were what we wanted, then they would not be "distractions" and we would greet them with enthusiasm and excitement!

Please don't be misled by this. It's good to serve others and assist them in their lives, just as it's good to have others assist us. However, when we *continually* accept *unwanted* tasks that have been unjustly hurled at us, then we feel unhappy, dissatisfied, and burdened because we have to do things that we don't really want to do. When our heart is not in our work, then we won't do it with excellence, which makes us feel even worse.

Pleasing people by doing unwanted work is not exclusive to home and work environments, it crosses all barriers: homework, sports, friendships, and pretty much every level of human contact. This is not limited to tasks, but it crosses over to *expectations* as well. It exists in every category of life, but not everyone experiences it as much as most of us do. This is simply because while they were growing up they had very good people around them, and they probably *still have* good people around them.

Doing things that we do not desire to do reaches far beyond other people saddling us with tasks that we don't want to do; it touches us at our very core—the deepest part of our being. There are a great number of us who do things that we don't really want to do, and the part that's frightening about this is that most of us do it to ourselves! Yes, that's right, *we*, ourselves, all too often, saddle *ourselves* with things that we truly would rather *not* do. All of us realize that some tasks will come up in our lives that we feel are unpleasant, that we still need to do regardless of whether or not we want to do them; this happens to everyone. We will disregard those *required* tasks for now and focus on the more prominent things that are longer-term situations; like our jobs, who we picked as a mate, our friends, and where we live.

Do You Live in Contradiction?

We live in contradiction when we do things that we truly don't want to do. Look around you and observe others: Are they happy? Do they have skills that are going to waste? Are they doing what *they* really want to do? There are a whole lot of us in this world who are just going through the motions in life because of the decisions we made in years past. Due to our emotional investment, our financial investment, and our circumstances, we usually cannot see our way clear to making the needed changes to eliminate the unwanted aspects in our lives.

Here's an analogy to make things a bit clearer for you: our personal, emotional, and financial investment in our circumstances is much like having an older car. Let's imagine you have a car that's getting along in years and is worth only about one tenth of what a similar style brand-new car would cost. Then, as you're driving merrily along one day, the brakes go out, so you think to yourself, "The car's been dependable for a number of years. What the heck, I'll get those brakes fixed. It's been such a reliable car."

Just as soon as the brakes are fixed, the windshield wipers stop working, so at the first sign of rain you get the message real fast to get the wipers fixed. A few weeks later, the weather hits all-time high temperatures and you find that your air conditioner promptly needs to be recharged. Then everything is fine until slippery winter comes along and you realize that your car needs new tires. While you're at it, get an alignment too, after all you don't want those new tires to wear out prematurely. Now, in a matter of a few months, you have just spent, on repairs, about what the car is worth to begin with. This is good! Now you have an affordable and reliable car that runs great and is all set to go for winter.

Then one snowy winter Sunday afternoon, you and your family pack up and go to the store to get some snacks for the evening only to find that your car won't back out of the parking spot as you try leaving. So you call for a ride and have the towing company bring your car to the garage to look it over. On Monday you get a call from the mechanic and find out that you need to spend more money on transmission repairs than the car is worth. And there it is, right there... what do you do?

You've already invested an amount equal to the value of the car into the repairs, which was fine until the transmission went out. But now you'll have to spend, again, that much more money if you decide to get the transmission repaired. So, how do you decide when to cut your losses and get a new car?

Some of this may depend upon your finances. However, the better choice is to get a new or different car because something else is likely to break after the transmission is repaired.

Life and relationships are no different. No matter what you spend on that car, its value is unlikely to increase by repairing it. If you spend too much, you would have been better off getting a new one to begin with. Life situations can be thought of in much the same way, and relationships can too. If you have a friend with whom you have a long-term relationship that's weighing heavily on you, and you have poured much of your energy into that relationship by fixing problems on a regular basis, then it may be time to move on if the repairs won't improve the relationship. While you can repair *your* parts of the responsibility in a relationship, there is little that you can control with regard to the other person's responsibilities in the relationship. If there are parts broken in the relationship and the other person makes those parts unavailable to you, then you are without remedy in correcting the *real* problem.

We are each responsible for ourselves. It's always good to lend a helping hand, but you should set limits for your own protection. After all, you're no good to the world if you have been depleted. In fact, some relationships are downright dangerous and bad for you. And the sooner you get out of those relationships, then the better off you and those around you will be.

In the example of the car repairs, it seems easy to see that it's time to make some changes and get a different car. In the example of a friendship, it is somewhat cloudier; but with a spouse, it's complicated even further.

I <u>do not</u> advocate divorce, but relationships should always be joyful. If they are not, then they need to be promptly repaired or terminated. A troubled marriage relationship can be thought of in terms of a valuable and cherished vintage car with regard to our prior example. As described in the cornerstone book *Red Hot Marriage*, a valuable classic car may need a complete overhaul and *restoration* with the help of *both* spouses, rather than junking it in the scrapyard of divorce. Where, on the other hand, some friendships may be more like an old beat up car that simply needs to be junked because no amount of money is going to make it right. In either case, things need to be dealt with sooner, rather than later.

We are Unhappy Because...

The most prominent area of contradiction in most of our lives is that of what we *are*, or rather what we *do*—which is to say, our job or our occupation. Our world is filled with people who are doing things that they do not want to do, and they are very unhappy doing so.

Why are we so unhappy doing these jobs? It's largely because we don't really want to be doing these things to begin with, or because we are dealing with people who we do not get along with or who are demanding too much of us. Of course, there are those who are just plain lazy, who don't want to do *any* job, or refuse to get along with anyone. But for now, we're focusing on ourselves more than others, so we won't concern ourselves with such extremes.

We get unhappy when things don't go the way we would like to see them go. I'm not referring to someone demanding their way. No, rather, I am referring to having life not happen the way we *expect* it to happen. These *expectations* include occupations, the people who surround us, where we live, the time frame involved, and other similar factors. Too many of us lack joy in our lives simply because we are not happy. In fact, this is rooted so deep into our own life-system and heart that most of us don't even recognize joy; and therefore, we don't even realize that we lack joy. Our culture is built on a joyless way of life. Sure, there are many little things that bring some fun into our lives now and then, and we remember those things because they are all too rare. But, what we don't realize is that we can have it better than that almost all of the time!

By now some of you may be feeling like there's no hope for you in your life. *You* may even be the cause of *your own* misery and feel trapped, or feel that your life is just plain unfair. You might feel that you have to accept life as it is, which is true, *but only for a very short period*—the truth is that you can change it right now if you want to. And you will learn how to do so in this book.

Life becomes a trap for most of us, especially after marriage and children. We get a job, buy a house, have children, and then work for years to pay for all of it; and often, it's our incorrect job that steals the joy from our lives. But even if we're single, over time we slowly get paid more, and because of our increased pay we typically spend more. We become dependent upon the higher income, plus it's hard to quit and find a job with similar pay that we would like better. The reason that this is a serious problem for us is because we don't want to make that big of a change, but mostly we feel that "we can't afford to take the pay cut." For some of us, we are holding out for retirement to get the promised pension. There might also be other similar reasons, but in the end, we are doing something that we truly do not want to be doing. Is this really how we want to spend our remaining days?

All of this is like the car example, where you have invested much value into the repairs for the car and would like to get the value of your investment back out if it. So, do you stay in the job that doesn't satisfy you, or do you take the leap that offers a chance to change your life?

I would like to encourage everyone to take the leap, but *I cannot*. This is because it is a decision that must run *deep* within *your own* heart. If someone encourages you to "Go for it!" and you're not thinking the same way deep-down inside then you will likely be headed for the same disaster that so many others have seen. My goal is not to encourage you to "go for it!"; but rather, my goal is to have you understand all of the details of how we each came to be at the place that we're now at, and after you understand that, then with understanding you can choose to change your life through your new understanding. This will enable you to take the needed steps in your own life in order to easily and quickly change things on your own with minimal discomfort to you.

In the beginning of this chapter I spoke about the feeling many of us have that the world is spiraling out of control. There is good reason for this: it's because this "spiraling" feeling has been in existence since the beginning of time. Culture shifts to-and-fro, and it seems that with each generation it gets worse; but it really doesn't get worse—it changes! There have always been criminals and people falling away from what they know is right. There's nothing new under the sun.

In our modern culture we have electronics; and electronic communication has the tendency to immediately show our actions, making things seem immediately bad. While we would like to think everything is private, it actually is not. Our actions and intent are now broadcast all over the world. For instance, advertising media is a response of what we respond to. To an extent, advertising is a reflection of us. Before this sort of advertising existed, our dark desires were hidden in the recesses of the shady parts of the village. But now it's all out in the open for the world to see and unfortunately to share in. This "spiraling" that we feel is within our own hearts and minds, and not in an imaginary way—because it's real. The spiraling is within us *and* our trust in those around us. Similar to taking a job we dislike, we often live much of our lives in that same way.

Every time we see a new step down into the abyss from what we each think of as good, we get the feeling that everything is coming apart at the seams and that the sky is falling. We all have expectations of what we would like to see our world be like. Generally, most of us envision our world in a similar way: we all want peace, love, and security; and we all know what is good and what is bad. Some of us have been desensitized to the less desirable aspects of our culture and are no longer bothered by those aspects. But the rest of us have not been desensitized, and when we notice those undesirable aspects we begin to be concerned. All of this is like the *decision* of changing jobs or getting a new car. Our happiness is the difference between what we wanted or expected, and what we actually got. Our **expectations** are truly the root of it all.

Our problem is that we have been conditioned to believe that we want or expect things to be a certain way; when in reality, we really don't want things that particular way. This is a clouding of our mind and of our expectations, and it is our true problem. We see this everywhere we look. But only a small percentage of people escape the plague of this problem, most of whom are well-to-do, very joyful, or better yet, both! Most of those who have escaped this have done so by accident without fully understanding *why* they are happy, joyful, and successful—*they* don't know the secret either.

Why is Our Identity Clouded?

The truth is that "the Secret to success" is not a *secret* at all, and this makes many joyful and successful people just as vulnerable and susceptible to this problem as the rest of us are. A secret is where some people know something and *won't* tell others. So, if I refuse to tell you what's in this book, then I would be keeping a secret from you. Thus, secrets to success are more like mysteries that we simply need to find answers to, like the answers offered in this book

Happiness is a way of life that some people have come upon by chance, or have been brought up with all of their lives. The rest of us (which is the vast majority of people) have a clouding of identity from all of the expectations placed on us by ourselves and others. This clouding of our identity is the root of our lack of joy, and it is the root of our dissatisfaction with our circumstances and our lives. It is the reason that many of us are down on ourselves, depressed, and even overweight. So what is the way out of this mess, and how do we make ourselves feel better and maybe even lose that unwanted weight? What do we do to change things so that our lives have the joy that we all seek and deserve?

Before we can answer those questions, we must understand more about the root of our unhappiness. Distrust and cynicism play a role, but they are more of an effect than a cause of the problem. Many of us are clouded in heart and mind about what we want and who we are because we have been sold a bill of goods that did not bear our name. Our identity has been clouded from birth on, and we have been trained to believe that we want a life that we really never asked for or wanted. From our earliest days as a child, we are being conditioned, by both our family culture and our societal culture, to believe things about ourselves that are not really true. The smallest and most insignificant things are being suggested to us on a regular basis. Every day, from birth onward, these seemingly insignificant suggestions slowly build our perceived identity.

Why it's Called Hot Water

Children need good guidance in order to go a good way in life, but because the clouded identity problem is so deeply rooted in our hearts, the problem unknowingly gets passed down from one generation to the next. Who we are is not genetic, but it almost appears that way because it tends to run along family lines. Why is this? As just mentioned, it is *deeply* embedded in our hearts and we don't know it.

To get an idea of how we can become accustomed to our environment, consider this experiment: Take three bowls of water, one *very cold*, one *lukewarm*, and one *hot* to the touch (hot, but that **won't** burn you). If you place your hand in the hot water until you get accustomed to it, and then immediately place your hand in the lukewarm water, then the lukewarm water will feel cold to you. Inversely, if you place your hand in the very cold water until you get accustomed to it, and then immediately place it in the lukewarm water, then the lukewarm water will feel somewhat hot. We often don't like this sort of sudden change in water temperature. And similar to the way a sudden water temperature change while showering will make us shout, so, too, are we startled at a sudden change in our own personal *Hot Water*.

This is much the way our minds sense life: As the temperature of our life's water slowly gets turned up to a boil, we don't feel the changes because the changes are small and gradual, and we continually become accustomed to the way we feel. It feels *normal* to us until something shows us different. This concept of becoming accustomed to things is like in the hot water example just given, and it is the central point of this book—a critical point we will be discussing in deep detail.

With the *Hot Water* example in mind, think about raising children: If you were brought up with certain behaviors surrounding you, then *that* is your hot water and you're accustomed to it. You don't even realize that you're *in* the hot water, and when you have children of your own, they are born into your hot water; so, to them, your hot water is *normal;* and they, in turn, will do the same when they have children.

In part, your hot water may be your religious, political, or philosophical beliefs. It may be your feelings about attending school, your work ethic, the cars you drive, or the house you live in. It can be the kind of friends you keep, or the way you feel about yourself. It can even be you yourself and your spouse. Many of the things that are a part of your hot water could have been, and are likely to have been, adopted from your parents' hot water. To you these things were normal because you were born into them.

It is important to note that your hot water is not necessarily all bad. Your "*Hot Water*" is simply what you are accustomed to. The things in your hot water have become a part of your thinking; and through that, your hot water becomes your actions.

How Expectation Built of Hot Water Allows You to Believe Lies

With regard to the effects that "hot water" has on children, what you will notice if you observe this in your own family is that a child will see something and get an idea from what they saw. Then, they will express that thought to a parent, sibling, or maybe a friend. Because of the hot water of the family member or person that they are sharing the thought with, the child will typically receive a reply that is not in harmony with the child's original thought or feeling. The child is usually looking for approval or satisfaction of their own thought. If the approval does not come, then the child will modify the thought so that it better fits with those who the child admires and shared the initial thought with. The modification to their own thought will cause the child to feel in harmony with the other person with whom they shared their thought. And in doing so, they become a bit more accustomed to the Hot Water. The initial response that a child gets from the other person is typically unanticipated, and is different from what they had hoped for or expected in their effort to get satisfaction about the thoughts that they shared.

When we share our thoughts and do not get the response we expected, then we typically leave feeling dejected and dissatisfied, which causes us to adjust accordingly. One major reason our expectations are not met is because we ourselves, or the other party, has chosen a thought or perspective that is not truly accurate or does not match our own. For example: would you be expecting a tiny three ounce drink if someone offered you a soda-pop? You most likely would be *expecting* a glass filled, a full can, or a full bottle.

Hope, expectation, and adjustment are how we learn. Adjustment due to expectation is not necessarily a bad thing. In fact, in general, this is a good thing. Without it no one could learn, and the world would be in utter turmoil. Where does the problem come in then? Well... while learning is good, learning things wrongly is *not* a good thing. The innocence of a child is often correct, but children are frequently told to think differently than their innocent way would have them initially believe. In a sense, children are often told to believe *half-truths*. These "half-truths" are the same as lies or incorrect information. A lie is a deliberate deception, where incorrect information can be the hot water we have become accustomed to.

Whose Fault are My Past Mistakes?

As we trek through our lives with this constant assault of contaminated hot water, we begin to make changes to accommodate other people's thinking. We try to be agreeable with them, or with society, and we don't even realize that we are doing it because being agreeable is part of our own *Hot Water*. This applies to every aspect of our lives, it is our *Hot Water* and it's our way of life. The longer we allow this in our lives then the worse the problem becomes.

Please read the next couple of paragraphs very carefully:

Sometimes we are thinking wrongly, and then we correct our thinking, and as a result, we are now thinking rightly, and that's good. But, all too often we are thinking rightly, and then we make what we believe to be a "correction" in an effort to accommodate other people, but now, in truth, we are actually thinking wrongly. This is because we made a *perceived* "correction." I put the term ***"correction"*** in quotes because I want to emphasize that it may not be correct, but rather it is only seen, or *perceived*, as being a "correction." And we do this without realizing it.

Even though we don't realize that we make these false "corrections," we do notice that something is slightly unsettling, but we usually brush it aside in our minds. When we do this enough times it begins to wear on us. This is when we begin to feel badly about our circumstances, both of the world and of the heart. Most of these incorrect "corrections" are seemingly insignificant and appear to have little effect on our lives. But given enough time and occurrences, they are sure to affect our disposition, and then eventually we become cynical and edgy, all of which becomes a part of our hot water.

When these false corrections occur with the small things in life, we don't give it much thought; however, when we do this with the larger things, it's more obvious and easier to realize, but our realization often comes only after it's too late. With the larger or more prominent occurrences, we often put in the category of "*mistake*." When we realize that we have made a mistake we usually self-*correct* in the proper sense of the word *correct*. Self-correction is done because the particular circumstance suddenly causes us a noticeable amount of pain, and the pain is what made us aware of our mistake. The mistake suddenly increased the temperature of our hot water causing us to immediately notice it, much the way we will notice it in the shower when someone suddenly turns on the cold water in the kitchen. To avoid further pain, we make a change to accommodate what *should* have been done to start with. The circumstances that caused the pain are like placing your hand from the *warm* water into the *hot* water, and in cases of extreme change it's like going from very cold water into very hot water.

Past mistakes are not exclusively caused by having bent our will and our desires to please others. Mistakes are also caused from *not* heeding to accommodate others and society. There are times when we are thinking wrongly, but the others are actually correct. If we take the stand and are inflexible in our thoughts when we are thinking wrongly, then we will feel the pain of the resulting circumstances and eventually realize that we have chosen a mistaken path. When we finally realize that we are on a mistaken path, we typically change to make the needed corrections in order to accommodate things properly and accurately. There are other reasons that mistakes occur, such as *deception* done or caused by others. But, most of our mistakes or errors are from following wrong influences or from failing to follow proper and correct influences.

For many of us, our own arrogance is a major factor in our perpetual misery. Often when we make a bad choice that defies good judgment, and haven't followed the expectations of those around us, we then have a tendency to deny our error and continue to try to prove that our choice was not a bad choice. This stubborn arrogance is a very common problem that most of us face, and it often runs undetected in our thinking because it is part of our own hot water.

To begin overcoming these foundational problems with our hot water we must realize that our hot water exists and that we are into it over our heads, both for good *and* for bad. With each passing moment of our existence most of us are continually modifying our perceived identity to conform to what we or others feel is best. The part that is a problem for us is that we don't actually realize that we're doing this, which is where our battle truly begins. And when we manage to personally escape this trap and make the needed changes, then our friends, family, and others, who might not even know us, often feel judged by our example, thus, causing them to attack us, even though no actual judgment has been made by us against them. For instance, making a decision like no longer drinking alcohol typically can make some of those who continue to drink feel judged by you.

Belief or No Belief
A Biblical Perspective

From a Biblical perspective, the reasons people don't like themselves is an age-old problem. Its root has been the cause of much discord for many thousands of years. To help us understand and better get to the core of feeling "off", let's visit the Bible for a moment. Whether or not you agree with, or believe the Bible, you must understand that the Bible has affected our culture in a very profound manner for centuries and even for thousands of years. For those who do not follow the Bible, whether or not it is a real account of what actually transpired doesn't matter in regard to the aspects of it that we are discussing here; this is because its effects still touch all of us and the world that we all live in.

Starting with Adam's error and Eve's error in the Garden, as the account of the story goes:

Because of Adam's choice to follow Eve's choice to obtain the knowledge of good and evil, we are all predisposed to being able to tell the difference, and can therefore distinguish intuitively, between good and evil. Even if you do not subscribe to the belief of the Adam and Eve story, you must certainly admit that we all seem to understand when something is odd or out of line. This is the knowledge of good and bad spoken of in the story. We often refer to this as common sense, we can think of this as emotional common sense. When people who were brought up living in *good*, or who have come to understand *good* on their own, live by that *good*, then they are generally happy. But, for the rest of us, there is something out of alignment in our lives; or to be more specific, out of alignment in our hearts, minds, and souls.

How Hidden Darkness Lurks in Your Life

Through the continuous parade of generations who seem stuck in darkness, our world has produced a frightening array of ills. Generation upon generation has bought into the lies of evil;

and as a result, each generation has perpetrated that evil on each subsequent generation, resulting in much discord, disease, and death. With these strong statements I would expect people to be picturing pitchforks, horns, and mayhem everywhere! While that darker side of life does exist to an extent, what I am speaking of is a "lesser" evil, but that is far more deadly.

Blatant evils are easy to spot. For instance, by simply observing young children in an unusual circumstance you will see that they will either watch with a peculiar intrigue, or be peculiarly frightened.

One day while visiting a local department store, I noticed a parent take their child, who appeared to be about one year old, on a tour through the Halloween decoration section of the store. The father proceeded to show the child a mutant human decoration, to which the child, with a look of terror (not just crying—but rather terror) began to scream and shake convulsively from seeing this "decoration." This was very obviously a horrid and frightening experience for this innocent young child because it terribly frightened the child by merely looking at the decoration and being in its presence. The child's father found this entertaining and laughed, and then he went on to demonstrate this reaction to the child's mother.

The peculiar actions by the father had an impact on the child to some extent. We will likely never know how much this sort of thing affects the future of a human being, but the very obvious immediate effect was that the child did not want to be near or see that decoration. As adults, we might not see certain things as a very big deal, but to the child, the trauma that they felt could be equivalent to what, for us, would be a horrific event such as witnessing a loved one get very seriously injured or killed. Ask yourself, what horrific event would make you convulse and cry as the child did?—That is your gauge of the possible effects that that experience had on the child.

Hidden evils, on the other hand, the truly dangerous kind, are far more subtle and they permeate our culture and all other cultures of world. These "hidden" evils seem to be mere harmless acts of ignorance (which we will get into later). These are small things like betraying a friend, gossiping, poking fun at an injured soul (or anyone for that matter), and so many other small things that we ignorantly do every single day in our world and life. These often seemingly insignificant acts do profoundly affect us all. Little by little they erode the self-worth of those to whom we dish these acts out to, and they erode our own self-worth as well. It is at this point of awareness that you get to make some decisions in your own heart and mind as to whether or not these things matter to you.

But before you make those decisions, consider this: Let's take gossip for instance. Gossip is probably one of the most damaging of the hidden evils. If you happen to be a gossip, then it likely doesn't bother you that people gossip, because that is the currency for your trade. Gossip is typically personal stories spread around by uninvolved people. These "gossips" are people who have no concern in the matter of the person's personal business who happens to be the subject of the gossiper's gossip. Gossip has the outward appearance of shock and awe for others about the business of the third party who is being gossiped about, often ending by degrading the victim in the minds of the hearers of the gossiper's news.

While it appears that the victim is being injured, and at times the gossiping harms the victim's reputation and the victim of the gossip, the true harm is to the gossiper. Slowly, a gossiper will self-destruct and become a laughing stock of the community, not even realizing that they, the gossiper, have single-handedly reduced their own credibility to the butt of many people's jokes. And sadly, most of them will likely never see or come to realize that this is so even when confronted about it.

When a gossiper is approached in request to stop their ill behavior, the resulting sensation for them is typically that of feeling insulted or attacked. Initially, most of us feel insulted when approached on our bad behavior, but often we will quickly correct our poor behavior because we realize that we must accept our error or face being wrong. However, too many of us allow this hidden darkness to lurk within our own lives, and slowly it destroys us. The word *insulted* is probably better replaced with the word *humiliated*. When we partake in any behavior, we typically know that the behavior is right or wrong via good old fashion common sense.

What the Word "Humiliate" Means and Why it Matters to You

Many people take offense at Biblical references for their own reasons, and thus, it's distracting to them. Yet, whether good or bad, it is emotionally and culturally intertwined with *everything* around us and throughout the world. Because of the level which the Bible permeates our culture, Biblical references have tremendous importance because much of our culture is based upon the Bible and people's belief of it. Understanding this very important point will help you understand why we believe some of what we believe, and *why* we do some of what we do.

Understanding the reasons for some of the words we use is critical in understanding our problems. For instance, the word *humiliate* has its root in the idea of *humble*, and the word *humble* has the same root as the word *humus*. *Humus* is earth or the soil of the ground. It also has the same root as the word *Human*. So, *humus* means earth, dust, dirt, and soil. The word *soil* is derived from *sole*, as in the *sole* of your foot which stands upon the flat of the earth, ground, or soil. Both *dust* and *dirt* also trace back to the *soil* origin. The undeniable truth in the origin of the word *humiliate* is that it is associated with Adam and earth, as in: Adam was taken and formed from the earth as a vessel. So when we are *humiliated* we are like Adam was.

When Adam partook in the fruit from the tree of the knowledge of good and evil, he realized something was wrong. Now, whether or not you believe this epic Biblical account, the origin and the concept of the word humiliate are both from the essence of that story. This is very important to understand when discussing humiliation. We can debate about the word's origin and which came first—*human, humble, humiliate,* or *humus*—but we cannot debate that these words are connected. It is the fact that these words are connected that is of importance to you.

Humiliate is to be a *human* like Adam. The story of Adam and Eve taking the fruit from the tree of *the knowledge of good and evil* is where you will find the roots of the word *humiliate*. What came first? I won't say because I wasn't there. This is a conclusion you will need to ponder for yourself.

In the story, Adam and Eve clearly did not follow the simple instruction given to them by God. This is why we relate getting caught in error to that event and become as Adam and Eve were in the story. Whether or not the actual story happened is irrelevant to our cultural reason *humiliate* is connected to *human* and to the Adam and Eve story. The fact remains that the story, true or not, is the likely source of our modern concept of *humiliate*. The importance of this cannot be stressed enough.

You might be thinking that much time was spent on something so trivial, but I will assure you that this is not at all trivial. In your future you will find that this will play a key role in a more full understanding of the actions of other people *and* of yourself.

Let's set aside the concept of the Bible being the "inerrant Word of God", and focus on this story just as a good tale to tell. Adam was explicitly asked, or maybe commanded, by his Creator **not** to take fruit from a particular tree; but, at the behest of his companion he did so anyway. If you recall, in the story, after eating from the tree, Adam and Eve heard God in the Garden and they hid themselves. Pressing the issue, God asked them, "Why are you hiding?" To which they replied, "Because we are naked." Then God asked, "Who told you that you were naked? Have you eaten from the tree?" (I'm paraphrasing here. To get a fully specific account please read it for yourself. It's in the first few pages of the book.) Then Adam replied, "The woman whom you gave to be with me, she gave me of the tree, and I ate from it."

In our story, Adam and Eve hid because they were humiliated. We understand this as humiliated, but to them, in this story, the concept of "humiliate" was invented at that very moment. I am going to go out on a limb and speculate that Adam and Eve were not very pleased with themselves at this point in the story. They would have changed their circumstances if possible, but they couldn't change what they did because it was too late and was already done. They separated themselves from God by following the advice of something other than God.

Now, back to "Why We are Not Satisfied with Ourselves." Whether or not you buy into the Adam and Eve story just mentioned, you certainly feel that "common sense" exists and that we generally *know*, for whatever the reason, when things are not quite right. Yet, through our years of growing up in this world, we become conditioned to ignore many of the commonsense cues that indicate to us that we should stop behaving badly. But the problem is, regardless of how much conditioning to the contrary we receive, we still feel the draw of our commonsense. It is our *defiance* of the natural pull and beckoning of commonsense that causes us to doubt, to fear, to be depressed, and to be unhappy.

An important point to think about while reading this book is that we *do not* have to make a dumb mistake to feel this way. Often we have been conditioned to believe contrary to our common sense. Even though we make the right choices to not partake in ill behavior, we will, nonetheless, struggle in our own hearts and minds with regard to the nonsensical information that we have been conditioned to believe is true, even though our common sense is telling us otherwise. This also causes us to be uncomfortable and uneasy about ourselves and about decisions we make that are actually good.

When we were young children, we were taught by example from authority. When this authority tells us something via their example, then we *expect* it to be right and proper—we *trust* them—but we don't specifically realize that we are doing this. Sadly, far too often, the so-called "authority's" information is out of sync and out of alignment with our own common sense.

When our thinking is in conflict with authority, then our nature to want to please authority steps in and overrides our common sense and causes us to *believe* thoughts that we are in conflict with. When we do this it causes us great confusion that is typically accompanied by low self-worth and, all too often, self-hate, even though no specific ill action has been done. Just the conflict within us of this inherent truth is enough to throw many of us over the edge down onto to the slippery slope of doubt.

You don't have to think about this subject long to see these truths become apparent to you once you have heard them. Take the time and effort to observe yourself and others when something seems amiss, and you will quickly see these effects show through. Passing the buck and lashing out typically accompanies the circumstances. (Please do not confuse "passing the buck" with "giving credit where credit is due", both for good and for bad). Be honest in your assessments. Passing the buck is trying to put the blame for your own error, or your part of the blame for the error, onto others who do not deserve it. Passing the buck, by wrongfully blaming someone, is an attempt to distract and deceive—it is a lie.

As we explore the next chapter, do not forget that the reason we are discussing this is to understand *where* our discontent and unhappiness are really from, and then to remove that source and fix the problem. When you approach life in this way, then *nothing* or *no one* can *ever* bring you down again.

Before you can rise up and stand firm, you must first *understand* how it all comes to be so that *you* are aware and prepared with the power to win this war.

Without the fundamental understanding and awareness discussed throughout this book you cannot be truly whole— **ever.** Religion cannot help, politics cannot help, money cannot help, and people cannot help. If those were the solution, we would all be living in a utopian-world free of pain, but this is not the case.

So far, we learned that the source of most of our unhappiness is from us doing things that we truly do not want to be doing. This includes our beliefs as well as our actions. (Please note: our thoughts *are* mental actions.) Through understanding how this all came to be, you will be able to easily change your situation, even overnight if you choose! But to do so, *you* must understand yourself and who **you** truly are.

Chapter 2

The Importance of Your Identity

You cannot permanently solve all of your problems, and you will never feel safe and confident, *unless* you understand the *root* source of your problems. *Completely understanding* a problem is the majority of the work in fixing any problem.

To begin, let's take a look at how we, as people, relate to the world. Everything that we experience in our lives becomes a part of us. All of the little everyday things that happen shape us and make us what we appear to be. Major events typically cause us to change abruptly, while the minor things work to slowly shape us over time. As we continually experience life, we become accustomed to that which is in our lives; this is the effect called "*Hot Water.*"

How Your Identity Affects the Way You Relate to the World, for Good or for Bad

Our behavior is our response to all that we have experienced and all that is currently around us. The people who are in our lives on a regular basis, and those who we meet as only acquaintances are affected by *how we present ourselves* to them.

And how we present ourselves to them is how we relate to the world.

Our relationship with the world is mostly guided by the effect that our hot water has on us. Our hot water ultimately creates our perceived identity. The sum of our life experiences is our hot water. It is this hot water that has dictated your perception of your identity and actions up until this point in your life. Your perception and actions are what you use to interact with the world—they have become your perceived identity. This simple logic becomes easy and obvious once we are informed that it exists and understand it. In general, most of us don't ever give the slightest thought to this at all.

No matter where you go, what you do, or who you are interacting with, your perception of your past affects your perception of your present circumstances. In turn, this will affect your perception of your potential future. An example would be: If you've had a rough time up to this point in your life, and it included people mocking and being cruel to you, then it's highly likely when you meet people, and they make a light-hearted joke aimed at you, that you'll perceive it as an attack and likely take it very personally. When this happens, the other person's perception of you is affected and that becomes a part of *their* hot water.

As we relate to the world through our hot water, we all have an effect on those around us for good or for bad. Hot water is not always a bad thing—it simply exists. If you are one of those who have been so blessed to be a part of a loving, kind, and supporting family, then your hot water is likely mostly good. This book is written for those who are feeling off and/or are hurting, so the term hot water is going to come across negative in this book. But in truth, your hot water is nothing more than hot water, and whether good or bad, your hot water simply is: What you have become so accustomed to that you tend to overlook it and do not realize that you are doing so.

Throughout the years I have had the wonderful opportunity to observe everyone around me and the way that they interact with others and the world. A common thing that I noticed in all of us is that we all gravitate towards what we are familiar with. For instance, if a person feels interested in sporting attractions, then they will frequent those events and also associate with others who do the same. This obvious statement demonstrates the sort of gathering of people that the saying "birds of a feather flock together" indicates. People who are of the same nature typically relate in the same way, and so they wind up in close association *because of* the way they think, what they do, and where they hang out.

What is not so obvious is that there are many cases where, deep down inside, many people are actually not particularly interested in something or some activity, but because of their hot water they continue doing things and thinking that they like something that is actually adverse to their own true deepest personal tastes. Again, because of their hot water, they will associate with people that they are familiar with and have become comfortable with or accustomed to while partaking in such activities.

The question that arises with—how we relate to the world—is: Can we change our interaction with the world? The answer to this question is an emphatic, *"Yes!"* But, to do so, you must achieve a true and deep understanding of all of the "whys" in *why* you do what you do.

As you continue reading, we're going to approach the hot water topic from many angles to drive the point deep into your heart so that you don't forget it—*ever*! Similarities you notice in various sections in this book all have a slightly different approach. Each approach points out an important difference and very important aspect of hot water, all in order to get you to understand the full depth and gravity of this age-old problem that too many of us have been unable to conquer. At some point in life the problem surrounding hot water has plagued just about everyone who has ever lived, including you.

When you're done reading this book, it's possible that things will seem confusing for a short time as you come to accept certain realities about yourself and those around you, and about your hot water. But, after everything sorts itself out in your heart and mind, you will quickly become understanding, self-assured, and confident in your ways like you have never before experienced!

Why Do We Allow Others to Create Our Thoughts?

As an example of the difficulty we encounter in trying to see beyond our hot water, consider the following story: One day as I was driving in the car with a close friend, we were having a discussion about my own life. I was complaining a bit and he asked, "What do you want?" He meant, "What do you want from life?" As I quickly began to answer, I mentioned all of the things I wanted to go away in my life; and what I had to do in order for that to occur; and that other people wanted things a certain way that were different from what I wanted. And on and on I went about detailing all that needed to be done to achieve what I wanted.

He finally stopped me and said, "But what do *you* want?" Understanding what he meant I, again, continued down the same path, only this time trying to tap into what it was that *I* actually wanted in my life. And, again, I failed; so, he asked me the same question, "But what do **you** want?" Once again I continued along the same lines, only, this time, trying to be *very* cautious of my answers. Eventually he became a bit frustrated with my apparent ignorance and got firm with me. You must understand that he is one of the kindest and gentlest men you will ever meet, so for him to become upset with me was not typical.

In telling you this story, you need to understand that he and I spent much time together growing up and I talked with him much about this very topic. So, why am I relating this story? It's because I want to demonstrate just how difficult it is to see through our own hot water. Even, I, the guy who does nothing but think about this sort topic all day long, has the very same problem that everyone else has because we **all** are *human*, and no one is exempt from this problem. Even when we're aware, we must stay vigilant to keep our own hot water in check.

We could say, "So, who cares? What does it matter if I can't really see what I want? I'm generally a happy person." Well, the answer to that is where our trouble starts to become somewhat more apparent. In my story, where I was having a discussion with my friend about what I wanted in my life, I couldn't even seem to get to the root of what I wanted within my own mind. Why? Because of my hot water.

I love to help people and that includes giving them what they think they want or what they think they need. I have often immediately dropped what I was doing to help someone else. This is admirable, is it not? Not really, or rather, not if it's done improperly.

Helping someone is fine, but changing the words that come out of your own mouth with regard to what *you* actually want is different. This doesn't mean that we should do everything that we want in the face of what others want, or in the face of how it might negatively affect them or us. Rather, what we are trying to establish here is for us to be able to *know* and *admit* to ourselves, and to others, what we ourselves *actually* want *regardless* of others and what they think about what **we** want. People who are "pleasers" (and most of us are), have a tendency to fail at admitting what we truly want throughout everything in our lives.

Because of our people-pleasing ways, we have a difficult time stating what it is that we want without our words being affected by what we think others want or expect of us. I'm not speaking of being demanding or selfish. I am speaking about having the ability to *see* **and** **admit** to ourselves, what we want *regardless* of what others want or think. What we truly want is an entirely different issue than *what we actually do* about what we want.

Our goal is to reclaim our ability to be able to state our own desires without adjusting those desires to satisfy *other people's* ideas of how *we* should think, or *their* idea about what *we* should want. Sadly, because of the power of our hot water, we seldom succeed in doing this. Again, this does not mean that we should do whatever we want despite what others want. At this point we are only referring to our ability to freely *think* about what we want, and then to be able to admit what **we** want to ourselves and, when needed, to the world as well.

If you recall, in the first chapter, we discussed how we have a natural tendency to try to please people and accommodate what *they* think so that we are agreeable with them. When we do this it initially appears to have the effect of making our lives more harmonious with them. Our hot water is why this problem begins to be very difficult for us to see. What happens is, in the same way that we help people, we also will try to change our thinking to be agreeable with or to them, just like was mentioned earlier when children adjust their thoughts to accommodate those who they look up to. It's important to point out that we *need* to adjust our thinking so that we are thinking *rightly* or *correctly*. Yet, there are many times when what we think is neither right nor wrong, but is simply something that we want in our own life, such as our personal preferences, like our favorite color, etc.

Because of our hot water we have become accustomed to adjusting our thinking to accommodate other people's ideas for us and their ideas of us. We often set aside our own true desires so that we don't upset the other people in our lives. Or we change what we like, so as to be seen as "cool" or acceptable. This usually happens because we don't want to admit to others what we really want because we don't want to feel embarrassed or humiliated with regard to our true desire. For some reason we feel inhibited or embarrassed to ask for things that are reasonable and good when we know people will be negative about what we want. Nor do we want to have to ask for things that are customarily common, if the others speak out against it.

This is all a very common problem for a specific reason: From experience, especially in childhood, most of us have learned that sharing our personal and deepest hopes, dreams, and desires will get us a swift bit of discouragement from others. When we were children, our discouragement came from our elders, such as, parents, teachers, and older siblings—all the people who we looked up to. We were told that *it* can't be done, or we may have been laughed at because what we wanted was beyond *their* ability to imagine.

The things we imagine as children and as adults, that we then decide to share, are too often met with much doubt and criticism from others. The feeling we then have is that of embarrassment and discouragement, along with a feeling of false humiliation and even rejection. When this becomes a part of our hot water we then adjust our thinking and actions. It guides us and causes us to voluntarily do things *on our own* that we really don't want to do; or worse, it causes us to *not* do things that we really *do* want to do. This sort of discouraging dirty hot water is a dream killer and a hope killer. It is evil, and it needs to be defeated.

How I got Burned by Hot Water and Why it is Important for You to Understand

The following is an example of how very important it is for us to understand that our hot water and our identities can cause each of us minor problems that lead to disagreeing perceptions that can result in troubles *far worse* than the following example illustrates. You'll find that the, all-too-common, failure of two different people to see things in the exact same way applies to *all* aspects of your life:

While growing up it was common for people of my generation to get cavities in their teeth, requiring the teeth to be drilled and filled. While at lunch one day, part of one of my filled teeth broke off but the filling stayed intact, so I left it for a bit. Then, a couple of weeks afterwards, while eating a cherry, the tooth next to is also chipped in the same way, causing both to be in need of prompt repair.

The hot water effect part of this story and the reason I am telling it is yet to come, but it is important to note that the hot water effect is also heavily involved in the reason that the unnecessary childhood cavities occurred in the first place. That is to say, my parent's generation had them, and so, when I was young, it was more-or-less expected that the children of my generation would get them too—but this does not need to be so.

After the second tooth chipped I went for a consultation about the two teeth. As an adult I take very good care of my teeth, and my philosophy on tooth repair is to remove absolutely as little of the tooth as is possible when repairing them. At the consultation I made very specific requests about this so that in the distant future, if the repairs failed, the next dentist would have something to work with. I asked how long that sort of work typically lasts and even went so far as to ask the dentist how long he expected to live and if the work would last a lifetime. I asked this in order to get an idea of the longevity factors in relation to needing the teeth repaired again later in my life. And I wanted to understand his life-view of the necessity of the duration of this type of tooth repair. (If a person expects to live to only seventy years, then a repair at age fifty will only need to last twenty years. However, if a person expects to live one hundred years, then a repair at age fifty will have to last fifty years. That is two-and-a-half times longer.) The dentist responded by stating that his grandparents lived into their eighties and nineties, indicating that was about how long he expected to live. I informed him that I expect to live longer, which is why I wanted as little removed from my teeth as possible.

He was agreeable to my request and clearly indicated that what I wanted was the preferred way to handle such repairs. At this, I felt comfortable enough to schedule the appointment. But at the appointment I was still somewhat uncomfortable about the situation because there is no going back once any tooth material is removed, I felt uneasy about whether or not the dentist fully understood *exactly* what I wanted. So, before he began, I stopped him and, again, told him that I wanted as little removed as possible from the two teeth, to which he agreed and reassured me that was his plan.

I don't like local anesthetic but he insisted that I needed it. This should have clued me in that I was not going to get what I expected, but for some reason I didn't put two and two together to realize he was saying that he was going very deep and it would hurt a lot without anesthetic. I was bothered by all of this; but, as my hot water of trusting the supposed "expert" or professional would have it, I just sat back and let him do the work.

When the prep-work was complete I felt the area with my tongue and immediately asked for a mirror. I was horrified when I saw that he had unnecessarily prepared my teeth for full crowns. At that point, nothing I said would have brought my teeth back to the way they were before he started, so I said nothing as he placed the temporary crowns, and then I left. The next day, I called back with concerns about the temporary crowns, and told him that I didn't like how the teeth felt and that I was concerned that the final crowns would not meet my expectations because of the way the temporaries felt; at this he was dismissive of my concerns and assured me that everything would be fine.

After thinking about it a bit longer I decided that I was not ready to trust him to work on my teeth again. So I searched for a dentist who would repair my teeth the way I envisioned and quickly found such a dentist; but, sadly for me, they could not do it the way I wanted because the useable tooth material was already unnecessarily removed.

What happened to me was that my regular dentist's business hot water and my hot water were two completely different temperatures, and when his water hit me _**I**_ got burned. He was an old school dentist who only did old style dentistry with full dental crowns. Where, on the other hand, the new dentist I found had modern equipment that could actually make a perfectly fitted puzzle piece of the missing tooth area and then cement it in while not removing any of the actual tooth material, other than for preparing the surface.

My old dentist's business hot water was that, the way he did things was the "industry standard." He didn't believe that he did anything wrong. In fact, what he did went perfectly and he did a fine job of an "industry standard" type repair. However, that type of repair was not what I had expected in my own mind. My expectation was exactly like what the second dentist does with the puzzle-piece type repair. Sadly, my hot water was taught to trust the medical professionals; but, as you can see, they are nothing more than people just like the rest of us are; and, like the rest of us, they misunderstand and make mistakes too. Teeth might not be all that serious of an issue, but imagine going to the doctor to get some stitches in your fingertip because of a cut, and then coming out with almost your entire finger removed. The moral of the story is that your hot water **_does_** matter a great deal! If you're not vigilant in life, then other people *will* be doing what *they* feel is best for you and your life.

Understanding that my former dentist and I had two very different visions in our heads about the repair is a very important aspect of *Hot Water*. We both saw life from two completely different perspectives with regard to the expected repair technique, but somehow we failed to communicate fully enough to each other to make the differences in our visions apparent. He believed what he did was proper, and I believed that I was going to get what I imagined in my mind. He was very dismissive of my concerns; but, wrongly, my hot water was trained to *not* challenge the "experts." During any consultation, if you feel at all uncomfortable with a doctor, or any professional for that matter, it may be in your best interest to immediately get up and walk out, and then go seek another person whose skills and attitude are more suitable to your needs, beliefs, and liking.

Our hot water is just like this: If someone is bitter in their own heart, then they will likely see the world as a bitter place. But if someone believes that there is a better way and that the world can be joyful, then *that* is likely how they will see the world—as joyful! When this is the case, a joyful person will typically not expect the ills that bitter people will perpetrate against them, just as I didn't expect my teeth to be handled as they were. This applies to *all* aspects of life.

Can You Stop Your Brain from Incorrectly Defining Yourself?

Our hot water isn't specifically our perceived identity, but it is largely what shapes our perceived identity. Our perceived identity is what we are, or what we see ourselves as; and *we* define ourselves *using* our perceived identity. This part of our hot water is something that very few people ever think about because it simply never even enters our minds to think about it. This is more along the lines of something philosophers might ponder, but you don't need to be a deep thinker, *your* thoughts count too, especially when it comes to *your own* well-being.

Very few people ever deeply think about—what they think of themselves as—or what they are all about. It's common to wonder about the world and where we came from, but seldom do we wonder to ourselves: "How did I get to be what I am, *and* what exactly am I?"

Revisit the thoughts you have about yourself throughout reading, or reread the notes you wrote about yourself and the feelings you had about yourself. Then add to those thoughts if you have any additional thoughts, such as, what you like, what you don't like, why this is so, and so on. If you feel that you need to add anything now, then do so before you read on. Writing or thinking about it right now will prove to be very helpful to you as you're reading. Be detailed in your writing and thinking. What you write down is really what you have been defining yourself as. But is this really who you are?

As we discussed earlier, others have influence on what defines you, but it's really you who gets to choose how you define yourself. The shaping of our perceived identity that happens during life, guides our path and what we will do, where we will go, and who we will meet. Then all of these interactions affect us, and, in turn, affect our actions. Our perceived identity defines us to ourselves. The waves of hot water that we each live in push us—this way and that way—until we succumb to their overwhelming force and change our thinking and our ways in order to fit our own expectation of the hot water.

Whether good or bad, we do things because of our hot water. When we do good or bad things, those actions become the perception that we have of ourselves. After we *say*, *do*, or even *think* something we are constantly evaluating our actions, but usually not deliberately. From this evaluation we define our own perception of our self-worth. Our self-worth is how we see ourselves, and it is greatly affected by our feelings about our own actions—Remember that your *thoughts* are actions too.

After our automatic subconscious self-evaluation, if we didn't like what we saw or felt, we then feel poorly about ourselves, which typically causes us to partake in the same behavior *again*, thus deepening the particular perception we have about ourselves. This is happening to us continually and it is defining us every moment of our lives. There's no secret in this, it's simply the way it works: day and night, three-hundred-sixty-five days a year, every year of our lives! It happens while you sleep, and while you're awake. It happens at work, at home, and at play. It's always changing ever so slightly, and the things that you gravitate towards are the things that become more prominent in your life and in your hot water. While it appears that we are stuck with this, the truth is that we *can* change things!

Identity is what You Relate To
Even if what You Relate To is Feeling Worthless

Many of us do not truly know what we like. Rather, we like only what we are familiar with; which is a summary of what we have been discussing so far—we like the comfort we feel as we bask in our own hot water, even though that hot water is often uncomfortably hot for us.

As we experience life, we see things, smell things, hear things, feel things, and taste things. This is *all* inclusive. What we eat, the things that we do, where we go, and the people we are with, are amongst the largest contributors to our experience of life.

When we meet a person, our natural inclination is to immediately find common ground wherever we can in order to strike up a good conversation. When we agree on much, then we have often found what we refer to as a "friend". This person could be a man or a woman, and if they are of the opposite gender they might even wind up being your romantic partner, and ultimately your spouse. As we converse with this person we get to know them, and if they feel familiar enough to us, then we will typically befriend them to some extent.

When we begin a friendship, we do activities with our new friend and everything that we experience with them becomes a part of us. If we are very compatible, then most of the experiences will be good because we're relating so well to each other. All of the smells, tastes, sights, and sounds become a part of our feelings toward that person. With each good feeling that we experience together with them, we will relate to them ever more positively.

In most cases, we're looking for someone who feels much the way we do about most everything in life. We are, in a sense, looking into the hot water reflection trying to find someone who looks like ourself—this is also how we relate to *ourselves*. We relate to what is familiar to us, which is more of our hot water. When two people with very compatible hot water mix their waters together, then there is little or no notice of temperature change or differences in water quality by either person because the hot water is so similar, which is what my first dentist expected. He expected that I would simply be happy that my teeth were fixed and that I wouldn't question his work and that I would accept his work as perfect as he was accustomed to other people doing, but I did not meet *his* expectations, nor he mine.

But, our relationship to *ourselves* is what we are working to get the focus on. We must dive *deep* into our hearts to understand how this all happens. The information won't have the intended profound impact on your life if you don't grasp **how** it happens. As our nature is revealed here, we will continue breaking things down so that you're aware of *everything* that affects your life. It's not that you need to keep in mind each small detail about what is being discussed here; but rather, you will learn the type of things that have been influencing any given direction or choice that you have made during your lifetime.

I want to shift the focus a bit from your hot water, and place it more on your resulting perceived identity, because it's really your perceived identity with which you connect to things and people.

Let's play a brief imagination game and imagine that we are a house. What kind of house are you? Are you a big house? A small house? Maybe a fancy house? Or just a plain old house with a white picket fence?

If you are a house from an oppressive struggling country of this world you may be imagining yourself as a tin shack. When you see yourself as a broken down house or a tin shack, then your perceived identity is likely similar to a broken down house because that is all that you have ever experienced.

Please note: We are not concerned about what kind of a house *you* are; we are imagining that the house can think and we are trying to find out what kind of a house the *house* thinks it is. When the house thinks of itself as broken down, regardless of what kind of house it is, then that is what the house is relating to; whether or not that is the case. The initial thought of the house will almost always be similar to its environment. If the house sees itself as a fancy mansion, then that is how the house relates to itself *regardless* of what the house actually is or what its environment is. Even a tin shack could be happy with itself, while an expensive mansion could feel unworthy.

The way we relate to ourselves is typically a reflection of what we are and do: the way we behave, the way we dress, the way we talk, think, work, and every other aspect of our lives. Just as we let our hot water shape us, we also relate to ourselves with this same perception. The way we relate to ourselves is similar to our self-image, but it is not the same thing.

How we relate to ourselves is a *result* of our self-image. Our self-image is *what* or *how* we think of ourselves, just like the one house saw itself as a broken down house in our example. It is what the house does in response that shows how it relates. If the house burned itself to the ground because it saw itself as a broken down shack, then it related to itself as unworthy and acted upon it. This is exactly what we do, though usually not so drastically.

When our self-image is good, we behave accordingly towards ourselves, but when it is bad we also behave accordingly towards ourselves and typically take action. These actions are the words we say about ourselves, the clothes we wear, the foods we eat, the amount we eat, the way we walk or carry ourselves, even our thoughts and so much more. Of course, sometimes outside pressures will force us to dress a certain way, but we're not talking about those situations, we are discussing the ones that *you* create, allow, and even enforce upon yourself.

How Your Identity Shows Others What You Are,
and You Can't Stop It

It is the actions *you* allow that show others what or *who* you are. Your actions are your interface or connection with others. It's true that people often get an incorrect impression of you which usually happens when someone speaks to them in a good or bad way about you. It's also possible that their first impression of you is based upon a brief interaction where you may have been very happy or very angry at the time and as a result, they used that particular moment as a starting point in forming what they think about you.

Regardless of how someone's first impression of you was formed, the first impressions are easily overcome. This is because most people have the capacity in their hearts to give us a second chance with regard to making our impression on them. If we take the time to get to know people—or in this case, take the time to have them get to know us—we will usually find a willingness and openness from them to share in what we have to offer.

When you hear the phrase "what you have to offer" you may think of a sales person selling their wares, but whether you are a salesperson, or just a person walking down the street, what you are actually selling is *what **you** are*. You're not selling it in the sense of a financial exchange; rather you are allowing others to see what you have and what you're all about. And you desire for them to accept what you're offering. This isn't something we do deliberately; in most cases it's simply other peoples' impression of us as *they* see us. We go out of our way to impress people when going in for a job interview, often making ourselves out to be more than what we actually have to offer.

We also see this "trying to impress" action done by stretching reality in the sales world. This is especially so in advertising where they try to make things seem better than they actually are. We're all familiar with these obvious tactics and usually we see through it all. For instance, when you get a frozen pizza, does the pizza in the box ever actually look as good when it's baked as the one on the box does? If only it did... Typically the products *in* the package are far less appealing than the pictures *on* the package. Having been involved in advertising, I can tell you first-hand that there is much deceit in the portrayal of foods in advertising to a point where, often, it is down-right dishonest.

But it's the more subtle things that make our true impression on those who we encounter. This includes the "sales shows" that we ourselves put on at times. People see through the show. And the fact that we put on the show to begin with gives them an impression of us—not the show itself, but the fact that we put the show on to begin with. This is especially so when they can easily tell that we are putting on a show. Our shows usually indicate inflation of reality to some extent.

It's the little things that your hot water has placed in your identity—things like *when* you smile, or whether or not you make eye contact, your facial expressions, your body language, your verbal language, the way you dress, the way you walk, your attitude, and so much more—these are the things that people base their long-term assessments of us on. Their assessments may be accurate or inaccurate, but no matter what their assessments are, those assessments are largely derived from our presentation of ourselves to them.

Our presentation comes from the perceived identity that we have allowed to grow within us. Their perception of us could be inaccurate due to their own perception of life. But still, no matter what their case and circumstances have been, the fact still remains that they make *their* judgment, right or wrong, based upon what we, or our perceived identity, presents to them.

If you like to wear yellow all the time because it makes you feel good, then others will see you in yellow. If yellow bothers them, then they may unfairly hold that against you. However, if they like yellow, then it will seem favorable to them and their assessment of you will be better. This applies to *every* aspect of your presentation, whether it's what you wear or what you say and do. It is an inescapable fact of life: No matter what you do or what you are, on the surface of it all, your perceived-will and your perceived-identity eventually show up in your actions, thoughts, and words. These things *will* affect the way people perceive you, and, try as you might to escape this truth, it cannot be thwarted!

In the long run, your perceived identity will eventually find you out, both for good and for bad, because it's difficult to hide what we ourselves perceive that we are.

The Critical Importance of Understanding that Identity is Your Relevance to the World

The world at large will view us only by our perceived identity. So what is "The World"? "The World" is the combination of people and circumstances that surround us all. When thinking of describing "The World" in this context, computers are a good example to illustrate problems that can occur. Your relevance to the world is assessed by the world in terms of how you fit into the world. During the late twentieth and early twenty-first centuries, computers had become a large part of determining our relevance to the world. Our relevance to the world is judged through credit scores, job applications, college degrees, applying for loans, financial status, and many other instances where your information is being fed into "The System." Ultimately there are people behind all of this, and these people are generally fine folks if you know them personally. However, once they sit down at their desk, they only "fill in the blanks." They do so because they don't want to lose their jobs. When we *fill in the blanks* we are "feeding the beast"—which is to say *The System*.

The only information that we can enter into the system is the information that has been made room for by the designers of each software program (Society). The elements that the programmers and designers created are there to make the job simple enough so that the business owners do not need to do as much training with their new employees who are collecting the information from us. This way the employers can hire college graduates with a degree in filling in blanks to easily do the job, thus, requiring little or no expense for training them.

The problems that arise from only filling in the blanks are most evident with government organizations, but are becoming increasingly evident at any bureaucratic operation such as hospitals, phone companies, public utilities, etc. This successful business model becomes very impersonal and is wide-open for abuses. The abuses can go in either direction; for example, those who abuse the government system of available entitlements. But it also can come back on the people, and the people can be abused by the system. If you're the type of person who does not like to give up personal information easily, then you become a target because the people who are taking your information are told that they *must* enter the information and fill in all possible blanks in order to do their job properly. People want to fill in the blanks whether it is putting your data in a computer or filling in the mental blanks about you and your identity.

When people can't fill the blanks in, then they feel that they are failing at their job and they will pressure you for your information. In this case, your actions have affected your interaction with the world, and *you* begin to become a victim of the world because of your interaction with it. Your interaction with the world is the result of your actions, and your actions are the result of your perceived identity. This example was not about filling in the blanks, even though that is a good analogy. Rather, it's about the interaction *between people* because of them needing to fill in the social blanks. This is all very important to understand for the many reasons we will be exploring throughout this book. You can think of the blank relative to the term "genre" with regard to music. When a singer is new to the public, we want to put them in a genre box, or blank. If we can't fit them in an existing blank, we either dismiss them or have a

difficult time describing the type of music they in the fit, that is
to say what is there relevance to us regarding music. What we are
addressing here is that your perceived identity is your relevance
to the world.

We need to examine the term "The World" more closely
because it is *very* important with regard to your identity. What is
"The World"? As indicated earlier, "The World" is the people and
the circumstances that surround us. In our example, computers,
or rather the available blanks for our information, are the
circumstances, but the circumstances of the entire world are vast.

When you walk down the street in your home town you will
find things the way you have always found them, only slightly
changing from year to year. Go into a different area or city and
the world circumstances are somewhat different.

What we see in advertising and entertainment does not play
out so well in our day-to-day lives. For most of us, the people in
the community would point and stare if women dressed the way
the women do in many advertisements that we see and accept on
a daily basis. For most people it just would not fit into the mold
(blanks) of what is *expected* in our local communities. Yet, we
often see these images as the way that we should be because
we're being told, through advertising and our culture, that this is
how we should be or behave. This includes how we act, how we
look, what we eat, what we drink, where we live, the things that
we say, and any other method of interacting with the world. This
doesn't mean that it's wrong to dress the way that women do as
depicted in some advertising, but it does mean that we would
typically not accept this as "normal" in our everyday lives.

When our perceived identity doesn't match the pressures that
the world places on us to conform, we become aware of this and,
often, we try to change in effort to accommodate the world's way.
If the world starts to lean in a certain direction and our perceived
identity does not fit in with the leaning or the sway of the group,
then, to some extent, we will be cast out if we comply, just like

becoming a target if we refuse to give out our information to be entered into the blanks on the computer screen.

As you can see, your perceived identity, which is yours to mold and shape as *you* see fit, is vital in your perceived acceptance by "The World." I say *perceived* acceptance because it is a false reading of reality. Your relevance to the world is affected by your perceived identity for sure, but the question is: Does that really matter to you?

Chapter 3

What is Your Perceived Identity?

Now that you have a good grasp on *your* hot water, we'll spend some time on your resulting perceived identity. *Your* perceived identity... what is it? We've established that it is largely formed because of our hot water circumstances, but we all still need to be able to learn to detect our perceived identity. However, because of our hot water, this is not an easy task.

How You Identify with Your Identity

The fact that we do what we do—largely because of our circumstances—makes what we do too familiar for us to readily notice. Therefore, we seldom detect or notice that we even have a *perceived* identity. So how do we detect our perceived identity? Simply by looking at *what* we identify with and *who* we identify with. While this is simple in concept, you still need to see outside of your hot water, and that is a difficult task for any one of us to do.

The first thing that I would like you to do is to think about your own hot water. Become conscious of the concept that your hot water exists and that *you* have *hot water*, which is to say, those things that are common and regular to your experiences in life, or what you might refer to as "normal." After thinking about your hot water for a bit, in order to get its existence to the forefront of your mind, you need to shift your thinking towards finding or identifying your own perceived identity. So, for now, I am only asking that you understand that your hot water exists.

For the purposes of this book you must *understand* your perceived identity. To begin that understanding, we will look at the things that we identify with. Hot water and your perceived identity are closely related, but are separate aspects of your life.

In order to begin detecting your perceived identity, you should be trying to identify *what you identify with* as you begin to look around. Start by thinking of your likes and dislikes in your friends, family, work, and leisure activities—basically anything in your life. What or who are these things? And why do you like or dislike them?

I want you to begin by focusing on some of the basic and most prominent things such as those that are easier to spot, like your house or apartment. Dig deep and ask yourself, why do I live where I live? Is it because of the location? Was it the only place you could find in your price range? Did you choose it or did your finances choose it? Did you fall in love with the layout and the color scheme? Was it close to your work? What were the things that made you live where you live today?

The following is not intended to cause friction in any relationship or between any friends. But take your best friend for instance: Does this person excite you? Do you like to be in their company? Did you choose them as a friend or did they choose you? Are they a life-long friend? Does this friend watch your back for you? Do you care? How much time do you spend with this person?

You don't need to answer these questions specifically, but they are a good start toward thinking about your relationships. In most cases, our best friend is a person who we can identify with to some extent. The same goes for our home or our apartment—our dwelling is typically something that we can relate to. Of course there will be people who have things that run contrary to their actual perceived identity; but largely, all the things in our life are things or people we identify with. These things often change when we have major life changes; for instance, when you get married it's common, and usually good, that your relationships with your friends change and maybe, in some cases, even dissipate completely.

With this understanding, think of the things or people in your life that are the most prominent. Then think about each thing or person and render some opinions *of your own* about those things or people. To do so you must ask yourself questions like those just mentioned, and then answer the questions honestly to the best of your ability. And finally, draw some conclusions about your choices based upon your answers.

In many ways, your conclusions reflect you and what you have become due to your hot water. The accuracy of your reflection will depend upon where you are personally at in life with respect to the types of things we are discussing. This rule-of-thumb is very strong, and it is as simple as this: Your perceived identity is that which you identify with.

So far in this section we only mentioned concrete items like your home and friends, but the effects of what we discussed in this section go far beyond that and touch *every* aspect of your life, including the abstract—**your thoughts**.

If you're not a good listener then you might not really know the thoughts of your friends. If this is the case, then you likely also find identifying *your own true thoughts* to be somewhat difficult.

How the Gravity of Laws Determine the Things You Are

When you have completed the mind exercise of asking about yourself, about your own thoughts about other people, and about the major things that surround you, then you should begin to see that you like these things because they are familiar to you. This basic inescapable fact is a simple truth so common that few, if any, escape this, and, thus, are never made aware that they are doing so. To better relate these things to your identity, recall the concept of your hot water. Your *answers* to the questions that you asked yourself about the people and the things in your life are a part of your hot water. One way or another, the specific *questions* you chose are a reflection of you, and, even more so, your *answers* are a reflection of you.

Some may find a few contradictions in this with regard to their own lives, but it generally applies across the board throughout the lives of most of us. In small part, it could be true that it won't apply to every detail, but most aspects of this are still a part of your perceived identity. For instance, if you very much dislike certain aspects of a person's behavior and still tolerate their actions, then the tolerating that you do of their actions is part of *you*. It's not so much what *they* do, but rather *your reaction* to what they do. Both what they do and your reaction to it are all a part of *your* hot water. This is not some secret that was created by anyone. Rather, I'm simply explaining the way things work; just like Isaac Newton's Law of Gravity explains the way we cling to the Earth.

Newton's "Law" is nothing more than a *description* of the way things work; and his "Law" is merely a statement of his observations. The way gravity works has absolutely no bearing on his statements and observations. This is because his observations are based upon the way gravity works, rather than the other way around. Newton didn't just make up arbitrary nonsense, he took careful measurements and observations; and after gathering his information, he then analyzed it and drew conclusions that could not be easily debated. After proving his conclusions, he made statements on his findings that are now referred to as "Newton's Laws." The "Laws" are nothing more than the current best description of how it all behaves. *Hot*

Water is similar to Newton's Law in that respect. The comparison to hot water is merely an observation and statement of the way things work with humans. In fact, this entire book is about the truth of the way things work in your perceived identity. The fact that we are referring to it as *hot water* and *perceived identity* has no effect on your life, but your *awareness* of the *Hot Water* concept is critically important for you to grasp. Hot water is simply a description of the events that brought you to where you are today. Better understanding this will bring you to where you will be tomorrow. And where you are tomorrow, can be a position in life of *your own choice* when you decide to do so.

The questions that you asked about your friends and some of the larger items in your life, like your home, should have brought a few answers to your mind. Your observation of those answers is exactly what Newton did. He observed and then he drew conclusions about the truth of what was happening during his observations, just the same as you have begun to draw conclusions about your own hot water a moment ago and as you will be doing from now on. We could call your observations the "Laws of Hot Water," but we won't because they are not really "laws," rather they are truths of the way this all occurs.

All of the things that make up your hot water have become you, and you have become them. If a situation is not agreeable to you, then it is your recurring *rejection* or *toleration* of the situation that is part of what you are. This is not some invented thing just made up, it is *what* you are—it is your *perceived identity*. As stated earlier, this doesn't stop at your home and friends, it extends to every part of your life, like the clothes you wear, where you bought them, the reason you made the choices you did, your religious and political philosophies—everything! All of this becomes the essence of you and your perceived identity. We could go as far as to say that your perceived identity *is* your essence, but we won't, and we will discuss the reason for that in a later chapter.

What You Relate to is Your Life's Resume

We relate to our own perceived identity in very intimate ways. These ways are so deep and subtle that we simply do not understand or notice that we are doing so. All of the major and minor aspects of our identities that we have discussed thus far are continuously weighing on us and affecting the way we interact with people and the way we see ourselves.

As our hot water slowly shapes our perceived identity, our blind perception is that we become it and it becomes us. This is a logical and expected result when analyzed. Our perceived identity becomes our self-description. It is as if it is our life resume. Other people will read our life resume (or our perceived identity) and will assess us based upon that resume. Our perception of this is blind because it is a part of our hot water. In the same way that our hand becomes accustomed to actual hot water, so too, our perception becomes accustomed to our environment.

How Your Perceived Identity Affects What You and the World See You As

No matter what, you and others who meet you will see you as you present yourself. This includes all of the subtleties that our perceived identities have. You *will* be judged on *your* perceived identity. When people meet you, every single aspect of you forms their thoughts about you—*everything*. The slightest blink, nod, and movement of the eyes, the way that you shake hands, how fast, how slow, how long—it all has an effect—the clothes you wear and how you wear them; are they neatly pressed or wrinkled? Everything about you makes an impression to those around you. In fact, it all affects *you* as well—and very profoundly at that.

Most of us look in the mirror several times a day, and every time we do so we are seeing what others see. This is our visual first impression to the world *and* to ourselves. We can dress very poorly and people will judge us for our initial basic appearance. We often judge visual appearance very harshly, but even if we dress poorly on a regular basis, people will likely change their impression of us when they have an opportunity to actually get to know us over time. They may soften towards us, and maybe even embrace the way we are. Though, in general, we don't get the opportunity to get to know people all that well, and so our first impression is typically all that we get to offer them because we will not see them very often, if at all.

Understanding your perceived identity is of great importance in order for you to be able to *accurately* interact with the world. This brings us to detailing how our perceived identity is formed.

We—that is to say, any of us, and children in particular— typically do not ponder the subject of perceived identity without first having attention drawn to the subject in some manner. We, sort of, just live our lives, which is a good thing to do, but when problems or tensions occur it's usually a good time to examine this subject.

By the time a child is about two years old, our perceptions of that child's individuality are often set firmly in our minds. To be truthful, this is unfair because we typically treat people as we see them, and in turn, often the child will begin to see themselves as their superiors see or treat them. This usually results in years of a given behavior by the particular child.

These behaviors, which can be good, bad, or rather bland, are the foundations that we all build our own perception of our own world or life upon as *we each* grow. Since most people are typically considered friendly and good, *most people* are usually not an issue. So instead, we will draw our attention to the more difficult personalities that we encounter.

People who make it their habit to irritate us have been conditioned, sometimes by us, to behave in an irritating way. Their behavior has become part of their perceived identity.

So what exactly is this "perceived identity" that we each adopt? It's simply our reaction to our perceived experience of the world. When a child is in the early stages of learning, (birth through about age three) they are conditioned as explained earlier. Regardless of whose fault that conditioning is, the good or bad behavior becomes a major role in their perceived identity. This good or bad *nature* that we adopt becomes a part of our own perceived identity, and it is our perceived identity that we will be recognized for all of our lives... *unless*, **we choose** to change.

Throughout our years we will build on the foundation of the perceived identity that we have been forging, and we will add to, or take away from, the perception that we and others have of ourselves. Some of us are fortunate and we catch our undesired personality traits early on in our lives. Then we quickly make changes before they become too deeply rooted and too difficult for us to easily change within ourselves. But the rest of us suffer from a voluntary self-blindness.

As we grow and move through adolescence into adulthood, we bring this perceived identity *foundation* with us and build our lives upon it. Often, people who are searching for worth, value, and of course a job, will attend some sort of higher education. That education will be set upon the foundation of our perceived identity that was put in place in our youth. If our foundation has issues, then everything built upon it will inherently express those issues.

As the chosen education assimilates into an actual job or career, it often becomes an integral part of a person's perceived identity. As you move through life you will typically be known for what you do: *you are* a mechanic—*you are* a doctor—*you are* an artist—*you are* a stock broker—etc... and thus the adult "perceived identity" is born, and it is built upon, and added to, your early life foundation.

It is important to mention that what we are illustrating here in this chapter is not about what *is* or *is not* good about perceived identity, nor is it about the way things *should* be in your life. Rather, it is about the way we all typically view ourselves and others with regard to our own identity and how it is perceived. Everyone sees things differently, which is a very important point to understand. If all of humanity had always seen all things identically, then our world would be a very different place today.

Through the events and methods described in this chapter, we and others create our perceived identities, and we carry these perceived identities throughout our lives and do with them as we are *expected* to do. Whether to our benefit or to our harm, based upon our individual perceived identities, we generally follow what we feel we are expected to do.

Chapter 4

Where Does Your Perceived Identity Come From?

In this chapter we're going to dive into the family model and break it down in order to more clearly illustrate each phase of life that assists in the development of our own perceived identities. This chapter has to do with parenting and the perspective view of a child, and walks through each life stage to better illustrate how we each have come to perceive our identity as we do. Depending upon your current life circumstances, you will be able to see yourself in several of the positions discussed throughout this critical chapter. Understanding the family dynamics described in this chapter is a *major key* to understanding your own perceived identity. If you do not first understand your basic family dynamics, it will cause you to miss much of what is discussed throughout this book in regard to your own identity.

We have discussed the method of how our identity is formed as we looked at our hot water and its effect on our own identity, but we haven't done more than make minor mention with regard to the circumstances that bring it all about.

How Your Early Family Identity Affects You

Let's imagine a young lady and a young man, still in high school, who are introduced by a mutual friend. At this point we already have three perceived identities at play in this scenario. The friend knows the young man and the young lady very well, and the friend makes the assumption that the two will hit it off. After their introduction, the two are attracted to each other and go off on their own and talk.

As this young couple gets to know one another better, several things are occurring: First, they feel familiar to one another. This offers them a certain feeling of safety too subtle to detect. The familiar feeling that appears to offer such safety is their hot water, which is to say, the hot water of each of their families.

The couple could be from different sides of the tracks, in that, she is from an upper-class neighborhood and he is from a lower-class neighborhood. On the outside, it would appear as if they are worlds apart—even to themselves it appears this way. Observers around them only see the superficial part of their identities and base their assessments on these superficial parts of the couple's identities. This is much the way we superficially observe as we watch the news of the rich and famous unfold before our eyes— judging a book by its cover.

In the example of the young couple, their mutual friend knew a different part of their perceived identities beyond the superficial, and it was this part of their hot water that the three had in common and which the friend recognized as similar between the two, thus bringing them together. might be trying to picture yourself as one of these people in the couple; however, for our purpose here, the couple is your parents.

Now that this couple has become acquainted, they will continue to get to know each other. With each meeting they have an affirmation of perceived identity. This affirmation feels to them to be a very rewarding thing. The feelings of *acceptance* from each other overwhelm them and they choose to continue their relationship. With each new encounter they grow more and more fond of one another as they share their life stories, interests, and mutual affections. In the beginning, they generally reinforce one another's perceived identities. This occurs mostly because they have an affinity toward one another that allows them to blind their eyes to the weak or undesirable parts of each other's' perceived identities.

As the relationship continues, they slowly slip into a comfort zone and begin to more fully reveal their own perceived identities; and thus, each will also more fully see the other person's perceived identity. This will begin to remove the voluntary blindness that they both had in the very early stages of dating. Now, because of their hot water, these new revelations about each other seem to be of little consequence to them and they happily continue their relationship. All of the things that they do and say to one another become, in some form, a part of their hot water; and in turn, this is adopted into their newly adjusted perceived identity, both individually and as a couple.

After marriage, while they are together every day, an even greater revelation occurs with regard to their perceived identities. Their habits, both good and bad, are now in plain view of one another and slowly begin to become a part of each other's perceived identities and of their perceptions of each other. They'll do things like choose what type of life to live together such as: will they have children early, or will they wait until the finances are in order? When their decision is made, their decision is added to their perceived identity. Our decisions become part of our perceived identities because we must commit to them and live with those decisions. These decisions typically deepen our feelings about the particular subject, and that causes us to make more decisions along that particular line, yet further deepening our feelings about the subject.

In our example, let's have the couple wait to have children; we'll say that they married at the age of 23, both got jobs, and had everything in order, and then around the age of 33 they began their family. Then we have to ask: Why did they wait? Was it pressures from society? From family? Fear of struggling? Or something else? Whatever the reason for waiting, one thing is certain: they had a reason, and that reason is integral in their hot water and in their perceived identities.

So, at the age of 33 they begin to have children. During the pregnancy, the expectant mother is bombarded by thoughts and opinions from siblings, parents, friends, in-laws, and in society about how a child should be raised. Some of the advice is good, and some of the advice bad; but all of this hot water affects the mother-to-be's perceived identity regardless.

As the couple anxiously awaits the arrival of their new baby, they may recount things that they liked or disliked from their own childhood. As they raise their own child they will try to change the few unfavorable things that they have actually become aware of throughout their lives. Their baby is born healthy and they take their newborn baby home and begin their new family life together.

Everything that the couple experienced up to this point has all affected their individual perceived identities. And because of these perceptions, there are certain expectations that they have of each other. Additionally, *because of what other people have told them*, they will also have expectations of their new baby. These expectations are the beginning of the child's perceived identity and are the child's hot water. The term perceived identity is not in reference to other people's perception of us, so much as it is in reference to our own perception of ourselves.

How Your Childhood Identity Was Formed

As the newborn child begins to sense the surrounding world outside of the protection of its mother's womb, the child experiences cold for the first time and will typically share that experience by crying; and by doing so, the child quickly learns to request to be comforted via crying. Similarly, crying when hungry will bring about the same result for the child. The child immediately begins associating crying with a desire of wanting to be satisfied. As the child grows, the parent or guardian will typically change their response to the infant and guide the child to a new level of communication. Most experienced parents have become very familiar with this process.

All of these early interactions begin to form an individual's perceived identity, and these early interactions affect the child's entire lifetime, for better or for worse.

As the couple brings their newborn infant home from a successful and happy delivery, they begin the monumental task of raising a child. The very first evening home, the excited young couple lays their beautiful child in her crib after feeding her, where she falls fast asleep—and so do the exhausted parents! Two hours later, the child wakes and begins to cry. Excited to care for their newborn infant, the parents rush to see what's wrong and they begin to comfort their baby, as they should. They change the baby's diaper, and then try to feed and rock her for a while, but she doesn't eat. When she has fallen asleep they lay her down and get some more rest for themselves, only to find that, three hours later, their baby wakes once again. This time she's hungry, so as is appropriate, they feed her. At this point, on the first night home, they have already begun to set up precedence with the child: It is good and natural precedence of expectancy. The child cries and gets an appropriate response from the parents, and with each parental response, the child's behavior or action is reinforced. This will continue as long as the parents continue to rush to comfort the child whenever she cries. This happens very quickly—within a couple of days after the birth of the child.

It is appropriate that they care for their infant this way. And the parents, having only one brand-new baby to care for, find it of little effort to comfort their beautiful new child, so they continue to do so whenever the child cries. The child becomes accustomed to the comfort that she receives from her parents and it becomes a part of her hot water even though she is only two months old now. As the months pass, her parents become less tolerant of this and begin to become frustrated due to their interrupted sleep. At this point the child has little perception of her own identity. This first child may have been you or maybe was a sibling.

Now that the parents have experienced parenthood for a number of months, the novelty of a new baby has mostly worn off, and they are feeling that their sleep is being deprived. They do a little research and reading and find a new word—*colicky*—and because their child often cries and many of the elements of *colicky* fit, they wrongly *label* their child as "*colicky*", generally, not truly knowing what *colicky* actually means. (It will benefit you to research the etymology of the word *colic*, especially if you have children.)

While the child is growing, and the parents are responding to every cry of their child, the child is learning that whenever she needs anything she can cry, and her parents will quickly come to comfort her. This is a very common situation with new parents who only have one or two children. Because the parents are new to handling a child that needs to be cared for twenty-four hours a day, seven days a week, they *must* make decisions with regard to how they should handle their child.

In our example the parents chose to go to the child **every** time the child cried as shew aged. In the long-term, as the child grows, this will begin to create poor hot water and a poor perceived identity for the child, which will require much of the parents' future time and energy. They will never be able to fully comfort their child by continuing to handle this situation in this way. This will continue, and when their next child arrives they will have the monumental task of serving two children in the same way.

When a child is allowed to get their way in opposition to the parents' best discretion, then that child learns the cruel art of manipulation. If this behavior goes unchecked then the child's new-found skill of manipulation will stay with the child all of her life. When a manipulative child enters the real world, (that is to say—outside of their home), the child will run into opposition that did not exist within her home. This opposition will come from relatives, teachers, friends, and any other interaction with outside people. This opposition to the reaction of the child adds to the child's hot water and shapes their perceived identity even more.

After feeling comfortable in handling their child by tending to her whenever she cries, the young couple feels ready and decides to have a second child. The second child is a baby sister.

Having received all of the parents' attention up until this point, the first child is generally content and served very well by her parents. When the second child is born, with excitement, the parents introduce their first daughter to her new baby sister. For the little girl it is exciting to see this new baby and she enjoys spending time with the new baby and her parents.

After some time home with their new baby, the parents notice a change in their first child. She has become more demanding and often misbehaves, but why? We will more deeply discuss this very important aspect of perceived identity and hot water later, but, for now, what is important is the *parents' reaction* to their oldest daughter's behavior.

With young families it is a common situation where the mother and father become overwhelmed when both children are demanding both parents' attention at the same time. The mother is usually the first one to crack because she is generally doing the most with regard the amount of time spent on the care and comforting of the children. (Thank you Mothers everywhere for being there, this has *not* gone unnoticed!) A very common outcome is that, in her frustration, the mother will often sharply react to the crying of the oldest child, and sometimes the mother might even sharply react to the new baby's crying. This can result in the damaging action of labeling the children.

It's common for a young parent to say things like, "You're always crying!" or, "Stop being a crybaby!" Different parents will say different things to their children, which will largely be dependent upon the life experiences and hot water of each parent. The parents' hot water might have been full of this sort of behavior while growing up, so it is of no consequence in their minds to do the same thing with their own children—this is done without truly being conscious of doing so. The behavior resulting from the parents' frustration is not something that the parents are much aware of. Rather, it is an auto response that they either learned, or they are unaware of the level of their frustration. But regardless of the cause, the frustration *is* a part of their hot water.

When parents label a child, they send messages to the child via the label, which serves to reinforce what the child is doing. Given enough repetitions—usually only a relative few—the parents will typically begin to expect this behavior from this oldest child. When this expectation exists and the parents do not resist it in an appropriate way, then the child will respond accordingly. This increases the expectation of the behavior, and therefore the response from the child will aim to support the expectation that the parents have. With each occurrence, this becomes more and more of the family's hot water and of the child's very own hot water.

This vicious cycle feeds itself in a circular manner. (It is a noteworthy to point out that, to some extent, the parents each had this in their own lives growing up. It, too, was a part of each of their own hot water as children.) As more children come into this young family, the effect becomes less noticeable with each child because the parents' attention is already divided up between the existing children. With each division of the parents' attention the effect is less pronounced, but it still has the same effect on each child depending upon the way the parents handle themselves and their children.

This reciprocal tug from expectation, and then fulfillment of that expectation, will continue until the children are independent of their parents, and it will still exist, to some extent, throughout their adulthood. The expectation, and reaction to the expectation, will continue throughout the life of the parents. Without completely understanding the effect of the child's own hot water, after the parents are gone, the hot water and the resulting perceived identity of the child are often too strong for the, now adult, child to overcome. It is this complete understanding that we are striving to achieve with the principle being discussed in this book.

A Detailed View of Your Early Perceived Identity

As you read, see if you recognize any of this in your childhood family or in yourself. The early hot water starting points of young children can send them towards a particular direction of behavior. As long as this behavior is reinforced it will continue to move in a given direction, and the behavior will typically intensify or amplify over time as that child grows. If a parent picks up a child every time the child cries, then the child becomes accustomed to getting his or her way, and this **will** continue to grow if it goes unchecked. When the child reaches the age of two or three, then the behavior evolves into a tantrum. The tantrum could come in the form of a child becoming irrationally upset after having the parents decline the child's request, for instance, for candy or a toy in the store. Children's tantrums can also be observed through their defiance and manipulation.

Just because a child has an occasional tantrum *does not* deem them as spoiled! An overtired or over-stimulated child will often behave in a difficult manner. In the case of an overtired or over-stimulated child, the parent usually knows this, and will get the child to bed or promptly distract them to sooth the situation. A well-seasoned parent *will not* give in to the child, but instead will work to quickly change the circumstances in order to meet the child's *true* underlying needs.

Regardless of who you are, what you have done, or what age your children are at, a parent will greatly alter their children's behavior, for good or for bad, by their approval via expectations and the level of expectation that results from their hot water.

When children actually enter into the behavior mode of manipulation-by-tantrum, then, we as parents, begin to expect it of them and often label them as "a difficult child." By labeling them we are reinforcing their behavior, and through this we help to forge a very sturdy foundation for the particular behavior. With every revolution of events in this nasty cycle, the child will behave as expected all the more, and, in turn, the parent will become more expectant of that behavior. This will cause the child to behave even more so as expected, and so the cycle continues. This is true with *good* behaviors as well!

A great many children have grown into young adults with little sense of identity, causing them to begin to search for something to identify with. This is what has made the advertising world thrive for so many years. From generation to generation, many parents have, by example, passed down their own vagueness of their own perceived identity. They have done this by identifying with their environment, never truly having a feeling of any sort of true fulfillment in their own lives. The negative and frequent effects of this are usually felt for decades, but are seldom ever fully realized by parents.

Your perceived identity and the way you value it (your self-worth) is the core of your mental worth, and it is tightly connected to your individuality. Whether our lives are peachy-keen or are totally destitute, our individuality is at the center of the topic. As young children emulate their parents, which can be both a very good thing and/or a very bad thing, they adopt the parents' behaviors, and these behaviors cause *expectation*.

When people interact with children who exhibit any particular behavior, they have *expectations* of those children because of the behaviors exhibited by the children. These expectations reinforce and affirm to the child that the behaviors that the child exhibited to begin with are proper. In turn, this deepens the child's conviction that the particular behavior is the way for them to continue to behave; which, in turn, deepens the expectations of that child by the people who are around the child. This terrible downward spiraling effect of events is a tragic part of life that seldom is adequately addressed.

Because birds of a feather tend to fly together, it makes it very difficult to detect this phenomenon. Our behavior very much runs in our families, which wrongly makes it appear as if it is genetic when it is actually not. When we are children we know no different than what we see around us, and in our earliest critical years "what we see" is typically our parents and our siblings. Since we know no different as a child, we have no other point-of-reference with regard to our behaviors and attitudes, which results in us believing that what we see at home is "normal" and acceptable.

Often, parents will become angry, both at children who are acting much the way the parents themselves do, and/or when the children respond exactly as expected with regard to the way the parents treat them; try recalling your own childhood in this regard. This means that if the parents perceive the child to be spoiled, then they will treat them as such, and the child will live up to the parents' expectations. Thus, if the parents expect the children to be bad, then the children will most certainly be bad. Then the parents become angry at the child because the child behaved badly just as the parents expected of them, and the child behaved badly because that was what was expected of the child's hot water. It's a terrible circular trap for any child, or parent, to be caught in.

Of course, these little children do have a temperament of their own, but a good deal of it has been formed by their environment. For some of us, this is a difficult thing to swallow. Like it or not, we parents are largely responsible for all of our children's behavior. This means that if the children's behavior is lacking, then it is likely that the parents' treatment and love towards the children are also lacking. This includes us and our relationship to our own parents, just as it includes us and our relationship to our own children.

Focusing attention towards a child's bad behavior with too many spankings, too many time-outs, or too much yelling, only serves to reinforce their bad behavior. Usually, bad behavior simply needs to be ignored, unless, of course, it is going to cause injury or is cruel to others. **Parents: No means no**! The cornerstone book *Strong Family* discusses how when a parent who wavers at the tyranny of their children, they will remain at the mercy of their children as long as they waver.

When a parent is raising a child they are better served thinking of it as **building** a child. Viewing it in this way will make you more conscious of the hot water aspects of you, your children, and your family as a whole. When we, as parents, regularly give in to a child, we are reinforcing the behavior of the child. Usually when a parent gives in we are giving in to a temper tantrum of the child. Every time we give in we are saying to the child that what they are doing is okay. Often, *but not always*, moms are the ones who give in, where dads are more firm-handed because they typically have a bigger bark. The temper tantrum problem typically worsens for some reason when the father is the one who always gives in.

Let's go back to when a child begins to discover that he or she exists, which tends to be between the ages of one and two. This is the time where most people form their fundamental understanding of life. What children learn during that age is the—what they will see life as for the rest of their life—part of the problem; that is to say, *their perception* of life. **Unless** at some point, of their own accord, they choose to fully re-evaluate and then see what is really true. A child's parents can assist in correcting the child's wrong perception, provided that they themselves understand that the child is perceiving things improperly to begin with.

Consider a child at the age of twelve months, usually just at the brink of walking, tottering as they stand being supported by the sofa or a chair while looking to their parents for validation of each step in this grand achievement. The encouragement from parents' goes a very long way in the child's ambition. Typically, parents are very encouraging to their children with regard to their children's first smile, rolling over, taking their first steps, and other special precious early-life moments.

It is around the age that children begin to walk where parents also become more easily frustrated with their children. As the child becomes increasingly independent it takes more effort to care for them, and often this tests the patience of a parent. There is a difference between *patience* and *tolerance*. If the parents become frustrated with a child, then the child will automatically make certain adjustments in his or her perception of life, causing the child to gravitate towards that perception.

Now let's add siblings into this mix. In a household that is filled with love, acceptance, and patience, from both parents, there will typically be very few problems with siblings; but, if the parents grew up in a household of strife, then they will be hard-pressed to notice it as unhelpful within their own lives. Even if the parents do notice that something is wrong, it is often a hefty challenge for them to eradicate the problem because they are so accustomed to that sort of behavior that they tend to not do much to correct it, they're also accustomed to *tolerating* that sort of behavior.

When strife exists in a household, the older siblings of the family will often be jealous because they have to compete for their parents' attention. This *attention* is better achieved through the parents' love and approval, but it often comes in the form of the parents' confused and ambiguous punishment of the children for misbehaving.

What happens in many families who experience this is that the misbehaving child, who is seeking the validation of parental approval, becomes jealous. This jealousy drives the child to go about trying to stay superior to their siblings, which might be done in several ways. When older siblings are born they get *all* of the attention from their parents because there are no other siblings to have to share their parents' attention with. As each new arrival to the family enters the picture, the oldest will have a portion of their parents' attention stripped away from them. If the parents themselves have grown up in an environment of jealousy, they unwittingly take actions with regard to their children that invoke more jealousy.

As the younger children reach the age of mobility when they begin to crawl well, much of the parents' attention is directed to the crawling child. At this point, as often occurs, the older child will try to find ways to regain their lost attention. And as is the nature with children who have poor hot water, seldom will they seek to regain this attention with love and affection toward their parents; but because the natural reflex of pain is to cry, they usually often make their first attempts to regain the lost attention by crying and with tantrums.

When these tactics get rejected by the parents, usually in the form of reprimand, it begins to set up an ugly precedent for the child. A person who is hurting from a lack of, or a *perceived* lack of, love, will often take what they can get with regard to attention. The reprimand translates as negative *attention*, but it is *attention* nonetheless and becomes the substituted attention for the child who is feeling deprived. At this point this negative attention typically becomes the goal for that child.

Children adapt to their parents' actions more quickly than most of us want to imagine. Newborn babies do this within a few days, and they very quickly develop a habit of crying in order to be picked up and cared for. When handled well by the parents, this is a very good thing, but when handled poorly it can be a bad thing.

Please do not misunderstand: It is very good to hug, hold, and show parental affection to your children of all ages, especially when they are infants. With proper and gentle action in the desired direction the parents will have this mastered before the child is six months old.

But, when a parent runs at *every* peep of their child, they will find the child quickly adapting to this, and then the child uses the only method he or she knows to convey his or her needs and *wants*—and that method is to cry.

The parents' effort to soothe the crying child sets a precedent for the child. When the child wants to be held, then the child will cry until he or she is picked up by the parent and consoled to the point of contentment. This period of time is the most difficult balance for young parents to learn: it is the balance of when to leave them cry, versus when to pick them up.

Please do not confuse this with touching, comforting, and holding a child. What we are discussing here is *only* in regard to picking up a child because the child is crying for no particular reason. Some children will outgrow this even if their parents did not hold their ground well on the matter. But, in many cases, this lack of fortitude that the parents exhibit is characteristic of those parents, and this characteristic often follows their child-rearing throughout the child's life in all areas of their child's life.

It is the first-born or oldest one or two children that typically experience this the most. After the third child, parents usually get the picture and promptly make adjustments. But, by this time, the damage is often already done with the older children, and they have already become demanding of their parents' attention in this negative way. This is where we, again, pick up on the earlier mentioned point of the older child becoming jealous.

The older children, wanting to maintain their status with their parents, will do as they have always done and will cry for attention. These crying spells often turn in to all-out tantrums. Parents are often stressed enough as it is due to having their attention pulled in so many directions from multiple children and life in general. Then when they have to deal with a child who is behaving with an unreasonable tantrum, the parents' frustration ensues and ultimately ends in anger and shouting directed at the child. Sometimes these tantrums are not shown with crying but instead use poor and disruptive behavior.

When people are frustrated long enough, they become angry; and when people become angry, the common result is to lash out. Usually this lashing out is verbal, and when that doesn't work, then a spanking or other punishment will often follow. Now, none of this is a problem in itself; the *problem* comes in when the parent chooses the wrong words and actions for the misbehaving child. This is one critical area where the perceived identity initiation can go very wrong.

Often the parent, for obvious reasons, will tell the child that they **are naughty** or that they **are bad**. This is the worst kind of thing for a child; they begin to get the attention that they crave from those people of whom they hold in the highest regard— their parents. When these people whom the child holds in such high regard begin to give the child attention by shouting in frustration and telling them that they *are* naughty, it reinforces that behavior. The child can now obtain this kind of attention whenever he or she chooses simply by misbehaving, and then each instance of this serves to reinforce the child's action. This has been happening to people since the dawn of mankind, and you likely recognize this in yourself or in your siblings to some extent. Adults also mistreat each other in this same way.

In our scenario here, the oldest child has now obtained the desired power and control over the parents' emotions, but is now marked as "naughty" or "bad" by the parent. To some degree, this exists even in the gentlest of families. The difference in each family is in *how* the older sibling chooses to obtain the attention.

In our scenario, the older child is now cast with a perceived identity of being "naughty" as expressed by the parents. Now that this "naughty" child knows how to manipulate the parents with this new-found ability, that child can draw attention away from the younger children by acting out, thus obtaining the desired attention. This is often done by taunting the other children, which accomplishes two ends for the "naughty" child: Because they have come to expect the negative feeling of the parents and have adapted to it, this becomes almost as a form of love to them. And when they taunt their siblings, the siblings will get angry and do just as the parents did. This has gained the child the attention of their siblings, and is likely going to grab the attention of their parents as well. With each occurrence of this situation, it even more deeply cements the perceived identity for the misbehaving child.

When a child receives the negative words of a parent, or even the negative words of their siblings, it is often very traumatic and impactful, and it will affect that child for many years to come.

Let's explore early relationships: What is a two-year-old to think when their siblings—some of the most important people in his or her life—inadvertently and subtly verbally beat the child down, and it goes unnoticed by the parents? Sometimes even the parents join in this behavior. At these younger ages it typically is not a calculated effort to destroy the child, but it is extremely damaging nonetheless. It's often difficult to detect these occurrences because everyone in the environment—in this case it is the family—is immersed in the activity, and they don't specifically realize that they are doing so or the damage it causes.

So what do we do about it? There is little that can be done, *unless* the person who is the recipient of the unwanted bad behavior begins to realize that something isn't right and decides to do something about it. To add to the problem, any awakening is often blocked by those who have been treating the person badly. Typically, as long as you continue to accept behavior that violates you, you *will* be subject to the person, or people, that are keeping you down by violating you. All of this continues throughout life, and it is all a part of our hot water. So, until we have the opportunity to experience a better environment with a different, cleaner, and more comfortable temperature water, we will never truly be able to feel the difference with regard to our hot water versus other people's water.

Your Teen and Young Adult Identity

When children are in their adolescent years, they interact with one another in individual and group settings. When they do, the children will commonly reflect each their own parents' expectations of them as they interact. The expectations that are a part of each child's hot water will be manifested in the child's behavior. In turn, the behavior of the children becomes the hot water between the children themselves, resulting in certain expectations of one another. This reinforces the behavior, and the behavior reinforces the expectations in a circular manner. This occurs with everyone the children interact with. Who they interact with often changes over time, but is greatly guided by their family's hot water. It is important to note that the parents' actual expectations of the child are usually not the same as the expectations that the parents profess out of their mouths with regard to the behavior of the children. That is to say, what parents *say they want* their children to behave like is often different than what they *expect* their children will behave like.

In the early stages of life—from birth to about five years old—the children are mostly exclusive to their siblings. The interaction with siblings also contains the parental dynamic. That is to say that, when a parent has expectations of a child and professes those expectations, either in word or in deed, then the other siblings of any one child will typically adopt those same expectations and treat that child according to those expectations.

Parents are the "parents" and are therefore usually on the watch for a child to mature and change, but siblings are not on the watch. Siblings often carry these feelings and expectations about each other for many years; these are typically the feelings and expectations that were started by the parents during the early years of the child's life. Depending upon the hot water of the family, the siblings could hang onto these expectations well into adulthood, and often will do so until they are finally forced to let go many years later due to their own deaths.

When the expectations of a sibling are happy and joyful, then there is little problem. But problems will arise when negative feelings are involved. When a second child comes into the picture it's typical for the first child to have some of the attention he or she was previously receiving from the parents be suddenly given to the newest addition to the family. And depending upon the hot water of the parents, the first child will exhibit behaviors that lead to jealousy. Most children do this to some extent, but the determining factor is often the parents' hot water and their behavior and attitude toward the older child.

If the parents' hot water is from an atmosphere of jealousy, then their hot water will blind them from realizing the necessary actions needed in order to correct the jealous behavior of the first child. Gone unchecked, this behavior will increase in intensity where the child can become a discontent rebel.

When children enter their teen years, their perceived identity typically becomes amplified. The more the children become aware of competing forces during their teen years, then the more they try to prove themselves. Some of this is to impress or prove themselves to others, but, in truth, they are actually trying to prove themselves to *themselves*. If a teen grew up with hot water that somehow indicated that they were not good enough, then they will work even harder to prove themselves to *themselves* and to others by trying to seek validation. This is what so much of the petty competition that we often see between high school students is all about. During the teen years this will also appear between friends and most commonly between siblings.

It's common for children to protest their perceived identities and rebel, only to step into a new perception that is even more difficult and often more damaging than the first. During the late twentieth century, *appearance* had much emphasis placed on it, and in an effort to make a statement of a perceived identity change, many people chose to get permanent piercings and tattoo markings on their bodies. This was regretfully done for the purpose of outwardly showing their newly adopted identities. In doing this, we often trap ourselves in a new perceived identity that cannot easily be changed because of the permanency of the method used. This has been going on for centuries, but during that time it was very common, and the frequency was increasing as well. An additional part of rebellion of perceived identity is unusual apparel, unusual hair, and unusual makeup. Those who wisely resist doing permanent alteration to their bodies can much more easily change their own perception of themselves because they don't have to see their later-unwanted permanent body alterations every day as they dress.

For those who choose the more permanent identity methods, such as tattoos, they will struggle far more to overcome that false identity because it is not easy to escape large, intrusive, permanent alterations to the body; thus, being reminded daily of past unwise decisions, causing them to feel devalued later in life. Clothes can be changed, hair can be changed, minds can be changed, but skin cannot be changed—you get only one skin, use it wisely. As these visual forms of identity change became more common, these permanent changes also became somewhat common for older adults who were also rebelling against their own incorrect perceived identities.

The perceptions that we are referring to here are not only the perceptions that others have of us, but this rebellion is mostly the rebellion of our own perception of our own perceived identities. Much of this is done in effort to stand out and get attention. In many ways it is a competition for attention with one's own perceived identity.

Your Adult Identity

As we enter our adult years our competing will continue. Competing identities are most readily noticed amongst men, but, throughout life, women certainly do compete as well. The intensity of this drops over time with most people. But at older ages, it is typically only when we feel directly threatened that we will we respond by competing. Yet, for some of us this will remain intense throughout most or all of our lifetime, and it will be a source of frustration and pain for us. Because this is our hot water, we are largely unaware that we are behaving in a certain way, while at the same time many of those around us see our behavior as peculiar.

When we were young children, not many of us noticed our own behavior because our family was the extent of our hot water. When we entered high school we were still mostly around people who we grew up with, and *they* were also a part of our hot water.

Community is a part of our hot water too. In many smaller communities, you only need go back three or four generations and you will see that many of the people are closely blood-related. Often the blood relationship was that of siblings in many of those communities. This means that your ancestor's hot water was shared with your friend's ancestor's hot water. However, because no one's hot water is identical, there will be some minor differences. But in close-knit communities, these differences are often very small and not easily noticed. In fact, community hot water is a big part of what makes them a *community* to begin with.

Hot water is also cultural; in fact, hot water is what creates a culture. If someone's hot water is 100 degrees and their friend's hot water is 101 degrees, then they will hardly notice the difference, if at all. This is the reason that they seem to get along so well to begin with. People in our own community all share certain parts of our own hot water as common without even realizing it.

Our heritage (or culture) is often only thought of as our traditions—religious, celebratory, or other. These traditions or customs don't stop at the level of a festival of some sort. This obviously includes the way we dress and the way we speak, such as our language and dialect, and goes far beyond that.

What I am referring to is not the obvious and overt cultural hot water, but rather the subtle cultural hot water. You will see this in almost any small city; good or bad, all communities have hot water attitudes. Because of the subtleness of the hot water of a community, the people within the community can go almost anywhere within that community and have no thought of any differences, especially in a small community (with the exception of the differences between individual families and their personal family hot waters).

The environmental hot water of a community is often built on family and generations of children and parents doing their hot water and continually passing it on to their children. In turn, the children grow up and pass it to their children and so on. Religion and politics are an enormous part of community hot water; this is most noticeable in smaller communities that remain tight-knit, because, as mentioned earlier, these communities are often heavily blood-related, thus they grew up in the same family of relatives.

People become aware of the differences of their hot water when they leave their community and venture outside of the safety of the communal hot water. We become aware, not specifically of the concept of the hot water, but rather that there is a difference between us and the new people we are experiencing. We typically notice this most when we travel. We will go into one city and think that the people were very rude, and in another city we feel that the people were very friendly, kind, and helpful. Then in another city we may have felt almost at home (whatever that may be for you), all of which is based upon each community's collective hot water.

Once we have left our teen years and we enter into the workforce we see this same effect. It's common for people to go away to college, and then when done they get a job in a place far from where they grew up, or they simply relocate for a particular job, any of which makes us become more aware of our hot water differences due to our new environment. Even if *you* didn't move away, but instead simply got a job near home, there will be others who you work with that came from another area with different hot water. Depending upon your hot water, and the differences between your hot water and their hot water, you might feel as if you want to either like or dislike the person.

For many of us, these differences are enough to get us to begin to understand that there are other people in the world that see things differently than we ourselves see things. Seeing these differences causes us to become aware and sometimes this causes us to start to make changes. Thus, as we get older, we grow out of our old hot water at least to some extent. This is simply because we meet more people who are different than ourselves and we begin to realize and accept this. The younger we are, the smaller our world of people who we meet. The older we are, the larger our world of people who we meet.

How Your Environment Affects Your Perceived Identity

With regard to religion and politics, (truth be told, they are truly inseparable) we have a tendency to think that the separation of Church and State is new to our era. The Church and State battle, has, in some form, been raging on for millennia, and it all has to do with communal hot water.

When our hot water is of a far different temperature or quality than another community's hot water, then as a whole, each community will somewhat be at odds with each other, just as individuals are. When this happens in a community, then the leaders of the community who all have their own personal hot water usually try to protect the hot water of their own community. To some extent this is good, but historically it has led to war and much bloodshed when taken too far.

People are outraged when a country chooses to go to war. Part of the reason is that the people do not want to be seen as "war mongers" like those who we have seen around the world throughout history who oppress people. The reason that people don't like this is because the personal hot water of a single dictator can impose his or her will, and hot water, on everyone through means of *using military force.*

When we see this kind of oppressive behavior internationally, we realize that something's not right. During the eighteenth, nineteenth, twentieth, and twenty-first centuries, the United States of America became a powerful nation for the very reason that its principal intent was to preserve the hot water of individuals. This was done by *not* allowing others to force their hot water on the citizens of the United States, which is what many of the United States' citizens died for in wars. In this particular case, the protection of individual hot water is referred to as "freedom."

During that era the United States of America had a very protective policy about personal freedom. This became a part of the hot water of the country from the country's birth onward, and even from before it was established as an independent entity. Eventually, certain expectations of what "freedom" is had arisen in the culture. When outside countries needed assistance in protecting the freedoms of the people of their respective country or land, then the United States would step in to assist them. However, in the late twentieth century and early twenty first century many of the citizens of the United States of America became confused and afraid due to the freedom and safety that was a normal part of their own hot water. Many saw it as oppressive when their leaders made decisions to assist other countries in protecting the freedom of the people of those other countries. Viewing this assistance as oppressive is because of the hot water of freedom. Freedom allows for us to do as we please, but without a very important key, freedom will always degrade. We'll discuss this critical *key* in a later chapter.

No matter what the level of community, whether it is global community, country or nation community, city community, family community, or personal community, the method that hot water uses is all the same. The circumstances may differ, but the method is *always* the same.

I want you to recall that the concept behind **your** *Hot Water* is that you have become accustomed to your hot water, just as your hand will become accustomed to *actual* hot water. You no longer sense it as hot, and instead it feels *normal* to you. This is not good or bad, it simply **is**.

Have You Become "The Bad Guy"?

Since this book is about understanding and improving our own lives, we need to understand that, depending upon who you are, or maybe rather, what position you are in with regard to the relationship examples we listed that might apply to you, you may now feel as if you are either the bad guy or the victim.

Regardless of which position you feel you are in, it is *you* who can improve your own life. This book will likely have a higher appeal to the *victims* who are being hurt, than it will to the so-called "bad guy." This is because a person who is hurting others does not feel the pain that they inflict upon others; and while they sort of know, they typically don't fully realize how much their words and deeds hurt the other people who they interact with. With that said, it is important to know that the so-called "bad guy" is often the one who is in more pain deep-down inside. This isn't because when they hurt you they feel badly for doing so—that goes mostly unnoticed by them. But deep inside they are usually in much turmoil, and it is that *turmoil* that causes them to treat other people in the manner that they do. This turmoil is their hot water and it is the source of their pain.

It is possible for the so-called *bad guys* to not even realize that they are hurting others. If this is the case, then we usually only need to explain to them that what they're doing hurts us, and they will immediately stop *if* what we are saying is true. If they do not stop when asked, then they have problems that reside deep within themselves that they're not dealing with. This is true for people at any age. The person who is doing the action that is hurting you has both a perceived identity of themselves, and a perceived identity of you. Depending upon your own hot water, your feelings about the actions of the person may or may not be valid. Sometimes we have to look deep within to find the truth.

While most of this, so far, seems to implicate the bad guys, there is another side to this which is that of *hiding*. When we make mistakes, we will typically hide those mistakes. When this becomes habitual, the hiding then becomes a part of our hot water. Then when someone calls out our error, we try to hide the error, possibly with shouting or belligerence. We attack the person who is pointing out our error to us, and we treat the notification of error as if it is a deliberate attack on us. When we do this, **we** have rendered **ourselves** **un-teachable** and have officially become the "bad guy."

All of your life-experiences, combined, have affected what you think, what you do, how you feel, and how you behave. All of the subtleties of your hot water have become your perceived identity. The good things and the bad things, together, have all formed the way you and others see **you**. This applies whether things are true or not true, and whether things are good or bad. It is in your political beliefs and in your religious beliefs. It is in the way you dress and in the way you walk. Everything you have experienced, done, had done to you, said, heard, what you decided upon, and chose—all of it has, in some form, become a part of your perceived identity. It can even be an opposite effect, where your response was in opposition to something you did, said, heard, or had done to you. All of this has affected the perception you have of yourself and the perception that others have of you.

Are You the "Inner-City Kid"?

At some point, most people have likely seen **or** heard a report where some inner-city kid was taken out of an economically and socially poor situation, and then was given the opportunities that many well-to-do people have. When there is an *expectation* of the inner-city kid to rise up and to be good and desirous of learning a new way, then, typically, they *will* rise to the challenge.

In some cases, a person who is transplanted into a new environment will fail by falling into past expectations and into their own self-expectations. This is where the importance of an individual's perceived identity is most profound. The reverse financial situation is also often able to overcome: When a person who has been brought up around money falls into a destitute situation, they are often able to overcome the circumstances. All of this is because of their hot water.

Living a status quo life is fine; most of us do this and live happily-ever-after. But, excelling is even better, especially when you contribute to the betterment of mankind. What is tragic is when people are *less* than they should be. Some people will get offended by the last statement because it could be interpreted as, "You're not good enough!" However, that is not at all the meaning. Whether you are a very successful individual, or you simply succeed by living your happily-ever-after life, you're still a productive member of society. But when you have been held down by your environment and have low self-worth from being held down, then you are living in an unfair and cruel world. This world is harsh and cutting at times, and the worse it gets, then the worse it gets. This effect is the central issue facing all of us.

The concept of what our perceived identity is, happens to be very important and it comes down to what others think of us and what we think of ourselves (or what we see ourselves as.) *What we see ourselves as* is a slippery slope and some attention needs to be directed to this subject.

We typically feel compelled, by some unknown force, to follow the perceptions that we and others have of ourselves; and we typically fulfill those perceptions no matter what they are. Our difficulty with this comes in when, deep down inside, we truly know that something is not right with these perceptions. I don't believe that people are losers or winners, but rather, that people have or have not overcome the negative perceptions of, and about, themselves. On the surface it seems easy to spot winners—just follow the money and the neighborhood, right? Ah, not so fast!

There are many inner-city citizens who are flat broke and live in not-so-great communities but are very happy, loving, and kind people. Conversely, there are many suburban folks who are affluent and are very unhappy, mean, and even hateful. They have their high-paying jobs, good schools, new cars, huge houses, and all the rest that accompanies affluence; yet, they hurt inside and often hate their situation, or worse, they even hate themselves and humanity. This is clear proof that money solves little in this regard.

We can clearly see by the number of problems in destitute, inner-city neighborhoods that, statistically, people in those neighborhoods have more problems. Lack of money plays a role in their problems, but more of it has to do with their perceived identity and personal hot water, and maybe more simply put, it has to do with their self-worth and communal hot water. Often, the self-worth is also the cause of their financial lack. Living in poor financial or poor mental conditions reduces our self-worth and causes a multitude of reciprocal and cascading troubles. This is often a considerable problem, with most of the end effect being mental poverty and/or low self-worth.

Mental poverty cuts across all classes, religions, and peoples. It knows no bounds, with the singular exception of true mental wealth. True mental wealth is the *only* thing that can stop mental poverty. The greatest part in all of this is that *it is free* and it can be obtained in an instant. When we can dig up the courage to become truly mentally wealthy, then we quickly begin to see and experience the importance of our identity. When we understand the importance of our identity, then we can overcome *any* future problems that we face.

What are Mental Wealth and Your Mental Bank Account?

While there truly is no difference in a person who is mentally poor who lives in the inner-city, and a person who is mentally poor and lives in the upper-class suburbs, it is usually easier to detect mental poverty in the inner-city than it is in the upper-class areas. This is because, in poor areas, the mental poverty cannot be hidden with riches.

Since we, as a society, tend to view everything, including ourselves, in a very superficial way, we believe that the big fat paycheck and a great big house makes us a success. Riches seldom hurt, but they also seldom help. What financial wealth can do, as just stated, is to hide mental poverty. Thus, as long as the bills are paid, the house is big, and the money is there, then the perception is that all is well, but in many cases "all is well" is simply *not* true.

Any of us who have been there, or know people in the well-to-do suburban lifestyle, know, all too well, that there is often much discord, unrest, and unhappiness in the homes and hearts of some of us who have had, or now have, a suburban lifestyle.

Even for those who have been blessed enough to have been brought up in mental wealth, all of what has been discussed regarding our hot water and mental wealth and poverty are often still unknown to us. Until we each ask these questions within our own hearts and minds, the message is very difficult for us to even begin to realize.

Don't let mental wealth fool you. Let's take a few moments to recognize some overshadowing factors. Money, lack of need, mental wealth, great social status, and other such aspects of life overshadow mental state, and then hide what is really going on in the heart and mind of a person. You may find it odd that "mental wealth" was listed in the lot of aspects. Mental wealth, in itself, is very good; the problem for people who are mentally wealthy is that they often do not specifically know or understand that they are mentally wealthy. While it's good to be mentally wealthy, unless you understand *why* you are mentally wealthy, you can easily and quickly spiral into mental poverty when troubles occur and, but sadly, you will not fully understand *why* those troubles occurred.

To get a better grasp on why this is a problem, you can think of being mentally wealthy like a rich kid who inherited a few million dollars after never having to pay for anything while growing up, and also never understanding the need to monitor the funds. For that child, everything is fine until the funds run out and troubles occur. Not having fully understood why the money was there and the need to manage it properly, the child will suddenly be in a situation that will leave him or her perplexed and destitute when all of the money has been spent.

What happened? Where did the money go? Well, mental wealth works the same way: As long as you are *un*aware that you are mentally wealthy, you won't know enough to monitor your mental bank account containing your mental wealth. Then when problems occur you'll wonder what happened.

You might be thinking, "If someone is mentally wealthy, then that won't happen." In a sense this is true, but there are many people who get by this way in life. They have a generally good disposition and all is well, but when truly tough times come upon them they crack and break down, often ending in broken families and broken lives. When trouble occurs this will happen with the majority of those who have mental wealth but do not have the proper and needed awareness *about* their mental wealth.

True mental wealth is unstoppable! This doesn't mean that you'll never experience difficulty. On the contrary, it is likely that you will recognize and face more and more difficulty in life the more truly mentally wealthy you become. The difference between *true* mental wealth and *typical* mental wealth (which is the same as mental poverty) is that *when* difficulties appear in your life, you will deal with those difficulties unafraid, confident, and ready for the challenge; thus, causing the troubles to quickly depart from your life. Where with *typical* mental wealth and mental poverty, panic will often ensue at the slightest sign of trouble, which commonly results in irrational behavior and irrational decisions. Those who have obtained true mental wealth can handle very difficult problems as if those problems are of no concerning matter to them; but those who are trapped in mental poverty will buckle under the pressure of even the smallest of problems.

To make this point stronger and clearer, there are people who are deemed "mentally retarded" or "mentally handicapped" who have more true mental wealth than most of us do. They have overcome their handicap and are loving and happy. Though they desire so, some cannot even feed themselves, and yet they are mentally happy; which is truly a wonderful mental place to be regardless of whether or not you have a "handicap."

Chapter 5

Do You Like Yourself?

After reading the previous chapter you probably have a good idea of where some of what you think, say, and do comes from. You have probably also realized what might be behind the behavior of *others*. In this chapter we're going to focus specifically on *you*. I would like you to pause for a moment and think of how you felt about yourself *before,* and how you feel about yourself *after* reading this book up until this point. (Look at the notes you wrote about yourself, and also consider what you have read here so far) Some people could feel better, and some worse. This will depend upon what you have noticed about yourself and others, but regardless of how you feel about yourself now, the remainder of this book will be of tremendous assistance to you. What you need to do is to ask yourself, "Do I like myself?" and then ask, "*Why* did I answer that question the way that I did?"

Are You an Aggressor?

This chapter addresses those who are not fully happy and are hurting and not pleased with their perceived identity. Because your hot water has been growing with you all of your life and changing with every new experience, including meeting new people, you likely have not thought much about your identity and likely did not realize that you have this "hot water" we keep discussing. This means that up until now, you have been mostly unaware and have been generally displeased with some things in your life. People make you angry but you're not quite sure why. You likely have an urge to conquer and beat someone in a competitive nature. You often feel down, sad, depressed, or unloved, especially if you are defeated in your competitiveness.

Those who were fortunate enough to have been brought up in healthy hot water tend to go through life with few problems or issues, and they seem to experience very little conflict. On the other hand, those who had difficult hot water while growing up have had conflict as a regular part of their hot water. Conflict is irritating, and it occurs when people do not care about others, or will not, or cannot, see that others may have differing thoughts and opinions. Conflict also occurs when we fail to admit our own error, to ourselves and, when needed, to others.

When we won't take the time to see others for what they *truly* are, then we have *chosen* to be blind. When we become discontent with our own perceived identity, we then come to expect conflict and often invite conflict into our hot water. This problem has two sides to it: Some people are antagonists and others are more passive, but both types generally have conflict as a part of their hot water. The antagonist will often be more confrontational, but will reject any confrontation made toward themselves. The more passive personality becomes accustomed to the antagonist's confrontations and aggression, and that then becomes a part of the passive person's own hot water. The aggressor also becomes accustomed to being able to be confrontational and that becomes a part of the aggressor's hot water.

In many families, this blindness continues and is accepted as normal because it is a part of the family's hot water. Tensions will grow if this is the case, and eventually the passive person will begin to resist the confrontations. When this happens, the aggressor sees the resistance as a confrontation and as a challenge to their hot water causing them to become even more aggressive towards the passive person. *If* the victim of this aggression backs down, neither the victim nor the aggressor can ever truly be happy, and they will both always be displeased with each other in the long run. Even if the more passive person, who in this case is the victim, actually does stand their ground, often the hot water of the aggressor is to treat everyone else in the same aggressive way. And, unless *everyone else*, as a collective group, holds their ground against the aggressor, the aggressor has no reason to change—**ever**.

Most aggressive confrontations happen in a small-group or in one-on-one settings; this eliminates the possibility for large group rejection of the aggressive behavior. If the passive person ever decides to stand up for themselves against the aggressor, then the aggressor's hot water causes the aggressor to blame the passive person and accuse them of being the aggressor. In the event that this is done in a more public situation, the aggressor will often point fingers and dig very deep for faults in the passive person. This confuses the bystanders; and for fear of being attacked themselves by the aggressor, seldom will those bystanders come to the aid of the passive person who is being unjustly attacked.

When the passive person chooses to step outside of their hot water, it will make waves with an aggressor. This will have a profound effect on the hot water of both people. Depending upon the strength of the passive person, it will either embolden them, or make them even more passive (the latter being more common with passive people).

When people back down from an aggressor, they feel weak and displeased with themselves. This becomes a part of their hot water, which forms their perceived identity, and they end up not feeling good about themselves.

Do You Find Joy in Your Identity?

Ask yourself, "Do I find joy in my identity?" Most people will have a hard time answering this question, not truly fully understanding its meaning. Because we have not been taught the importance of *understanding*, this question might be taken as "Am I happy?" But that is not at all what it means. When you evaluate yourself, as you have been doing through these first several chapters, do you see any places of *joy* and *contentment* in your own hot water?

Most people who pick this book up are likely doing so because they don't have any *true* joy in their hot water or in their resulting perceived identity. When first asked the question, "Do You Find Joy in Your Identity?" we often go into a rant about how bad our lives are. Then after our rant to air our feelings and a bit of discussion, little burning embers of joy may begin to glow.

I use this analogy of "little burning embers" because much of the original hot water of our personal, family, and cultural parts of life have mostly snuffed out our joy. When we were children, we wanted to be firemen, doctors, nurses, mommies or daddies, and much more! Then a world of contaminated hot water poured down in us and told us that what we wanted was not acceptable or that it was impossible. After enough repetitions of this we came to believe it—or at least we thought we believed it.

When we're hurting, most of us don't feel that we have any joy in our lives. For many of us, it seems that every time we do find glowing embers of remaining joy, someone is right there to stamp on it and snuff it out. It's when this happens that you need to understand that you still have joy hiding somewhere in your identity, so don't ever give up. Find reasons to draw that joy back to the surface and fan its flames! We will discuss how you can reclaim your joy after we fully understand our hot water.

This book is about *you* getting to the bottom of *your* sadness or discontentedness of life and of others. With that in mind, *you* must, then, observe others around you. Do they seem to have joy in *their* perceived identities? And, what part of them are you looking at?

When observing others, you will see a great number of people who are looking at what other people have, and they make the assumption that the other people "have it made." We do this and believe that they're happy and that their lives could not be any better. It is the all too common "the grass is greener on the other side" problem. We can also observe people who have plenty, but are watching those who have little while thinking, "How good it would be to live a simplistic life."

While situations exist where someone has much wealth and is living in joy, or that they lead a simple life and live in joy, the reality is that far too many of us are still troubled because of our own hot water. We don't realize the troubles others feel deep inside, and because of our lack of recognition of this, when we look at them, we often feel that their grass is greener, when, typically, it is not.

The grass on the other side is often just as dry and full of miserable and unhappy weeds as it is on our own side. But somehow, through their hot water, they have learned how to *ignore* the things that hurt them in their lives, and so they appear happy through their mastery at ignoring things. Many people paint their dry brown weeds green with the green of their money and call it lush and green grass. Part of their hot water includes their method of coping with heartache and discontentment. When this is in our hot water it affects our behavior, and our behavior affects our hot water.

People who *appear* well-to-do are often simply living on borrowed money just like people with a lower financial standing. They are struggling to pay their bills just the same as the person who has far less, and they both feel the same pain—it's just that the money numbers are either larger or smaller. Many people who have a lot of money and little or no debt, still struggle in life due to their hot water, especially those who have had their money given to them and did not have to work for it and do not understand.

We often look at the rich and think how good it would be to have their money, but, for them, money is a part of their hot water and is often an enormous problem because it has the effect of disguising their pain, much like painting the grass green disguises the dry weeds. The luxury that money brings can sooth some of their pain, or it can at least appear to sooth it. But, this doesn't mean that everyone with money has poor hot water. Our hot water has more to do with our understanding and views of life. However, money is very proficient at hiding the true problems that most of us have.

When observing others, realize that you are not doing this to judge, mock, or ridicule them. You are doing it to better understand them *and* yourself. When you take the proper approach in doing this, you will soon see who is actually hurting and who is not. Some people have a lot of practice in hiding their pain—*hiding* pain is a part of their hot water. It gets to a point where we don't realize that we're hurting to the extent that we are. When this is the case, as it is with most of us, it's more difficult to see what's beneath the surface of what we see in the perceived identities of those around us.

We need to look deep and understand that most people have people and/or circumstances in their lives that steal away their joy. Believing that someone is living in a state of joy, when they are not, is simply an unintended lie. When we fall prey to believing this unintended lie, then we will often feel worse about ourselves than is reasonable or needed. You should not be reveling in the fact that many rich people are in great pain too, but rather, realize that regardless of how things appear, you're not living in pain all alone while the rest of the world is living in joy.

Most people are *not* living in joy. Sure, we all laugh and have a good time now and then, but a great amount of the population is hurting because of the nature of their hot water. Don't believe the lie! Believing that everyone else is living in joy when they are not will make you feel worse than you need to feel about your own hot water and its resulting perceived identity. We see the signs of discontent in those around us who do not have joy, but we have learned to ignore those signs. We, instead, focus on their tangible things, such as their money, and then we subconsciously choose those things that we feel bring joy.

Do not mistake this section to indicate that no one has *true* joy, because the truth is there are very many who do. But, on a percentage basis, it is the minority of people who actually have *pure* and *true* joy.

Do You Smile When You Look in the Mirror?

A good indicator of your perceived identity's feeling of worth is seen when looking into the mirror. Most of us do this every single morning when we get up. Do you ever smile when you look at yourself in the mirror? Do you have a difficult time looking yourself in the eye? It may come as a surprise to you, but people often do not look themselves in the eye when looking into the mirror. We comb our hair, brush our teeth, and shave or put on makeup, but seldom do we take a couple of seconds to look ourselves in the eye.

Many people specifically avoid looking *themselves* in the eye and often won't look others in the eye when speaking to them. If you look at yourself in the mirror and say to yourself, "*I am awesome!*" it should bring a smile to your face or at least a happy grin. True smiles are partly a sign that a person has at least some real joy in their life, but the real evidence is in their actions.

A *real* and *true* smile is the *result* of what is going on with a given aspect in your identity. Some counselors tell depressed people to smile, or even to just pretend, because, "It will make you *feel* better." This is often false and of little use, but in ways it's better than grumbling all day long. I am not going to tell you not to smile. In fact, sometimes just forcing ourselves to smile can snap us out of the doldrums when we only have few underlying problems.

Culture has created vices with regard to our hot water and our perceived identities. We have a difficult time believing that we will ever feel joy without buying something that some company wants to sell to us, and/or we have a difficult time believing that we could ever feel joy without taking some sort of mood enhancing medicine, or other emotionally altering substance. Smiles, faked, are not true. Faking a smile is like putting a bandage on a wound. A bandage may stop the bleeding for a while, and the wound may even begin to heal, but if the thing that cut you to begin with is still there, then you are certain to get wounded again whenever you're near it.

Maybe this analogy is better: If a mole is undermining a dam, you can patch the holes that are causing the leaks, but if you don't remove the problem, then the leaks will continue to appear because the cause of the leaks is the mole's digging. Faking a smile is nothing more than patching the hole. The problem with this is that the *reasons* that you are not smiling with true joy *still remain* in your life, just like the mole still remains in the dam.

The reasons that we don't smile as much as we should, are strictly because of our hot water. Our hot water is **our** hot water and we are accustomed to it; and therefore, we don't realize that we're not smiling; and more importantly, we don't realize why we are not smiling. This is our hot water, and our hot water has formed a smile-less perceived identity.

It's not wrong to simply choose to smile when you're hurting inside. But it certainly is not the solution to solving your pain. If you're in a group setting it's good to smile and be kind and courteous to others. But if you smile all the time when you're not really happy then, in a sense, you are faking your smile or, maybe better stated, faking your joy. You are lying to others. And what is even more damaging to you is that you are lying to yourself. This will not help you, nor will it allow anyone else to help you.

If you're deliberately lying to yourself and to others, then you're giving the false impression that everything in your life is good when truly it might not be. When we do this, others are observing us, thinking that we have it made and that we're always happy. They believe that we have very green grass on our side of the fence... Sound familiar?

When we choose to fake a smile we often take an all-or-none approach and we try to give the impression that we're always happy and that things are wonderful in our lives. When we observe this from the outside, we make the foolish assumption that all really is well whenever we see these fake smiles. All of this becomes a part of our hot water and a part of other people's hot water, and it becomes a part of the shared hot water between the observer and the person who is using a false smile.

We see through the fake smiles, but this is usually done unknowingly by us. Most people can detect when things are not quite right for another person, but the hot water of the world is to ignore and avoid conflict. When we see the subtle inconsistencies in the tiniest of details and in the smiles around us, it causes conflict within us; but our hot water has led us to ignore this conflict, and we say and do nothing about it. Smiles can be faked, but are generally a good indicator for yourself as to whether or not you have any joy in your perceived identity.

My aim is not to have you smile because someone told you to smile, but rather to get you to smile as a result of the pure joy you are about to have in your life. This is a smile that no one can *ever* take from you!

Do You Like What You Have?

Many of us buy things as a quest for joy. Has this ever happened to you: You decide you want something that you have seen somewhere, so you make the decision to actually purchase it. You can't buy it right away because you have to save some money in order to afford this new thing that you want. During the time when you are saving, you're excited about getting the new item and you speak with great enthusiasm about it to your friends and family, often telling them how good it will be when you finally get the item and how *then* you will be happy.

You save and save until you finally have enough money. Then you go to make your purchase and bring the cherished item home. After playing with it or using it for a couple of days, you feel empty or maybe disappointed. Not in the item itself, because it's doing everything that it promised, but rather, you feel disappointed in your expectation of the fulfillment that you felt the item would bring to you.

That scenario is very common for people all across the land who are looking for joy in an item. I am not saying you shouldn't have good things or be excited about getting good things. But the things that you have are nothing more than *things*. When you make a purchase you should be happy with your purchase. If you buy something and you have an empty feeling shortly after the purchase, then your hot water is causing the problem. Is there a cure for this? Yes there is!

Look around your home and at your life in general. Take a few moments to absorb all of the *things* that you have. Then begin to ask yourself, "Do I like these things? Do I want these things? Why did I buy this thing or that thing?" Recall how you felt when you got the items: Were you excited? Did you like it then? Do you like it now? How many *items* or *things* do you have? *Grasp it—it is many.*

You don't need to get an actual count, rather get a grasp on how often you bought things and were excited, and then how often the fulfillment dissipated shortly after the purchase.

Buying things is not wrong. In fact, it's good. It keeps people working and can ease much in life and make life more comfortable and more pleasant to live. It's our *true* reason *behind* the actual purchase that's a problem for us—the cause of that problem is our hot water.

Culture is now, and has been for a great many years, built upon the consumption of goods. Ever since the concept of bartering has come about, consumption has had its hold on the citizens of the world. When common coinage and currency came about, the *value* of—what you had to do for what you received—became of less concern to people.

When our hand is filled with cash, we quickly forget what we had to do in order to earn that money and our eyes are, instead, set upon all that we can do with the cash in hand. In many ways, the money becomes devalued in our hearts, and this is a part of our hot water. Almost everyone works for a wage and receives currency in return to spend as they see fit. We save and buy, and save and buy. This whole situation gets even worse when we *borrow* money to make similar purchases. And we can add to this that many people don't actually ever even see the cash because most purchases are made with checks, cards, or by other electronic means.

We accumulate many things that ease our lives, but many of us place our focus on some *thing* that we believe will make us happy. We then anticipate the purchase and, finally, make the purchase. Then, shortly thereafter, we feel sad, let down, and often remorseful that we made the purchase to begin with. *Things* can make us comfortable, and in part, occupy us; and so we allow ourselves to believe that *things* can make us truly happy—**but they cannot**!

Most of us purchase in this way to some extent, but when we look around us, how many of those purchases that we were so looking forward to making, do we now feel the same happiness about as we did on the day that we bought them? The answer is likely, very few if any at all.

Then, should we sell everything and stop buying things all together? No, probably not. That has to be a personal decision. When we buy things for the wrong reason, it's not the things that are the problem; the problem is our underlying purpose for making the purchase to begin with. If we decide to stop buying things or even to sell everything, doing so will not change the cause of our actual motives. So choosing to sell everything, or to no longer buy things, will not solve your problems; nor will the usual completing of purchases and buying things to satisfy yourself.

Reconsider next time you want to make a purchase, and take a moment to recall all of the instances where you made your purchase and later regretted it, or felt disappointed and let down after you bought the item. This effect is far worse for us when we buy an item on credit and still have to pay for it after we are no longer feeling the brief rush of happiness that was created by making the purchase.

We often have deep regrets for buying things because we often still owe for an item that we truly no longer care about. Take the time right now to think, "Do I like what I have?" This can include clothing, cars, your house, even friends, and also your very own perceived identity. Many things in your life will seem good, but it is the *motivation* that caused you to buy those things that we are actually bringing to attention here.

What is More Important to You, Your Comfort or Being True?

Make a decision: What is more important, your comfort or being true? If this seems to be an implicating question, that's because it's meant to be. I want you to really think about what all of the *things* in the world mean, and whether or not they can actually bring real, true, and lasting joy into your life. Everywhere you look, possibly including your own life, you will see many people buying and buying, trying to make life more comfortable with their purchases. We even go deeply into debt in order to feel comfortable or excited or happy. The resulting debt is usually a very heavy burden for many of us and is a source of much of our grief. For far too many people, the debt still remains long after the item of comfort has been thrown into the trash.

The part that's difficult for people to understand is that this is all a part of our hot water. This is just the way life is for most of us, but we don't quite realize it in those terms; it has permeated every ounce of our being and we simply don't grasp the fact that we often torture ourselves in this way. It's a relative few people who have tapped into being able to be true to themselves and are able to avoid this.

You can research almost any religion, and you will see certain sects of that religion's group who have given up material things in an effort to find true and lasting joy. Some may find it, but most still have the same problem of not being truly joyful after everything has been given up. They might have relieved the stresses that ownership brings with it, but their hot water is still *their* hot water; and they cannot find the pure joy that they seek because they're blinded within their own hot water. We can meditate and hum for relaxation and distraction from the world, but we cannot truly achieve pure joy without grasping the principle that we are discussing here in this book.

Even ridding ourselves of comfort items can be an act of comfort in itself. If we have many things in our lives, to the point where those things become a burden to us, then getting rid of them to ease our burden is an effort to make our life feel more comfortable to ourselves. But when all is completed, the underlying condition still exists. The underlying condition *is* the hot water which forms our perceived identity. Taking this comfort approach to our problems will not solve our problems. The underlying hot water *still* exists whether we are buying in order to make ourselves feel more comfortable, or liquidating in order to feel less burdened and therefore feel more comfortable. When we finally grasp this, then we no longer need to *pretend* that we're better after we *have things*, or after we *relieved ourselves of our things*, because it will be real and true.

Why We Do This

There's often an urgency that accompanies either case of: obtaining items, versus ridding ourselves of items. This urgency is an effort on our part to feel better *right now*. When we choose to make drastic moves then we often do temporarily feel better, but that feeling is fleeting. When we allow this behavior to become our hot water, the behavior becomes and acts as if it were an addiction, and we will repeat the behavior over and over to experience a brief and fleeting feeling of comfort. What happens is that we've replaced any feelings of true joy, security, and contentment, with temporary and often fleeting comfort.

With regard to replacing true joy with fleeting comfort, we must realize that rarely in our lives do most of us actually feel true joy. A part of our hot water is our lack of true joy, *and* our lack of recognition of that true joy. We all seek the true joy that I keep referring to, but as circumstances would have it, our hot water has blinded us from understanding that this is so.

Trying to fulfill our absence of joy with *things*, or even with *actions*, such as occupying yourself with activities like trips and vacations can possibly bring temporary satisfaction, but it will never truly fulfill us because our *true* purpose is to find joy. In the end, we will always want more and more, and never find fulfillment in any of it. It's good to get out and experience the world, but how much better will it be when you are in a state of true personal joy? What understanding your hot water offers you is **the map to your key**—a *key* that unlocks the treasure of true personal joy and the treasure of your true identity that no one can ever take from you.

Throughout our lives we are being told to settle for less than what we want, and to accept something other than what we want. This happens to the point of becoming part of our hot water. We become so accustomed to settling that we don't even recognize that we're settling—it just happens.

If we settle, then settling was almost certainly in our parents' hot water, and in their parents' hot water. Our hot water can be like a disease, *or* it can be like a healthy life filled with joy and contentment! But sadly, our hot water being like a disease is far more common to many of us, which is why, in this book, we are learning to detect and eliminate the evil roots that make our hot water so bitter.

The rare few that have escaped this effect have mostly done so by default. To them it was accidental—or maybe better stated, it just happened and they didn't realize it. These individuals have been the fortunate recipients of very strong healthy hot water, and because it is their hot water, most don't realize just how good they actually have it. They likely know that they are often happy and content, but seldom can they relate to those who live in infected hot water. It is only when someone points things out *in a detailed way* that we can see, with perfect clarity, *why* there are differences in people's hot water. We can certainly see the differences, but to us they are only differences, and those differences are a part of our hot water. We *won't* know why the differences exist or how they came to be **unless** we choose to begin to question these things.

To try to get a better grasp on your own hot water, imagine the following: If you were a drop of water dripped in to a crystal clear spring-fed mountain-lake, you would mix in and quickly become accustomed to the other lake water and you would become a part of it. Similarly, if you are a drop of water placed into a sewer, you will also blend in and become a part of the sewer water. You will become contaminated with everything you mix with; you become a part of it and it becomes a part of you.

But if you choose, you can become a drop of expensive oil that will not mix with the other water. You will resist and you will only mix in with oil of pure Truth. In doing so, you will always be separated out from the water, and this will allow you to be able to quickly and easily detect unacceptable differences. You will be like a brilliant star, shining brightly in the night sky. Space appears to be filled with endless darkness, yet a star so very far away is still noticed because it shines its light just as you will.

By now you should have a firm grasp on the term *your hot water*, what is meant by it, and how your familiarity of your own hot water blinds you. You also should have a good feel for the effect of your hot water on your perceived identity. Later we will discuss a deeper truth about our identities, which will give *you* power over your own life like you have never before experienced.

Before we move on with regard to how to make yourself shine as a star in the darkness, we must further explore what happens when our perceived identities go down the wrong path.

Chapter 6

Identity Heads Down the Wrong Path

So far we have discussed the methods of hot water and the effects those methods have on our perceived identities. We can chase this subject down a genealogical trail to the beginning of time, but doing so will only get us right back to where we are right now in the discussion. We'll see how our parents' hot water affected us, and how their parents' hot water affected them, and how their parents' hot water affected them, and on and on we could go all the way back to the beginning of time. And, when all is said and done, we will be left with one question: **Why?**

Why did our hot water become our poison and blindness to begin with? Well... the blindness part is for two key reasons: First is the fact that it is our hot water and we have become accustomed to it, which we have discussed at length. We can pin the blame about the condition of our hot water on our parents, and our parents can do the same to their parents and so on.

The other key reason is *ignorance*. What really is ignorance? While ignorance can be a *part* of our hot water, as we grow older each day *we* are still ultimately more and more responsible for our own hot water. We tend to ignore things in our life that we don't like, and our deliberate ignorance is most prominent when we feel that we will be rejected. So, let's take a look at the word *ignorance*.

Ignorance is to **ignore**.

Ignor-ance.

Why do we *ignore* something to begin with? There are a couple of key reasons that we do so: The first reason we ignore things is because we don't want to deal with a particular problem. And the second reason that we do it is because we're afraid—we fear. But the first reason is usually because we fear something having to do with our problem, so it's really *fear* that is the underlying root of it all.

We're not speaking about small things like, when people don't want to deal with something that's broken on their car so they ignore it. While people do ignore those sorts of problems, here we are referring mostly to problems between people. We fear dealing with the problems between ourselves and other people, which leaves us to ask: Exactly *what* are we afraid of—what do we fear? In a word, we fear *rejection*.

Do You Fear Rejection?

The fear of rejection is the foundation for almost all of the problems that we face in our world. We don't like being rejected on a personal level, because it hurts. Some people have become proficient at rejecting others, and other people have become proficient at seeking acceptance from others. When we seek acceptance from other people in this way we open ourselves up to their rejections. Rejection is why so many of us have gotten to a place in our lives where we don't have much in the way of aspirations.

Rejection and failure run hand in hand. In most aspects they are one and the same thing. Rejection makes us feel lowly about ourselves, as does failure. The fear of failure and the fear rejection are core to our problems. People who have become proficient at rejection have largely done so as a protective measure for themselves. You may wonder, "Protection from what?" Protection from being rejected of course.

Those who have become proficient at rejecting other people are usually not very accepting, and they have a tendency to come down very hard on others in judgment of them. They themselves have likely been exposed to much failure and rejection in some form and at some point during their lifetime. Sometimes their proficiency at rejection was formed while they were young, where they merely observed someone older who was close to them being hurt through rejection. The fear of being hurt through being rejected teaches us to reject in an effort to protect ourselves. By doing so, we do get some amount of protection; but, we also have cheated ourselves out of a full and robust life when we do this.

The fear of failure is a similar story; often, someone fails and is made to feel badly about it because family or other people mock them. This mocking is *rejection* to the person being mocked. This is because the other people are not accepting the circumstances; and rather than supporting the person, they condemn them and make them the butt of their cruel jokes.

Fear of rejection via fear of failure can also be from *observation* rather than being from *direct experience*. A child, who sees their parent, or maybe their sibling, made to be the butt of other people's jokes and condemnation, will typically take some sort of evasive action in order to avoid the pain they see the other person experience. All too often this is done by withdrawal or low ambition; and the deep-down reasoning or logic we use to choose this unfruitful path is that—if we don't try, then we cannot fail. In other words, we are afraid. While this is true, it gains you nothing in the long run and you *will* live a lackluster life when taking this approach to life.

This petty fear that has paralyzed our world for thousands of years can be overcome with a single key thought. It is arriving at this single thought that is difficult for us to do. The *fear* that we're speaking of is the core problem in *all* of humanity and in *all* of creation. I call the fear petty because it truly is petty; however, to those who are experiencing this fear there is nothing petty about it—*fear* drives our lives. In the way, when we have fear as a part of our life, then *every* decision that we make is built upon that fear. It's very traumatic to us, and most of us either have experienced this at some point in our past, or we are experiencing it on a regular basis as we live.

You acquire the ability to crush fear when you understand the principle that we are discussing in this book; and, as a result, you can gain total control over your life.

When we're unhappy, and we don't *understand* things, we become confused and often try to change our behavior. But we don't know what changes to make in order to make our problems go away. And when we live in fear, we then live unhappy, discontented, and unfulfilled lives.

In previous chapters we discussed the gravity of our hot water and the method that the hot water works on our perceived identities that brings us low in heart, mind, and soul. Because of the hot water effect, we don't understand exactly what is happening in our lives; and even though we see and live it every day, in the end, many of us are left dissatisfied in our day-to-day lives. When we're *un*-happy, it's much more difficult to see our way clear with regard to the problems in our life. Being "happy" also makes us blind to seeing that others are facing the same or similar battles in their own lives—we simply do not understand.

The hot water effect of our lives paralyzes us through our lack of understanding until the day we see the light. Here's the part that's really sad about this: Even those who have been blessed with great hot water can still fall into desperation. Why is this? It's because they don't understand that they, too, are in their own hot water. Even though they've got a jump on life, because, while growing up, they had clean hot water that was happy, ambitious, and showed little fear; they still suffer from the very same blindness that we all suffer from—this blindness is our hot water. Those who have been fortunate enough to have healthy hot water are where they are and they don't really get it, just the same as people with contaminated hot water are where they are and don't really get it. We simply do not recognize this because it is so normal to our everyday life.

If those who have healthy hot water *slowly* migrated into different, but poorer, circumstances, then those new circumstances slowly become a part of their hot water, and they won't realize the changes until it's too late because they didn't detect the subtle changes in water temperature. Only after reflecting on their past will they fully grasp the mounting changes; but then the change is often attributed to all of the wrong things. This is typically because we are prodding in the dark when we try to understand how we got to where we are in life. It's only when we *fully* understand this that we can gain control of our life. But until full realization enters our minds, we are bound by the shackles of our contaminated hot water. This "*understanding*" that I keep referring to is the foundation of rock that *true* and *lasting* success is required to be built upon in order to be *true* and *lasting*.

It is because we are blinded with our hot water that we do not understand. Our lack of understanding causes us to react differently than we would if we had full knowledge of what was actually occurring. We base our decisions *only* on what we *perceive* in our personal world. Proper conclusions cannot be made without *all* of the information. When we make decisions in our lives without full understanding of the fact that our hot water actually exists, then we make poor decisions more often than not. These decisions are a part of our behavior and they also affect our behavior—they are part of our hot water.

What is a poor decision? A poor decision does not need to be utter failure. Think of decision-making like this: Let's say that you want to take a vacation *and* learn something at the same time. You have a choice to explore the pyramids of Egypt, go to Hawaii, or go to the local beach. No one of these options is wrong; in fact, each one of them has its own merits. The pyramids offer information about another culture long ago, interesting engineering feats, a warm climate, and maybe a visit to the shore of the waters of the Nile, and many other sight-seeing opportunities. Hawaii offers island culture, opportunity to investigate active volcanoes, and warm sunny relaxing beaches. The local beach offers the comfort of home, relaxation, the potential of meeting a new friend from the local area, and refreshing water to frolic in. There are boundless opportunities in each choice *if* you look for such opportunities. Even the choice to not go at all is a choice. While there certainly are things we can do to make bad choices, in general, choices are simply choices provided those choices do not unjustly take from or harm others.

A "poor" choice is any choice that is based upon *fear* and stops you from doing what you truly want to do. A "bad" choice will harm both you and others. Our problem is our inability to look beyond our hot water to find what we each truly want in life.

In our vacation example, you might feel that money is an issue, so we'll dispel that and make the assumption, that for the person making the choice, that money is of no consequence. Let's imagine the person has a keen interest in ancient Middle Eastern history, but then chose to go to Hawaii because of *concerns* about flying far from home because of a tense political climate in the Middle East. Whether or not you think this decision is wise, the fact still remains that the person made a choice that they really did not want to make. Wise or not, they changed their behavior because of *fear.*

This example was drawn to get you to understand that people *do* base decisions upon their fears, and in this example it was done overtly so and for the safety and best interest of the person. What I want you to grasp before you move on is that we all do this same thing every day because of our hot water. And, also (think carefully as you read this next sentence), because of our hot water, we *do not realize* that we are doing so because of our hot water. When we make our decisions based upon fear, then our decisions are *poor* decisions. This doesn't make them wrong, but a decision could have been made that would have enhanced the life of the person making the decision and affected everyone around them for the better. If a decision hurts no one, then it is not a "bad" decision; although, it may be a "poor" decision.

Your Roots of Frustration

When we function by making decisions that do not best serve our needs and desires, we stall our lives and we don't live up to the gifts and true joy that is trapped in the abyss deep within us. When we do this day in and day out, a feeling of falling short of what we truly want in our lives grows deep within us and replaces our hidden natural gifts and joy. This too is a part of our hot water and is the cause of much pain and a source of *major* frustration for most of us. Not everyone feels this because to "reach for your dreams" is a part of some people's hot water. When I discuss this subject with people, often either their eyes glaze over because they can't quite seem to understand the concept, or they become frustrated simply by talking about it. If someone is far-removed from their problems, or their problems are currently not affecting them much, then they won't relate as easily. It's common for people to become frustrated and defensive when this subject is discussed. And with some people their eyes glaze over *and* they become frustrated and defensive. This typically all occurs because we do not want to address or deal with our actual problems, so we suffer the consequences of our unwillingness to address the problem directly. The consequences are that the best parts of our lives are greatly delayed for us, or even worse, the best parts of life are never achieved at all.

The defensiveness that people exhibit when discussing this topic is a false protection that we all attempt to use in order to protect our investment in our wrong and/or poor choices that have ultimately led to our frustrations that are the topic of discussion when we become defensive. You could compare this to someone defending their choice to keep fixing an old worn out car in a situation similar to the earlier car repair example, where the repair investment rivaled the value of the car. Our defensiveness is a reaction to our feeling of being attacked—it is our self-protection. None of us like to feel attacked, but even if our feeling is unwarranted, we still typically feel attacked when discussing *any* of our own shortcomings.

Additionally, we often feel foolish and exposed because of our wasted emotional investment. The frustration from making poor choices has an additional problem, which is that—frustration leads to more frustration—and this causes us to place barriers between ourselves and the *assumed* source of the frustration. There are certainly other reasons that cause people to become frustrated, such as other people actually doing us wrong, but we're not discussing that here. This section is about *your internal* frustration caused from *your own* poor choices, and what causes this and what it leads to.

In the years that I have had the opportunity to be alive on this earth, I have seen many people be frustrated in the ways just described, where they truly do not understand why they are in such a state of being. And I have seen people be very defensive about their choices that have led to this particular form of frustration. Those same actions are done to some extent by *all* of the people who experience this type of frustration.

Where Does Your Anger Come From?

Regardless of the type of frustration, frustration will always lead to anger when allowed to continue—*all* anger is frustration fully manifested. Even if the frustration is not the personal, internal type, the same is still true—*frustration* is the cause of anger. If someone is harming you in some form and you can't seem to communicate to them that you are displeased with the situation, and they obliviously continue to inflict the unintentional pain on you, then eventually you will become frustrated with them. When your frustration is allowed to continue long enough you *will* become angry with them.

Uninvolved third-party persons are often the victims of our anger when it's caused by other people who are oblivious about their harmful actions. We fear fully confronting the person who is actually frustrating us. There are several reasons for this: One reason is because we don't want to hurt them. Another reason is that we don't want them to hurt us by telling us that they will not comply with our request. And last, we fear that they will be angry at us. When we eventually allow our frustration to show itself in the form of anger, our anger is often released through some sort of aggression against some poor soul who had nothing at all to do with our frustrating situation.

We, as people, must do that which is in our hearts. And if we do not, then we eventually become frustrated. When frustration goes unchecked it turns into anger.

In a manner similar to when *someone else* causes us pain and we lash out at the innocent, the same is true of our internal frustration from *making our own* poor choices. It's easy to spot the problem when someone hurts us, but when we are doing it to ourselves, only *we* truly know it; and because of our hot water, we are blind to it.

It is the fact that we are blind to it that causes us to be frustrated and angry, which is because we don't understand. In the Bible it says, "My people perish for lack of knowledge." How true this is! When we have walked our hot water's *path of frustration* long enough, our anger comes to the surface, and is usually taken out on those who are closest to us. But it can be taken out on anyone who crosses our path in any way. It is in this misdirected energy where our real problems reside. This undeserved and poor treatment of our fellow man is the source of the bitter hot water that too many of us have within ourselves.

The source of the bitterness in our own hot water is not as much the problem as is the bitterness that we each place in other people's hot water when we unfairly direct our frustration with a particular person onto other unwitting people who do not deserve our angry attacks. The frustration that is manifested into anger is *our* hot water <u>and</u> *their* hot water—it is much of what we discussed earlier in this book.

The bitter waters that are passed from generation to generation to generation slowly become the hot water of each subsequent generation. The hot water expectations that arise are that of *bitterness* and *want*. We have a tendency to attempt to use *activities* and *things* in order to fill the void left by this bitter unfulfilling and consuming fire. While tangible items and preoccupying ourselves can be enjoyable, in the long run they will always leave us feeling empty when they are obtained or done for this purpose. All of these elements put together add up to, and become, our hot water.

This can feel dismal because it seems as if it is a problem from which there is no escape. This is true **when** *you do **not** know the answer* to this mystery. We will uncover the answer to the mystery later, *after* you have been made aware of what the source of the problem is to begin with. Merely mentioning the answer will do you no good because we have all heard it many times before, but it had no impact on us because we did not grasp the fullness of it that is being revealed throughout this book.

There's a part of the concept discussed in this book that is a make or break part: If you have very bitter hot water in you, <u>***you have to make a choice***</u> of whether to *move ahead in life* **or** *to stay as you are* by continuing to live in anger, confusion, frustration, unhappiness, oppression, and/or depression.

Our lack of understanding is the foundation that our fear is built upon. Once we have obtained robust understanding, we no longer fear anything; and by grasping one important key, we wipe away all of the uncertainty and problems that so many of us face every day of our lives. The catch is that, the closer we get to understanding the source of it all, then the more our hot water seems to govern our direction. When we allow our hot water to guide our direction in this way, it compounds the problem causing the bad hot water to gain even more strength and power over the good hot water. Our end goal here is to *consciously* and *deliberately* **choose for ourselves** the temperature and purity of each our own hot water.

Bitter waters are built upon the following: We have not been taught and therefore we lack understanding. This lack of understanding is the source of our fears which have developed due to our circumstances. Our fear causes us to make decisions and choices that we would not have otherwise made. When, for a long enough period, we take part in poor decisions that are based upon our fear, then we become frustrated; and when enough frustration builds up we begin to become angry, and then we have the horrible tendency to unjustly take it out on those in our lives who are immediately around us. This effect usually happens slowly over long periods of time—here a little and there a little. It becomes part of our hot water, and as a result, it forms more of our perceived identity. Then our perceived identity creates the expectations that we have of ourselves, and the expectations that others have of us due to our perceived identity; all of which only serves to further deepen our contaminated hot water. This causes us to make decisions that we truly do not want to make, causing the cycle to start all over again only to end in the bitterness, about which this paragraph began.

You Might Think that You're True to Yourself, but are You Really?

When we go down this circular path, we are not being true to ourselves, and this causes us to continue to be dissatisfied and discontented. We can see this happen in a very rapid form when dealing with children. If you have children, then you are fully aware of the difficulties that can occur when raising a child under the age of three years old. If the child begins to cry, they are often frustrated because they want something and cannot quite figure out how to convey their needs or wants to us. If the crying goes on long enough *we* become frustrated and even somewhat angry with the child, which will only frustrate the child all the more. It is at this point that we can see the make-or-break emerge: If the parent tells the child that the child is being naughty or bad, only because the child won't stop crying, then the parent has just confirmed some of the child's hot water. In this brief scenario, which can be as short as only a few seconds, we see this whole model of *the lack of understanding*, fear, poor choices, improper action, frustration, anger, hot water, expectation, and perceived identity all unravel in a moment, and all in just one single simple interaction.

The brief example just given, in itself, has little to do with not being true to one's self. What is important to understand about the example is that it leads to the child not being true to themself when the parent begins to cast the child as spoiled, a cry baby, or some other incorrect and unfair perception. A parent must certainly take proper disciplinary action with a child, but it must be done with loving guidance.

If a parent raises their children in a cold and iron-fisted manner, then the children will *absolutely* have issues that will most certainly result in rebellion of some sort.

Being true to yourself is mostly seen only superficially by most of us, it is a part of our hot water, and therefore, we miss its true essence. Of course, some of us will take it at face value and understand its concept immediately, but for the rest of us, we miss the mark because of our own hot water.

Our perceived identity is only **_perceived_**, and it is the understanding of this particular point that will allow us to begin to pull our own lives together.

This point is very important: Revealing the solution to the problem does little good without understanding the problem itself. For now, you are already a good portion of the way there in understanding, because you are beginning to grasp the fact that—the effects of your hot water and the hot water of those around you are there, and that those effects exist in your life, *and* that hot water exists in general. You are also a good portion of the way there in understanding because you are beginning to grasp the fact that *because* your hot water is there, you do not notice things. You also now understand that you have become far too familiar and too accustomed to your hot water to even notice its high temperature and murky condition unless you are specifically looking for it.

Hot water is kind of like a small decoration in your home that has gone mostly unnoticed for an extended period of time. You know it's there, but you walk right by it every day not giving it any thought. Sometimes the decoration is even the type that you have to walk around every day. In fact, it could be the coffee table that you don't really notice, even though you use it daily as it sits in front of, or next to, your sofa. You might even place your feet up on it to relax. It makes you comfortable. It has become a part of the hot water of your home. Take some time to look at this item and notice its nuances, study it and appreciate it, and appreciate what you do with it. Would you notice if it was suddenly gone?

This is exactly how our hot water within us works—we walk around it. For some, it could be the coffee table in the living room, for others it may be a pile of clothes in the hallway, or maybe a box of junk that needs to be sorted through that sits in the closet. These things trip us up, and if we choose to avoid them, we will needlessly be walking around them for a *very* long time. They will *not* go away on their own, and eventually they become so common to us that we barely notice them at all— until we get tripped up by them and fall. Then we become angry and often curse at and even "damn" what tripped us up. But typically what trips us up is people and behavior and ourselves.

When we ignore or overlook things in this way, we are being partly lazy and partly blind. We can easily deal with the lazy part, but the blind part is technically impossible without *understanding*. This is because we simply do not notice it and therefore are not specifically aware that it's there. In either case, the truth is that we want the things that are causing us pain to be out of our lives. But, often we do not understand, so therefore, we have little power over the problem. This causes us to make decisions that are not truly in accordance with our deepest desires, which, in turn, means that we are not being true to ourselves.

This chapter discusses the central point around which all problems throughout the entire globe rotate. Being true to ourselves brings with it responsibilities and personal accountability. The fear that we discussed earlier includes the fear of *responsibility* and *accountability*, and they *both* are a part of the issue of fearing rejection. When you are responsible or accountable, then others can point fingers at you if you fall short in carrying out your responsibilities to the intended outcome. If you do fall short, then other people's rejection of you will typically quite swiftly follow. Joyful, successful people have developed a keen ability to step mentally and emotionally beyond this swift rejection.

Your Own Errors, Crimes, and/or Other Undesirable Behavior

When we wrap the *understanding* of all of these things into the neat little package referred to as "*Hot Water*" it can have profound effects in our lives. Good hot water is good; you can experience much happiness when you have much *good* hot water in your life. If this is the case in your own life you may feel that this book will be of little help; but, in truth, it is *equally* vital for *you* to understand what the principle point of this book is; because without it, you will most likely eventually get caught in the same trap as so many of the rest of us have been caught in.

And, as discussed throughout, you won't understand it until it's too late, and then you might still not quite realize what happened to cause you to feel the wrath of the bitter hot water, rather than the previous good hot water that you were born with.

Most of us have seen, first-hand, where a person, who seems to be really good and has it all together, suddenly or slowly falls from their happy position into a lowly state of being.

Bitter hot water gone unchecked will lead to very undesirable behavior in ourselves and in those around us. You could have the feeling that someone else's hot water is not your problem, but that's simply not true. In fact, other people's hot water is somewhat more *your* problem than it is *their* problem. If someone's hot water is terribly bitter, then their behavior will dramatically affect *you.* This can happen even if they are not in your circle of people with whom you have regular contact. For instance, when this happens in a political atmosphere it is very much your problem. As world history has repeatedly proven to be true, it has meant life or death for multitudes of people. How many civilizations have gone through major wars, killing soldiers, women, and innocent children? This undesirable behavior is all from the particular region's hot water and the personal hot water of their leaders; and often it is only **one** iron-fisted leader who causes so much pain for so many people. So, as you can see, *it* **matters**. Even if you are far removed from the person with bitter hot water, it can still greatly affect *you.*

To bring the problem a bit closer to home, you only need to consider the instances of crime in your very own community, such as robberies, muggings, murder, or any other crime against another person. This does not stop at violent crime; it touches just about everywhere in our lives, with rudeness being the dominant bad behavior. We have certainly all been victim to someone's rude behavior at some point. Normally, we can handle this and we simply ignore their behavior, but there are times when rudeness is dangerous. Rude hot water follows people in everything that they do when they carry it. This rudeness is especially dangerous when driving. I understand someone simply missing a stop sign because they were distracted; but even though *missing* a stop sign can result in death, it is still partially accidental. With rude behavior, we are deliberately running through the red light *and we know it*. We do this because we feel that what *we* are doing or where *we* are going is more important than stopping. This goes mostly unnoticed and unreported. We see this sort of behavior frequently, and sometimes *we* are one of those who partake in the careless behavior. As long as no one else is in the intersection when this occurs, then no one gets hurt; but all too often, that is simply not the case.

All accidents that are *not* caused from mechanical failure or unanticipated or unusual conditions are caused by people violating the traffic control signs, roadway laws, and common courtesy rules of the road. These so-called "*accidents*" result in many personal injuries and deaths every year. Truth be told, these are not "*accidents*" at all, and calling them "*deliberates*" may be more appropriate. When a person is preoccupied while driving, they have made the *deliberate* choice to continue driving instead of pulling over to complete the task. Whether it is rude driving behavior, or allowing yourself to be distracted while driving, all of these instances are part of each person's hot water. So as you can see, our hot water affects others, and other people's hot water affects us—this is a basic truth.

Another aspect of our hot water that goes hand-in-hand with poor decisions is that of obvious errors. Errors are not necessarily the same as poor decisions, but are more of a result of poor decisions. When you choose something that is less than you truly want, then you have made a poor decision, and, in doing so, you are not living to *your* fullest potential—this in itself is an error. It saddens me when I see all of the people who have not been living to their fullest potential because of their own hot water. To me this is very sad because of all of the wonderful inventions not invented, the beautiful music not written, the touching songs not sung. How many wonderful things have we been deprived of cannot be known, but there is no doubt that the number is staggering. If we do not consider this an error, then errors do not exist.

There are also the overt errors when we simply make an unhelpful decision. Or we can also err when we choose to do something because our hot water has conditioned us so. This happens to the point where we become ignorant of a circumstance. When we make decisions without knowing or understanding that a particular circumstance exists, then we will have error in our judgment because all of the facts were not able to be considered due to our ignorance of the circumstance and certain facts. Please recall the *true* definition and origin of the word *ignor*-ance.

Together, *everything* combined that comes into our lives affects us—both for good *and/or* for bad.

Are You Mentally Wealthy?

The worse it gets then the worse it gets—Only truly mentally wealthy people can hope to avoid this path of destruction. No matter what your social and/or economic class is, when life comes along and decides to give you a run for your mental money, then the worse it gets—the worse it gets, until life finishes its cruel tests on us and leaves us destitute. Unfortunately, for some of us, these tests will send us into mental or moral bankruptcy, with some of us never being able to recover—but anyone **can** recover! Every last one of us, **no matter what** and **no matter who**, we can recover if **we** so **choose** that straight path!

So let's take a closer look at a typical type of situation: Let's say that you are an average social status person. Now, you're living your life and something occurs that harms you in some way. Let's say raiding invaders come into your land and take everything you have, and now you are left with only your family. You have no home, no land, no food, no money, and no place to go.

So, of course you're frustrated and angry at this, and you focus your energy on how deal with the problem. You can't quite see a way clear, so you try harder and harder to change your situation.

No matter what you do, it just keeps getting worse. With every cruel blow, you feel worse about not being able to care for your family as you had previously been able to care for them. *Everything* that you had worked so hard to build up with your very own hands has been taken from you by the invaders. As you repeatedly fail to regain your status, your children see your attitude and begin to feel the effects of your "failures" along with you.

They can even lend to your failures, only serving to deepen the situation and begin to not care about things as much, and, as a result, you allow yourself to spiral down even more. Your children see this, and, because they respect you as their guardian, they begin to adopt your attitudes and behaviors. Slowly, bit by bit, any mental wealth they had is being eaten away and consumed; thus, the parents' and the children's mental worth is being depleted.

As the children grow they see the invaders succeeding and advancing in life, and as a result they might begin to see these invaders as good examples to follow, which is due to the children's current and very unpleasant experience of destitution, which will likely be the comparison that they will utilize to make their judgments of their life's direction moving forward. The apparent success by the invaders has a definite appeal to them. This is *the* critical point of choice for this generation. Do they choose to follow the apparent dismal path of the parents, *or* the apparent successful path of the ruthless and offending invaders. At this point, for the children, it is very compelling to follow the example of the invaders. All too often, this is the choice that is made by the children; we see this in areas of the world where war is common.

In the eyes of the children, the choice is only either to adopt mental poverty as displayed by the father, or to embrace the illusion of good created by mental bankruptcy as displayed by the invaders. Sadly, the children are seldom presented with the third, easiest, and most powerful option of *true mental wealth*.

The invaders or "Takers" are usually people who have been brought low by circumstances, and often these takers are children of one or several generations of people who have experienced mental poverty—many of these takers ultimately have chosen mental bankruptcy in the end. They are people who are sometimes outwardly thieves by profession, but more likely they are *your* family or friends, neighbors or relatives, teachers or authorities. Of course, not all people in these categories have gone down this path. No, it's simply that any people who are mentally bankrupt, or who suffer from mental poverty, are usually very close to you—it may even be you yourself.

After absorbing all of this, if you are coming upon the realization that you may have become a "taker" who is mentally bankrupt, or if you are realizing that you suffer from mental poverty, then get happy! Because the likely reason that you chose to hear or read these words is a clear indication that you are hot on the trail of your own personal secret goldmine that is richly full of true mental wealth.

Because the basis and appeal of this book is about feeling better about yourself, the assumption is made that you had been feeling either mentally poor or mentally bankrupt. The first thing to do in order to change this is to begin to be able to recognize the signs of low mental worth or mental poverty.

Before moving on, it is important that you stay keenly aware of how your perceived identity may have headed down the wrong path. Also, stay keenly aware that hot water, mental-poverty, and mental-bankruptcy all exist but you can be quickly *changed by you*.

Chapter 7

Don't Allow Others to Define Your Identity

Through the years I have been acquainted with people of differing classes, nationalities, races, creeds, and colors, and in most every instance the same thing happens: There seems to be no difference in any group with regard to inner behaviors showing through while under the influence of alcohol. Their perceived identity begins to crack and often a true part of a person begins to be revealed. Why is this? It's because we allow *others* to define *our* identity at all ages. This occurs throughout the entire globe. Typically, people who are more true to themselves tend to change less when drinking or are under the influence of any substance. But when we hide our true underlying feelings and emotions in our day-to-day lives, then, as a rule-of-thumb, we begin to reveal those feelings when we feel the mental relax of alcohol.

Did You Define Your Identity With The College Lie?

Depression appears to increase with each generation within people of all ages. In the late twentieth century and the early twenty-first century, there was an increase in the number of college students who experienced depression. Their lives had never been more luxurious, so then why the increase in depression? It's because of the *behavior* that has created *The College Lie*. This is not to say that college is wrong, but when we allow *others* to define *our own* perceived identity, then low self-worth and depression are typically the result.

Many of the college students of the late twentieth century had been taught by their previously-attended school system, by their culture, and by their parents that the only way to succeed and be happy was to go to college and get a coveted college degree. And thus, their "happiness" has been equated to this magical degree. Many students very quickly find that college is not truly what *they* want. Students are being told that in order to be valued, they must do something that they truly *do not* want to do.

If this is the magic formula to happiness, then why are there **any** "educated" and well-to-do people who are unhappy?

By thinking back to the earlier chapters discussing perceived identity and expectations, we can see that our perceived identity affects us profoundly. Our expectations of ourselves drive us to take certain actions as we move ahead in our lives. Because various important parts of our life are commonly being ignored, or altogether missed, we tend to follow the *expected* direction.

Many parents who lived through financially trying times, even if those times are only within their own family, typically do not want their children to repeat their experience and suffer at the heavy hand of poverty. Poverty can be a very cruel taskmaster, and so, many parents will show their children how to work hard. And they *expect* their children to get an "education." In addition, the school systems seem to be placing ever more emphasis on "higher education." We will call this emphasis— *expectation*.

Many children are *expected* to attend college. Guidance counselors and/or school systems often pressure students to *choose* a career to pursue after they finish college for that chosen occupation. Seldom will the students be encouraged to pursue *their own* passion regardless of what it happens to be. All too often, a child is told that the particular passion that they have is too difficult and that they are unlikely to be able to make a living doing that for a career. Students are also influenced to get educated for jobs that are currently in highest demand. This seems logical, but it is often very wrong for any particular student. It's not wrong to get an education, but working at a job that doesn't require vast amounts or overpriced education, might be a better path until the student figures out what they actually like to do.

The college example is only one small example of this problem. There are many other examples of such expectation that occur daily, though most are of a less significant nature. To get to the root cause of this, we'll wind back the clock a bit and start from a human's beginning.

In earlier chapters, we discussed some of the basics of how our hot water and perceived identity came to be. Now we're going to go deeper and be more specific in order to better understand what may have happened with the circumstances, that surrounded *you* personally, that conditioned your hot water, and, how that hot water formed your perceived identity, giving you the understanding that you need.

Did You Begin Learning in the Womb?

Though it may appear so, the following is not about child rearing. This section is to make you aware of the early formation of *your own* hot water. Understanding this early formation equips you with the needed understanding to remove this bad water from your perceived identity on your own.

There are differing opinions on what goes on in the womb and at conception. But if you ask any mother, without hesitation she typically will tell you that her children did not have the same temperament as each other in the womb. Some children are more active in the womb and others are more still or relaxed. From experience, we find that many children tend to somewhat follow this after their birth.

Depending upon your theological philosophy, you may or may not carry the belief that we have a spirit or a soul. If we do have a spirit, then the child would likely have a combined spirit created in the image of its parents' spirits. Since, according to the Bible, "the life is in the blood" it would stand to reason, then, that the spirit encompasses the entire body in the same pattern as the blood follows. If this is the case, then the children *are* created in the image of their parents in a physical *and* spiritual sense, just as we are all Created in the image of God.

To take this thought a bit further, we can also assume that the hot water that the parents each had in their own lives at the time of their child's conception, would also become a part of the child's spirit. Even if you don't have a God theology belief, the blending of persons is still of tremendous effect to the newly conceived child because the child is undeniably made from both of the parents.

If you have children, then depending upon the era of time when you may have raised them, or may currently be raising them, you might have seen people making sure that the pregnant mother listened to soothing music and/or was relaxed. Some mothers even went so far as having the sounds of educational information or music directed to their womb in order to have the developing child hear the information or the soothing and pleasing sounds of the music. Whether or not you subscribe to the belief that people are created beings made in the image of their Maker, the inescapable fact still remains that the child is a combined result of both of the parents. Whether or not you feel that they actually learn in the womb is your own opinion. But it becomes obvious when you pay close attention to that sort of thing.

People who subscribe to "a woman's right to choose" tend to wrongly believe that the baby in the womb has no ability to feel or understand in any way—even many months into the pregnancy. Everyone is entitled to their own thoughts and opinions on this subject. My personal feeling is that babies in the womb *do* feel the *entire* time. My conclusion on this is based upon the observation of various pregnancies. Gently placing some light pressure on the belly of the pregnant mother typically induces an immediate response from the child who is inside the mother's womb. Because the regularity with which this occurs is so high, we cannot ignore the connection to the fact that the child senses this when he or she feels the pushing from the pressure applied from the outside world. We could make the claim that this is not proof, but consider this: when a baby is born, only a truly foolish person would deny that an interaction occurs with regard to the newborn child and those who are interacting with the child. This same child could have been *born three months prematurely* and have interacted in the much same way immediately after being born; thus, the interaction just *before* birth of a full term baby is deliberate interaction on the baby's part.

I have seen newborn babies smile only a few days after birth. I cannot say that the smiles were from joy, but the evidence was plain that the child was interacting with the parent. People attribute such early smiles to gas, etc., but it is more likely that, during the interaction, they are either mimicking the smiles of their parents, *or*, the more likely possibility, they are actually smiling which is as natural as crying.

Parents who have had a child who had its nights and days mixed up can attest to trying to incrementally adjust the schedule of the child by keeping them awake a bit longer, or waking them earlier to get them accustomed to the parents' choice of a proper sleeping schedule. I have seen this done within the very first week and also several months after the child's birth. This includes premature babies, and it doesn't seem to make much difference what the age of the child is.

If a baby is born one-and-a-half-months *early* and is able to interact with its parents, and the baby learns or becomes accustomed to the care and sleeping and eating schedule that the parents create, then we also have to believe that the same is true and that a baby *can* be stimulated and influenced by interaction *within* the womb with a *full-term* baby one-and-a-half months *before* it is born.

This is compelling evidence that a child has the capacity to be influenced within the womb. The only questions that arise are: At what age does this begin? And to what extent does it occur? To answer these questions we only need to consider premature babies. The same interactive effect happens at nearly any point prematurely at which a baby is born and yet lives. Similar interactions are seen when feeding or touching a premature baby.

My own assessment is that it happens during *all* stages of gestation. For years I have observed active pregnancies and then their subsequent births, and I have been observing the temperament of the resulting children. When observing the circumstances and mental disposition that the mother and father were in around the time of conception and during gestation, it seems clear that it affects the child's original disposition somewhat. I cannot say this about all children simply because I have not experienced all children. What I observed indicated that the parents' disposition and environment around the time of conception and gestation *does* matter. Observe this yourself as you go through life and see if you conclude the same.

This might appear small matter, but the reality is that if this affect is so, then the resulting impact can be enormous because it all becomes a part of the child's hot water. If the child has a difficult temperament the moment he or she is born, then the parents will *immediately* treat that child a certain way to deal with the child's temperament. This becomes a part of the child's hot water. Think of this initial temperament as a particular kind of seed. If the seed planted in them is troubled, it can be removed and replaced with a good seed. The earlier this is done the better off we are. The quality of the hot water of the child (the water that the seed is watered with) can also change the course and quality of the seed planted in the child.

How You were Formed as a Baby

After they are born, babies will interact, on a daily basis, with their parents and others who surround them. Before and after their birth, babies have little say in what happens around them. The only way they appear to know how to communicate their needs is by crying—and it works! The problem for them and their perceived identity is that they have little option of what hot water they are being filled with by their parents and the surrounding environment.

As children age, they slowly begin to learn to interact and communicate with the people in their environment. As this amazing learning process occurs, their hot water is being created and shaped, and it is molding the child's perceived identity.

There are two main issues that direct how this child will be handled: First, each parents' individual hot water. And second, is the temperament of the child. As the child's perceived identity forms, there are greater and greater expectations of the child's behavior. The more their perceived identity is formed, then the more these expectations are cast upon the child. The more these expectations are cast upon the child, then the deeper their hot water becomes *and* the more reinforced their perceived identity becomes. This was true for you, just as it is true for the children you now have or may have in the future. This goes beyond parental interaction; it includes the interaction of friends and relatives as well. The friends and relatives will naturally have a more neutral expectation of the child *unless* the child's parents pre-place hot water expectations in the hearts and minds of those friends and relatives.

Expectations are commonly being placed on a child through what the parents say about the child to friends and family. It is nearly impossible to avoid these positive or negative expectations. And because infants are likely unaware of all of this, and mostly incapable of expressing their thoughts and/or feelings, there is little that the baby can do about these expectations. The expectations are reinforced by the baby's actions since it is the baby's actions that formed much of the parents' perception to begin with.

In the earliest days of a baby's life, the baby is most affected by the parents' expectations. Siblings have less impact in those early days, but as the baby ages, the impact of the interaction and expectations of the siblings carries greater and greater weight. Depending upon the parents' type and amount of interaction with the siblings *before* the new baby arrived, the siblings will notice a change in the amount and quality of attention that a parent gives to them when the baby is born and, possibly, even during the pregnancy.

The change in the type and amount of attention from the parents will greatly affect the hot water of the siblings of the new baby, and, therefore, will affect the siblings' interaction with the baby. This interaction will then affect both the baby's hot water and the reactions and expectations of the siblings. If the parents do little in the way of intervention, then the likely result will be jealousy, which typically results in aggressive behavior towards the baby or the parents by the siblings. The behavior that is displayed by the siblings becomes a part of the baby's hot water as well as a part of the siblings' hot water. Picture yourself in the position of the baby or the siblings to see how all of this relates to your own life—The effects are profound!

If aggressive behavior is displayed by the siblings, then *aggression* will be the expectation that the baby begins to have of the siblings. If the baby cries in response to the sibling's interaction, then the crying will also become the siblings' expectation of the baby. And neither of them will be realizing what is actually happening. All of this is hot water; and together, their children's combined hot waters with the parents' hot waters become the hot water of the family. This common situation is difficult for a family to escape because the parents likely experienced it themselves as children. It is a part of the parents' hot water, and therefore, they are simply blind to it. It happened in their family when they were growing up, and, gone unchecked, it will likely happen in their children's families when their children decide to have families of their own.

There is little that very young children and babies can do about this problem. It is only at the age of about one-and-a-half to three years old where, to a limited extent, a child begins to realize that he or she can alter his or her own environment. They are not specifically realizing that their hot water can be changed. Rather, they begin to have an awareness of what *they* want. Then they make attempts to have things that are important to *them* their own way. This is a very important time in the life of a person, and a person's hot water is very much affected in any particular life-long direction during this time in their life, although any direction can be changed at any time *when* we become aware and choose to make the change.

The initial major determining factors will be the parents, the siblings, and the temperament of the child. Depending upon how it is handled, this can be a time of blessing or a time of curse in any person's or family's life.

The examples set, and the interactions of the family, will teach the child some survival mechanisms. If a child is taught to stand firmly in their ways, it can be good or bad depending upon what they are allowed to stand firmly for. If it is a matter of the child getting their way about everything, then it will be a bad thing; but if it is the child learning to not back down from—they themselves not allowing others to push them around—then it is good. In general, we have a difficult time discerning any difference between these two positions, but these positions could not be more opposed to each other. One of these behaviors oppresses, while the other stops oppression.

I'm Going to do What I Want!

It is around the age of two that children begin to become self-aware, and it is this self-awareness that can give them the power to stop others' expectations from adversely affecting themselves. The difficult part is that it's hard enough to convey this to a reasonable adult; trying to get a young child to understand the logic of it is nearly impossible, though, a child can be easily taught *how* by an understanding parent's behavior. It is the *why* part that is difficult to explain. There's a fine line in this problem, which runs between **"You can't tell me what to do"** and **"I am going to do what I want."** Understanding the *why* is what will give you the power to discern this. Where, knowing only the *how* is not lasting; but the *why* is lasting, and that is much of what this book is about.

Most children, and most people for that matter, are oblivious to the **"You can't tell me what to do"** versus **"I am going to do what I want"** dilemma. This is an area of great concern with regard to the subject of this book. The **"I am going to do what I want"** group could be re-labeled as the **"I am going to do what I want, *and so are you!*"** group. This places excessive expectations on everyone. The, **"I am going to do what I want"** group will expect and demand others to do as *they* say. When the victims of the demands are children, then the children will likely become expectant of this behavior, and if they are not protected in their early years, then they will likely accept this within their hot water and become complacent and accept what the group demands of them; this is very common in all societies. The only remedy for the victim of this behavior is to join the **"You can't tell me what to do"** group. The positions and attitudes for these two behaviors are taught at *very* young ages, and unless a parent is specifically teaching their children to stand up for themselves, the child will have a much more difficult time in avoiding becoming a victim of the oppressive **"I am going to do what I want"** behavior, which is predominantly found in older siblings, but not exclusive to them.

Your Path as a Young Adult

As children reach their pubescent years they begin to become very aware of themselves, and depending upon their nature, they can be very shy, very outgoing, or somewhere in-between. This is where the **"You can't tell me what to do"** and the **"I am going to do what I want"** dispositions become very pronounced. Siblings play an enormous role in this, but it does not stop there. Friends and peers can cause young adults a great deal of trouble in this area. We touched on this in an earlier chapter; however, it is important to note that our focus is markedly different here.

If a person does not have one of these two dispositions, then they will be complacent and the **Complacent** people usually are enslaved to the **"I am going to do what I want"** group. The **"I am going to do what I want"** group also has the **"You can't tell me what to do"** disposition, but the **"You can't tell me what to do"** group does not necessarily have the **"I am going to do what I want"** disposition. This is because you can't have **"I am going to do what I want"** without *also* having **"You can't tell me what to do"**, logically, it is technically impossible for that to occur.

The hot water of children in their teen years gets filled with these dispositions, either as one who adopts one of the dispositions, or as one who is the subject of others who have one of the dispositions. In either case, it all becomes a part of their hot water. Now, while this happens in early childhood, and has a profound impact at that age, the teen years are the point when it becomes a position of *their own* choosing.

In the early years it leans more towards the circumstances you are dealt in life. And because you have not yet reached an age of good reason and awareness, you are mostly subject to your hot water circumstances. This is different when you're in your teen years. In the lives of most people, it is during our later teen years when we choose which position we will likely live by for the remainder of our days. This is where these three dispositions are chosen:

- **I am going to do what I want**
- **You can't tell me what to do**
- **Complacent**

The choice is largely dictated by the disposition that you enter this age with, and it is *usually* the one you will keep all of the rest of your life; but this is dependent upon the quality of your hot water, and it can be changed at will, *when **you*** understand this.

As stated earlier, the key to everything is *understanding*, but *understanding* alone is mostly useless *unless* we make the effort to act on that understanding. Choosing your disposition is the act of doing something about it. It's in the teen years that most of our transformations appear, but transformations can happen at all ages. This chapter is named *Don't Allow Others to Define Your Identity*, and we stop others from defining our identity by understanding where our identity definition begins, which is with the three dispositions of **I am going to do what I want**, **You can't tell me what to do** and **Complacent**.

Here is How it Works

The two, **I am going to do what I want** and **You can't tell me what to do**, groups will *always* be at odds with each other. Much like in politics where one side, usually the more liberal faction, often embodies the **I am going to do what I want** disposition and the conservative faction typically embodies the **You can't tell me what to do** disposition. It is the **Complacent** group that sits in between the two groups who gets to determine the feel of the hot water of any setting.

The "**am going to do what I want** children are typically aggressive and will force their desires and views on others, essentially demanding their own way even if it adversely affects others. The **You can't tell me what to do** group will never succumb to the **I am going to do what I want** group, but the **Complacent** group will easily succumb. The complacent group is about fifty percent of people, higher in some areas and lower in other areas depending upon the hot water of the community. The more demanding **I am going to do what I want** group, will inevitably *always* attempt to impose their will on the rest of the people, and the **Complacent** crowd will almost always acquiesce.

When the **Complacent** group does comply, then they hand all of their power over to the **I am going to do what I want** group. This makes the **I am going to do what I want** group feel empowered, and then they feel even more permitted to impose their will upon the rest of the people. This is how a bad leader's dictatorial leadership is allowed to get to the extremes that it typically does. This is seen in more simple forms in schools across the face of the globe; the schoolyard is a plain example of this. Think back to when you attended school: Do you recall seeing these dynamics? You even may have been a part of it. The **I am going to do what I want** teens often dictate who will be on what team, who can walk in what halls, and other seemingly petty young-adult rituals. The **Complacent** group either complies or feels the wrath of the **I am going to do what I want** group. And the **You can't tell me what to do** group will often be at odds with the **I am going to do what I want** group.

This doesn't stop at simple petty high school antics, but crosses over to verbal assertions at all ages. It is my goal to reveal to people the skill of *choosing*, and to become part of the **You can't tell me what to do** group without also becoming a part of the undesirable **I am going to do what I want** group. An important point to be made is that the **You can't tell me what to do** group, in its pure form, will *not* impose their will on others, except to stop the **I am going to do what I want** group from harming people and forcing their will on them. This is very much a part of people's hot water; and therefore, this is not typically recognized by any of the groups in the way that it is described here. We often label these dispositions as "*demanding*" and "*complacent*" but those labels are only generalizations and are often of no consequence or help to our understanding of the problem.

This behavior starts at home when parents do not understand that *no* means *no*. Parents simply need to stand by their decision *without backing down*. As discussed in the cornerstone book *Strong Family*, backing down will cause the child to be obstinate and obnoxious and to demand their way. When obstinate children are older, they often get the impression that they are liked; however, believing so, when it is actually the fear of the particular person's obstinate behavior, is not a good way to get through life and no good will come of it. Nor is it good to be the one who is afraid in this case. The sooner the parents stand firm in "*no* means *no*," then the easier it is to eradicate this problem in your family and in the lives of your children and yourself.

How this Affects Your Adult Life

In the adult world the problem with the dynamics between these three groups is extremely prominent, and often the groups are confused, both, when viewing each other and when viewing themselves; this is because of the hot water that we have allowed to enter ourselves over the years. Earlier I mentioned politics and generalized the groups in comparison with liberal and conservative tendencies. This general rule-of-thumb holds true, but politics are not bound to that rule because there are cross-over people who are opposite, though, they are relatively few in number.

The real confusion enters in with the adult **Complacent** group, often disguised as *pacifists*. When we are in this group we will be claiming that we want peace, but then violently protest in order to demand our way. This makes us both from the **Complacent** and the **"I am going to do what I want"** groups, but actually is only guided by the **"I am going to do what I want"** group. This combined radical *pacifist* group then actually has all three behaviors in their disposition. This is a part of their collective hot water and perceived identity.

The **Complacent** group is commonly the most angry and frustrated of all of the groups. Understanding why this is, can soothe many a heart. By the time we reach adulthood we have the full ability to turn in the face of our perceived identity and make a new way of life for ourselves—*intentionally.* In the teen years a change in people will often happen, but, typically, it's not deliberate; it is more of a decision that is *made* but is usually *not contemplated.* This is usually different when the decision is made during the adult years. The later in life that the change is made, then the more likely it is that it was done after a great deal of contemplation and reflection.

The same dynamics that we just discussed for young adults occurs in aged adults also, with politics being a very prominent place for this to occur. The workplace also is a common place for adults to experience other people's expectations of them. By the time we enter our mid-twenties our hot water is well-established, and therefore, so is our perceived identity. This perception shows in every aspect of our being and is reflected in the way we carry ourselves, in our body language, in our tone of voice (the way we respond or communicate), and even in the way we dress. All of this gives an impression to those around us, and causes them to have certain expectations of us. Two people can have two completely different expectations of you because of their individual hot waters, but, in general, their expectations of you will be close or similar because, in large part, *their expectations* are formed from *your* hot water.

To fully understand the essence of this chapter, we must also address how *their* expectation of *us* matters—*their* expectation, *not ours.* It matters because, they will interact with you and treat you in the manner that *they* see fit based upon their expectation of you that they assessed from the way you presented yourself to them. And secondly, their expectation will project itself on to you, and then it often becomes a part of your own expectation of yourself. This is where a strong will can prove to be a surprise, both to you and to everyone around you.

Make no mistake about it, your perceived identity shows up in nearly everything that you do, but it is important to note that this is only your **perceived** identity. Your perceived identity consists of the hot water you were filled with as a youth, along with the projections and expectations that others have of you, and the expectations that you have of yourself. When these elements are inaccurate, then succumbing to them will inevitably cause you frustration and will create your resentment toward those around you and even towards yourself. If you have children then you will need to take care of this in yourself before you can conquer it in your children. If you fail to properly address this problem, then you doom both yourself and your children to much frustration and pain until you figure this out and make the needed changes.

The surprise comes in when we allow the true nature of ourselves to rise above the expectations derived from the perception of our identity that others place on us. This may all seem to be confusing, but when we break the mold and truly be *ourselves*, then we surprise the people who have drawn conclusions based on our *perceived* identity. Rising above your perceived identity is only going to happen when you have a good grasp of the three groups we discussed in this chapter: The "**You can't tell me what to do**" group; the "**I am going to do what I want**" group; and, finally, the **Complacent** group.

Have You have been Defined or Labeled by the World because of Your Perceived Identity?

People generally see the three aforementioned groups as one and the same thing, and I suppose at times they are, because *if* you are not oppressing anyone, then it is of little consequence. The difference is this: When your attitude is, "**I am going to do what I want**" then you have little care of those around you, and you will impose yourself on them, and/or *you* will do what you want to do *regardless* of how it harms others. It is an extremely selfish and undesirable way to live.

The "**You can't tell me what to do**" disposition is different in that it is *not* going to demand of others, rather, it is simply saying, "Leave me alone and don't tell me what to do." The problem is that the "**I am going to do what I want**" group sees the "**You can't tell me what to do**" group as telling them what to do *when* they say "leave me alone." This is because the "**I am going to do what I want**" group does not want to leave them alone, and they often demand that other group acquiesce and follow their unreasonable demands. Any defiance is seen by the "**I am going to do what I want**" group as an attack.

The **Complacent** group fills the complete spectrum between the two extremes. This large group is often negatively influenced by the demanding "**I am going to do what I want**" group and they are often angry because of this, but do not understand or realize that this is so.

In the adult world, this usually runs along religious and political lines. In the beginning of the twenty-first century this was more noticeable in the political realm than in the religious realm. The political stand that the **Complacent** group and the "**I am going to do what I want**" group take is mostly guided by their perceived identity.

There is much manipulation of the **Complacent** group during the promotion of political candidates. In fact, in general, the blatant manipulation of perceived identity is the center around which the advertising industry, as a whole, rotates. Often, the advertisers' goal is to manipulate your perceived identity. In the case of advertising, it is a blatant and aware attempt at their manipulation of your perceived identity. As we discussed earlier, a perceived identity has the subtle expectations that occur daily, such as expectations about *you* based upon the way you carry yourself. Political and advertising manipulation of your perceived identity is a vile, heinous, and cruel attempt at getting you to do what *they* want you to do.

We sense this, but we still have difficulty placing our finger on why certain things irritate us. The reason that this irritates us is because we sense the manipulation. If we want red then **we** *want* to *want* red because **we** *chose* red, not because we were manipulated into wanting red. Not all advertising does this. If *they* show you a red car and you think it is very attractive, and then you go to buy one, then *you* have chosen, of *your* own free will, to buy that red car. But if *they* tell you that all other colors cause cancer and *they* can get you to believe that, so that you buy a red car, then *you* have been manipulated even if you like the red car.

The example of the red car does little to help us understand how this affects our perceived identity, but it does show the principle of manipulation. For instance, it crosses the *perceived-identity-manipulation* boundary line when you are being told that you personally *need* a medication, or that you are not "cool" unless you have some *thing* that they are trying to sell to you. It is in the worst way that this is done to us with political issues.

In politics, it's common to attempt to tell you that you are helpless, and only with the aid of the government will you be able to move along in life. Believing that this is true will drastically manipulate your perceived identity and hinder your life in ways too numerous to account for. It may be that some people already felt this way; and to those people it simply reinforces their own existing perception of their own identity. All of this is part of their hot water and the hot water of the community and the country.

A trap that many of us fall into that causes us a great deal of pain and agony with regard to the three groups is this: We have the right and ability to choose what we will allow ourselves to believe about our perceived identity, and we should exercise that right. But, we must be careful *not* to refuse ourselves that which is *good* just because someone is trying to manipulate us into that very same thing. If we refuse ourselves that which is good, it is the same as if we **do** let them manipulate us. If you want red, then get red because *you* want red, even if they are trying to manipulate you into choosing red.

Their reasons may be selfish and greedy, but yours are pure as long as your choices do not hurt or unjustly take from anyone else. To deny a pure choice that is of your own making is foolish and is allowing others to define your perceived identity, just as is allowing them to manipulate you. To deny yourself something that you truly like, because someone just so happens to be trying to manipulate you into the same decision, is a foolish and prideful move, and no longer can be considered to be from the **You can't tell me what to do** group. This is because you are trying to *force* them to not manipulate you and you are saying **I am going to do what I want** in the face of what *you* yourself truly wanted. That is arrogant and vindictive, and doing so will *never* bring joy into your life.

Knowing that this behavior exists in ourselves is the beginning of the power to eliminate it from our own lives.

We started this chapter discussing how all of this can cause depression. Succumbing to the pressures that surround us will *never* make us happy. Doing what we want *regardless* of what it does to others will *never* make us happy. And *forcing our will* on others will *never* make us happy. Happiness happens to us when *we* choose to do what we want *when* it **won't** harm others.

There is a catch to this, and it is that we *must* realize that we are not responsible for the happiness of others. If they do not like what we want to do, then it should be of no concern to them *provided* we don't hurt them or anyone else in the process, or force them in any way to pay for or suffer for our desires and choices. There can be a judgment call in this regard, because they could claim our decision *will* harm them. But we have to look at why this is, and if it is justified. The **I am going to do what I want** group causes much misery in our world for themselves and for those around them. If we're from this group, then what we typically will do to others is to manipulate or force them into doing things the way we want.

As explained earlier, there are many places in life where depression is seen, but college students were prime targets at the turn of the twenty-first century. Here's why: The "**I am going to do what I want**" group, which usually includes the students' parents, teachers, and a fair portion of society, was telling them that they would be *failures* if the student did not attend college and get a degree. If a student declined, then often the parents of the student would become angry and attempt to force their child to comply. Students whose opinions and views were not in agreement with their professors and teachers were also not allowed to express their own political or religious opinions without retribution.

This crosses the line with regard to identity. When this happens the "**I am going to do what I want**" group becomes the "**I am going to do what I want, *and so are you!*"** group. To put this in context, if the student made a decision to *not* attend college, it has no bearing on the demanding parents, but the parents are giving the message to the student that the student let them down and that they are hurting the parent because the parent had their heart set on the child actually attending college. But, what has this to do with the parents' lives? The student should do what he or she sees fit for their own life; the child should certainly consider the parents' thoughts and reasoning, but then go to do what best suits and creates a constructive, joyful, and productive life for him- or her- self and accept the consequences of their own choices and actions.

With regard to college, most students are directly and/or indirectly told that happiness and success will accompany their life *if* they attend college and get the coveted degree. This attitude was built up all through their childhood schooling, but what many found when they got to college was an empty promise that yielded only discontentment. This is not to say that some people don't find it joyful. In fact, for many students, who, of their own volition, choose to attend college and do find happiness in attending college to learn a trade because it was what *they* truly wanted. It can be difficult to detect what a person initially wants because we have often been told and influenced for so long that—we should not want what we truly want—that it has become a part of our hot water. This happens to the point where we actually believe that we want something that we are averse to—we have allowed others to define our perceived identity. This situation is especially problematic for those who want to be stay at home mothers.

Earlier we discussed how our identities begin to be formed. In our examples, where the person is old enough to readily reason, that person can choose to diminish the perceived identity that others attempt to place on them. Only their own awareness can truly solve this problem.

Take our example of the young family where the older sibling is on a subtle and regular mission to assault and diminish the younger sibling so that the older can feel better about him- or her- self by garnering the attention of the parents: When this older antagonist is regularly making negative comments about the younger sibling, then the younger—who is typically respecting of the older sibling—will often become angry. Some will lash out immediately, and some will hold it in for a very long time, and others will withdraw into themselves, but few will firmly hold their ground.

Those who hold it in and are tolerant of these assaults will become angry and are often the ones who lash out suddenly and violently. When a parent gets properly involved, then they will encourage the younger child, and attempt to put a stop to the antics of the older aggressor. This goes a very long way in teaching the young abuse victim the needed skill of *not* allowing others to place a false perceived identity on them.

At any age, when an aggressor launches an assault at their victim, if the victim is the type to hold it in and tolerate the unwanted and unwarranted remarks, it is likely that this person will, at some point, snap and lash out in some manner. Our self-awareness of this is critical because *we* can *choose* to let it go. All too often, when people hold the offenses in and have *not* come to the realization that *they* can release these assaults from their own hearts, then the aggressors have power over them, and, therefore, the victims cannot alter their own perceived identity.

When someone refers to another as a "loser" or any other derogatory remark that is unwarranted, they steal a small part of that person and they cast it aside as if it means nothing. Piece by piece and bit by bit the aggressor steals parts from the individual until their victim is utterly beaten down and has little self-esteem. The *only* way to overcome this is to take the power back, and then pick up all of your pieces and rebuild yourself. "How do I do this?" is the common question. The answers will vary depending upon your circumstances. And depending upon the quality of relationships in your life, *your* understanding of this will vary; it will also vary depending on whether you are the *aggressor*, or the *victim*, or even both.

There is a catch in all of this, and it is that, often, an aggressor was treated in the manner that they have adopted to treat others; this behavior is woven deeply into their soul. If they were beat-down as a child, then the probability that they will repeat this behavior with their own family and other people is high. Typically, aggressors don't fully realize what it is that they are doing or the amount of torment that they inflict on the other person; although, they often do know that they are inflicting something on the person, which is usually why they do it to begin with.

A very dangerous identity crusher for young people, or any person for that matter, is derogatory terms of endearment. Sometimes these are given to the children by a parent, sibling, relative, or a friend. This type of remark or name is commonly heard in high schools between male friends. While these terms generally seem to be harmless vocal utterances of affection or friendship, if the person who is receiving these ill-placed statements of affection does not like the references, then it can be a *very* big problem for them. These unwelcome statements will wear on the recipient until the recipient is either crushed and withdraws, or lashes out.

Giving the victim the power to overcome this is the kindest thing we can do for them.

With siblings, these terms of endearment often are challenged, and when the terms are challenged they commonly come with even more force whenever there is a jealous or antagonistic friend or sibling in the mix. And, they will typically increase the frequency when asked to cease. The best method in dealing with this type of jealous or antagonistic person is to simply distance yourself from them and ignore them. Any reaction will often invoke their perceived wrath, but even ignoring them can upset this type of person. You just need to outlast them; and when you do resist them, then you will find your power return and they will no longer have power over you.

Never allow this type of person to define your perceived identity—**ever**. Your identity is yours, and it is yours to do with whatever *you* so choose—it is not for anyone else to control. Antagonists are controllers, or at least they think they are, and they try to be controlling. They want attention and will do whatever they need to do to get the attention that they so crave. Giving in to their method of getting attention only serves to prolong your own agony. Whatever you are willing to tolerate *you will* **never** be able to remove from your life! If *you* tolerate it, then *you* are feeding it, and *you* are stuck with it!

This is **you** that were talking about here, and *no one* should be allowed to take *you* away from yourself—***ever***.

Subtle Ways Others Define Your Perceived Identity

Another common way people often affect our perceived identity is subliminally. This is not done deliberately, and almost all of us do this to our closest friends and loved ones. Because of this perceived identity confusion that we all live within, we allow people to tell us *what* we are. With other people's identities being so distorted in our own minds, we assume certain things about the person who we are interacting with. For instance, if a person wears a certain shirt with some sort of advertising on it, we often assume that the person associates themselves with the product, or as is often the case, a musical group presented on the shirt. Based on the assumption that this person likes this group, we make assessments about the person—judging the book by its cover as it were. When we do this, we indirectly make comments that are subliminal.

Let's assume that the person went as a companion with a friend to a concert and bought a shirt at the concert. Of course, they probably enjoyed the concert and liked the group somewhat to begin with, but that may be the extent of it. So, the person is now wearing their new shirt with the group's name on it. Let's assume that the shirt has a design and colors on it that are very appealing to the person wearing it, and they occasionally wear it because they like the colors it has on it and the way the shirt looks. Another friend, who did *not* attend the concert, may coincidentally see this shirt being worn by the person each time they happen to see them. So the assumption is made that their friend likes the band very much because nearly every time they get together the person happens to be wearing the shirt.

What occurs is that the observer will make comments about how much the person liked the group and will say things like, "I know you *really* enjoy such-and-such a band and..." Because this is a small thing, the wearer of the shirt will seldom say anything to contradict the statement *if* they even noticed the remark to begin with. The lack of response serves to reinforce the observer-friend's perception and understanding of the shirt wearer's likes and dislikes. This begins to become part of the person's perceived identity. If this goes unchecked it will become a regular occurrence, and eventually the wearer of the shirt might begin to identify himself as more of a fan of the band than he actually initially was.

This sort of situation is very common in young adults. And depending upon what the perceived identity is, it can become frustrating to the person who is receiving the perceived identity remarks. Often the person will not understand why they feel irritated. This is because the thing that is being said to them is not entirely wrong, which makes the problem far more difficult for the person to detect within themselves.

People don't like to get angry at friends, and when this type of event occurs we, in slight frustration, let it slip by while not really ever realizing that we are giving a pass on it. It's difficult to detect these comments because the comments are usually not the subject of the statement. Someone might make a statement like, "Hey, let's go to the record store to check out some new songs. I hear that such-and-such band's new album is out." The focus in this statement is the record store, and the recipient of the statement is simply interested in going to the record store with their friend. For him or her, the fact that the band's new album is out has little significance, but it can subtly irritate the person nonetheless. And because they understand that the initial aspect of the statement is intended for them as accompaniment of friendship, the other intention in the statement is ignored.

This very common type of perceived identity statement is not specifically intended, nor is it calculated. These types of statements are more of an on-the-fly comment, and are an unintentionally added tidbit that is perceived as a point of interest to the other person. It is an assumption based on presentation, and perceived identity. Our lives are full of these kinds of instances; others do it to us, and we do it to others *every day, all day*. This example was given to get you to grasp that this exists, and that it is always happening.

This becomes a much greater problem when it is something negative. In this case, a person will precondition a statement, saying something such as, "I know you won't like this, but..." or "I know you're not crazy about so-and-so, but..." These comments are almost always fashioned in this way as a protection method for the recipient of the information or comment. The recipient of this information is then being influenced by these subtle pre-conditioned statements. If this repeatedly occurs over a long period of time, to some extent, it usually alters what the recipient perceives he or she feels about the situation or person being spoken of. So, "I know you're not crazy about so-and-so, but..." turns, in to you thinking that you don't like the person even though that is not likely true. This seems harmless, but when it is stated in a negative manner in this way, it can cause the person to begin feeling that they dislike a certain person, a group of people, or some *thing*, even though, in truth, they don't feel that way at all. This is a very common problem that you will readily notice *when* you're looking for it. This pre-casting of thoughts is both wrong and dangerous, especially for younger people who are still forming their thoughts and perceived identities at those early ages—most notably before age three.

People who gossip often use this tactic to get others to agree with them, but in some cases they don't even realize that they are doing so.

Don't allow your mind to allow others to define your perceived identity by accepting pre-cast statements about you or anyone else. We all must come to the understanding that we are all meant to be filled with hot water. But, the problem is that, often, the water that's pouring into us is filthy. When we allow bad water in to us it's like filling ourselves with a flow of contaminated water. Then we fight it a bit by tugging the hose that fills us with the dirty water because we feel that something is not right, and we feel that putting more of this dirty water into us will help, so we pull the hose closer to us. When our tangled hose kinks as we pull on it, then the flow of painful dirty water slows to just a small trickle or stops altogether. Then we wonder what changed and we look into the end of the hose to see what changed but when we stop tugging to examine the hose we release the tension and then we get a face full of filthy water as it begins to fill us again. We need to learn to walk away from that hose and find one with clean water.

When others try to define us through a flow of unwanted filthy hot water, in our confusion, we often stop to check things or distance ourselves from people—releasing the tension—then, because we let down our guard caused by the tension, the water flows again. We repeat this over and over but we never figure out that the filthy water belongs on the ground. We get accustomed to getting the contaminated hot water sprayed in our face, and that becomes a part of us as it fills us up with filthy water.

Chapter 8

You are Not Your Job or Property

Our perception of ourself starts early and flows throughout our entire lifespan. When we believe that we are what we are not, it causes us a great deal of trouble.

How This Began in You

In our older years we come into the ability to overcome some of the undesirable hot water in our lives, but in our youth it is seemingly impossible for us to do this ourselves. As young children, our family, and especially our siblings, cast us in a certain way in their own minds. This can be as simple as their perception of the child sucking his or her thumb or carrying a blanket around all day long. If the hot water casting of these habits goes on long enough, the child can carry this stigma for a very long time. The people around them will begin to adopt that stigma as a part of the hot water of the child, and will have expectations of the child because of the child's relationship with the item.

When an expectation is cast on a child, the child will begin to adopt it as their own hot water. The *expectation* is reinforced in this way and slowly becomes a part of their perceived identity, thus, the child's blanket becomes a part of them in their own view. This does not stop at a child's blanket; and it becomes far more predominant as life moves on. The early occurrences of these types of situations are the precursors, and become the hot water for these kinds of actions to happen all the rest of our lives without us ever even realizing that it is happening. Though, provided that it ends at a reasonably young age, sucking your thumb and carrying a blanket around is typically not a problem. But, other things that we associate ourselves with, such as our job or our house, stay with us for a very long time.

As children age and come into their adolescent years, these tangible *things* run more along the lines of sports, music, and clothes, but the same affect holds true. If a child takes interest in something, then it is often the case that the peers of the child will associate *them* with the *thing*. A "*thing*" can be a sports team, singer, clothing, or any other such element of life—It can even be your belief system.

How This Affected You as a Young Adult

With children, the effect of this is not very noticeable; but when we reach adulthood it is of a more weighty nature. In our young-adult years, of age fourteen to about twenty-two, "*things*" play a very big role in a person's life.

From birth onward, we are inadvertently taught that *we* are *things*. This is difficult for humanity to grasp, and it is predominant in all cultures, including those cultures that we refer to as "primitive." From all indications, even "primitive" cultures suffer from this same social scourge.

You might be thinking along the lines that I am indicating that people are saying, "I am my house or car." I will concede that few people, if any, think that they are actually a house or car, so let's get a little bit less tangible and consider your job. You could do the same here and think, "I am not my job." This might be true, but when asked, "What do you do for a living?" most people begin the answer to the question with, "*I am a* [*insert occupation*]." Understandably, we know that we are not actually some thing or occupation, but the root to all of this goes deeper than we see on the surface. Of course, saying, "*I am a* [*insert occupation*]", is not the cause of the problem, but rather it is an effect of the hot water/perceived identity problem.

When you decided to get into a particular field of interest for a job, or even simply a hobby, you then began to build a set of outward symbols and signs to others that connected you to that particular preoccupation. This is usually done by sharing exciting stories about your new-found interest or job.

For many professionals, a new job brings a specific status to the conversation, and this becomes the central point of that particular part of our perceived identity. As we proudly share our perks and stories about our newest experience or job, we embed in our minds—and more importantly, in the minds of those around us—the specific details of that new part of our life. As we do this, others respond by receiving this information from us while, at the same time, making the assumption that it is very important to us. This is to be expected because that is the reason we talk about something in the first place—it's important to us. We do it to share and explore what is important or of interest to us and to others.

Along with our very own name, given at birth, these new experiences become part of the perception others have of us. As described earlier, when people perceive us a certain way then there is *expectation* on their part; and this *expectation* of us includes our activities, ourself, and our actions—and we seldom disappoint! This is not a rule, but merely a strong rule-of-thumb, because anyone is truly capable of changing in the blink of an eye.

For some reason, most of us feel compelled to fulfill the expectations that others have of us, both good and bad expectations. This is why your perceived identity is so *very* important to deeply understand.

When we identify ourselves so strongly with a particular *thing*, be it an occupation or something very tangible like a house, then we quickly find much of our conversation and thoughts will be about this "thing" which we have developed. There's nothing wrong with discussing your house, job, or any other *thing* in your life. However, there is a problem with it when you have no personal substance beneath that thing.

Lack of substance is predominantly noticeable in young boys and young men who place the whole of their being in a thing, such as a car; or in a person, such as a sports hero or rock star. Girls and young women do this as well. As long as this model item or person is in good order and proving to be worthy, then the young person will feel exultation.

Their friends will like their new sports jersey and the young person feels on top of the world because their team just won the championship. This gives them a feeling of elation and superiority, and thus, they feel accepted as a part of something larger. This is because they are *allowed* to *freely* take part in something that millions of fans think highly of, and thus, they are not rejected for doing so. He or she is accepted!

Now, take that same team and have it lose, or worse, have the sports hero fall from grace via some sort of an addiction or crime, then that young person who idolizes the hero will be crushed. Wearing a symbol of their hero can then become a scourge, and if they continue to do so, it will invite ridicule from their peers and also from the media indirectly via the negative reports about their misbehaven, fallen hero.

How This Affected You as an Adult

Consider the person who sets his sights on riches. Let me be clear here: In *no way* am I saying that a person should not be wealthy. No, rather, when a person places their identity in a house, for instance, this house will become the "*who-they-are*" part of their life. Society often places this false identity on the person as well. This happens because it is the way of our world. Because we live in a very superficial world, we have many different media outlets promoting "cool" via what you have and do. I enjoy good or so called "cool" things too, and I enjoy talking about them and sharing in them, and sharing them with others.

Now, let's consider what happens when someone is fully invested in such tangible riches. Many people derive their value from *things*, which can be money itself, a home, your family, or any other item—and even your own beliefs. When these things are stripped from the person, then the person becomes down or depressed and has nothing to fall back on. We need to examine this negative effect more thoroughly.

Let's ask ourselves, "Why would someone become depressed because their money is gone?" Many of us would say things like, "Because they're broke now, and they had so much before this happened." That's a fair enough answer, but it begs the question, What does that really have to do with being depressed? Is it proper for a person to become down and sad because their life's savings were stripped from them? I have to answer—only for a short period—much the way you would grieve for a week or two over a loved one who just passed away. But beyond that, the person should pick up the pieces, and then restart and do it over again with all of the lessons learned from the first go-round.

Many of us are able to do just that, to pick up and start over again. This is done by placing our perceived identity in that which we do. This cycle can go on for many years, and often people die with their pile of goods only to forfeit it all at their last breath. All of their life's work is spent chasing this false dream, or, I suppose, false god of goods, as their perceived identity. Little can be done for people who have immersed themselves in this manner of existence. However, getting people to understand that—they are loved for *who* they are—is the best and only way for them to see clearly.

A very bad circumstance that we face in this problem is that those around us also place their identities in *things*. Most of us believe that our value is derived from things, so *we* feel that *others* have value if they have things and status. This means that we are *all* causing this problem by feeding it. People who fall from financial grace will quickly find out who their *real* friends are. *Real* true friends are rare, and they are more valuable than anything else in your life. (Real friends can include people from your own family.)

Things and jobs can become dangerous snares to people who fall prey to this misplaced identity. The reason for this is that the people who are in their inner circle, and those in their outer circle, reinforce the feelings of acceptance that are due to their things. This is because they praise the person for their good items or their good job or occupation. Praises of acceptance build upon the false understanding we get from our perceived identity, and we begin to proudly strut our good stuff.

The sad twist in this, which makes matters worse, is that false admiration is often a contributing factor when things begin to unravel for a person who has a false perceived identity. False admiration is when that person who has adopted *things* as their identity, gets a feeling of acceptance and admiration from friends, acquaintances, and family *because* of their *things*. But, when the "*things*" go away, then, typically, so do the friends, acquaintances, and sometimes even family who are built upon the *things*-foundation. This type behavior serves no one, and it is truly a horrible thing for people to do. Such fair-weathered friends are not to be trusted, and they will use you at every interaction when given the opportunity. With regard to your hot water, you are best served by distancing yourself from such people.

Sadly, the person holding the false perceived identity is to blame just as much as the fair-weathered friends are. This is because the holder of the false perceived identity can quickly gain acceptance by having these items, and they are rewarded with accolades by their new-found friends or followers for having such items.

These superficial type relationships are never lasting. In many situations, such as with family, this can be a serious source of pain. This is an extremely common problem that we feel in the world, but it is ignored because we *immediately* feel better when we are accepted in this way. This is the same type of acceptance that someone would receive if they hired a prostitute to serve their needs; and in fact, we are indeed prostituting ourselves *if* this is how we handle life. We are, in a sense, buying love. Few people would argue about the validity of that type of "love."

How do we overcome this? The answers will unravel in the following chapters, but, to start with, we *can* do something that probably might not feel very good at first: We can cut off the supply of our goods to people, and then only spend time with them on a personal level that has nothing to do with our money or things. Yet, even that can have a false sense of honesty depending upon *your **status***.

It amazes me the amount of times I see someone's prestige or status being used by people so that the people will be seen as someone special because they are seen associating with the person of prestige. Enter the world of media... Do not mistake the following statement for people helping people. Of course it's okay to get help from someone if you truly respect that person and will give them the time of day. However, if you're the type of person who will not consider speaking to the person *after* you get what you want from them, then you are a truly misguided person and you need to promptly change this aspect of yourself. When you realize that you're being used by people, the best action is withdrawal of your goods, services, and reputation from them so that you are not being used by them. If they stand by you then

you likely have a rare and good friend. We are discussing
personal relationships here, because in business things and status
are often why the relationship exists at all.

I was once given a book discussing the physical needs of
people in a relationship; in this case, it was about marital
relationships. It was a good book and was filled with many useful
thoughts on getting a relationship back on track. It discussed the
give-and-take parts of a marriage, and what the needs of each
partner are. It had a good analysis of people's marital oversights.
But while the book had many good points, and has likely helped
many struggling couples become closer, it overlooked something
that has been the scourge of couples since the dawn of time. The
book had thoughtfully laid out each person's needs, which is very
important; and when addressing the needs of each other in this
way the problems can be solved. However, an important
underlying foundation was missing from the book: The result of
this foundation being missing in a marriage is typically the cause
of their future generations of children to seek marital separation
and divorce. When the needs of identity are not being properly
met, then accommodating each other's needs simply to be
tolerable to one another *will* cause a lackluster relationship—*no*
relationship should be this way. Many couples likely have been
aided by such books and rekindled their own relationships, but I
suspect most who follow that method have now entered into
more of a business-agreement-style relationship. If you give *me*
this, then I will give *you* that. It is, in a sense, paying them to get
what you want. The foundational problem that we are discussing
here, which is found in most marriages, is discussed in-depth in
the cornerstone book *Red Hot Marriage.*

If both parties tolerate this and are okay with it, and often
they are, then what's the harm, right? Well, the harm comes in
the after-effects. Anyone who is looking for answers to better
relationships in this world will spot these businesslike
relationships a mile away, but, typically, they won't understand
what is specifically wrong in the relationship. In this sort of

relationship, one person is usually doing all of the effort, and to get something in return they *must* negotiate. This is simply not good, but it is often the *only* way the giver will actually receive *anything* out of the relationship to accommodate his or her own needs and desires.

If this sort of business relationship suits you, then that's okay for *you*, but consider this: *All* relationships are transparent and are being seen and experienced by **everyone** around. These superficial unions **will** affect the children of the union. What these children experience **will** affect them as they move into all types relationships of their own. The insincerity that they observe **will**, by natural habit, become what they seek in a relationship. Often this results in their marital separation in the long run because it has become a fundamental part of their hot water. The discomfort felt in such relationships causes much pain regardless of whether they separate or not. This type of insincerity may even have been experienced by you as a child.

So what does all of this have to do with perceived identity? When we see ourselves as "*things*", then we believe our desire for these *things* can be satisfied by more *things*, either very tangible things, like a car, or less tangible things, like the act of sex, or even something like a reputation for how much alcohol someone can handle drinking while out with friends.

Men are often identified by their mates as demanding of affection (or sex). Women are often identified by their mates as demanding of assistance, security, and conversation. These things are all well and good, but when a relationship is on the right track, the fulfillment of these needs is a natural *result* of the proper foundation of the relationship. Discussing marital relationships is a good place for us to get to the nitty-gritty of identity issues and other troubles in a relationship as discussed in the cornerstone book *Red Hot Marriage*. But briefly, much the way a person who has many riches will typically have "friends" flocking to them, so it is with a couple when they both have something the other wants. They will often shower them with offerings of whatever it takes to get what they want. Of course it's okay to give and take in a relationship, but when the relationship is based primarily on things and fair exchange, then there is an underlying problem in the relationship. When this is the case, an empty relationship exists. In a situation of premarital sex, the ramifications of this are very apparent as can be observed in the landscape that is littered with the broken hearts of people who hoped for more than a one night stand—with special notice to the fact that many children are without fathers because their mother gave herself away too freely.

No relationship has to be balanced with goods or things. Those are only outward signs of what is truly beneath the surface. If a person is falling short, then they are not adequately addressing the identity of their spouse. Since identity is not a *tangible* aspect of humanity, *things* are often adopted as bargaining tools. When this happens, the relationship is in peril in the very same way it is when we are being used for our things or our prestige by acquaintances, friends, or family.

Have You Replaced Your Original Self-Worth?

The "things" that we have been referring to are nothing more than "things," and they can bring much enjoyment when you understand *who* you truly are. If a person is fully invested in the tangible things that they have, or even less tangible things, like their political beliefs, they may find much happiness in it, but when the thing fails them they will be devastated.

To illustrate this better, consider two people: Both have homes that are identical to each other and they both have similar jobs. For both of these neighbors everything is going along smoothly and they both appear equally joyful and content in their situations. Later, some opportunity arises and they are asked to leave and go to another place that is better than what they now have. One of the people happily moves, and the other neighbor can't seem to let go of his former home. Why is this?

Assuming they both have similar financial situations and similar new homes, why does it matter? The reason is that one of the people has invested his *whole* being into the place or thing, and when he is requested to leave, he then feels like he's tearing a part of himself out of his perceived identity—which he is indeed doing.

The problem with this is that these *things* are not truly a part of us; and in the example just given, the person uses the house to fill the void felt in his life, or better put, in his *perceived* identity. Those who do this have typically had this mindset as a part of their hot water for a very long part of their lives—likely from birth. It is a taught behavior that is so deeply embedded in our hot water that it is nearly impossible for us to see that it is a problem.

The reason that this occurs to begin with, is that our self-worth has been replaced with *things*, and these *things* have then become our perceived self-worth. And the way we feel about life and ourselves, rotates around the *things* in our lives. We have replaced our native self-worth with *things*. Try to evaluate your own motives relative to the *things* that are in your life. Not just the purely tangible, like a house or car; but also *things* like your job, and the less tangible things like your religious and political beliefs.

Religious beliefs are a major point of concern with regard to perceived identities. When people place their religious beliefs where their identity belongs, then the likelihood that they'll come crashing down at some point is extremely high. When this happens they can lose all faith in their belief and turn away from their religion altogether (this is frequently seen with college students leaving the nest). When we elaborate on this a bit later, you will see how replacing your native self-worth, with things, puts you at great risk of tumbling down from a *false* feeling of acceptance.

What Really is a House or a Job?

This effect permeates all cultures and is the cause of *all* human problems. The "things", both tangible and intangible, are *things* and nothing more than *things*. A job is some***thing*** that you do; it is ***not*** a part of you or anyone else. A house is no***thing*** more than well-organized dirt and trees that someone masterfully made into a home. All tangible items come from the ground, *including* people.

If you do not believe that there is a higher power, then that is up to you, but the fact still remains that we all *feel.* And when we build our perceived identity upon *things*, we are then *subject* to those things and we proceed to *serve* those things.

Take an athlete for instance. All of their worth may be wrapped up in their ability to excel in speed and agility. It is impressive that they can do what they do so well, but what happens if they lose that ability from a tragic accident that paralyzes them? For any of us to be paralyzed is a truly awful thought, but how much more would it affect someone who uses their body in such a way that the paralysis would render them unable to function in their normal job? This example truly cuts to the core of the issue, but we can take it one step further.

Let's take the example of someone who makes their living by being the subject of photographs for public viewing in magazines. If the woman model somehow is disfigured so that she is no longer as physically appealing as she previously was, then the likelihood of her still being hired for such work is very low.

She might not be considered hideous from her injuries, and she stills look quite attractive to most people, and can still function perfectly with the rest of us. In this example, the picture perfect face she once had is no longer "picture perfect", and it prevented her from continuing to use her former beauty for her work. If her perceived identity is wrapped up in her physical beauty, then she will likely become very depressed and begin to have low self-worth. Her perceived identity was her beauty.

In reality, the types of situations in our hypothetical examples just mentioned do happen every day, and so do many other similar situations. When observing these situations you will typically notice one of two outcomes: One outcome is that the person will become depressed and withdraw, often giving up and doing nothing to change their life. The other outcome is that the person renews their strength and does something else with the same vigor that they had used with their former occupation. Why is this? Their attitude all has to do with how they have come about their identity. The hot water problem plagues us all, but we seldom see it because it is our hot water. We don't realize the condition of our hot water, and, therefore, we can't *see* what we allow as our perceived identity. Or maybe better stated, we don't *realize* what we allow as our perceived identity.

Your Expectations from Other People and Your Expectations of Other People

As you go through your day, try to get into the habit of observing yourself and your actions. Why do you do the things that you do? How much are your choices and actions influenced by others? Do you have expectations of other people based on how you perceive those people? I don't mean your expectation of what they do, but rather what you think of them. Do you reinforce those expectations? And have you ever noticed that your expectations affected someone's reaction or behavior? You will likely answer "yes" to this after making observations and thinking about it for a while.

Now, consider that this is happening to *you* from *their perspective* as well. Just as you have affected them, they are affecting you, and you likely never really have noticed it in this way. We typically do notice these influences to some extent, but we don't understand what is happening. If the expectations are of a negative nature, then we become angry, frustrated, or depressed, and we often take it out on those around us.

When we allow our hot water to create our perceived identity as *things*, such as our house, job, degree, or even things that are for security such as gold, money, and weapons, then we have set that up as a god that we serve. We *fear* without those things, or rather, because of our hot water we fear, therefore we have obtained those things.

Chapter 9

Jealousy and Perceived Identity

Whether we are the jealous person, or the person who is the subject of the jealousy, jealousy in our perceived identity is an enormous source of pain and suffering for us. Jealousy is seen in marital relationships; for instance, when a spouse gives a certain type of attention to someone other than their mate, then jealousy will often ensue. But that's not the type of jealousy to which I am referring. Here, I am referring to the kind of jealousy that is based on *things*, rather than on human feelings and actions.

When we invest ourselves in what we have, as many of us do, then when others have something better than us, or when they have more things than us, it tends to evoke a feeling of jealousy in us.

Think about our earlier sports hero example, where the sports hero falls from grace and crushes the young follower. This young person is so wrapped up in the hero that it causes a major let-down when the hero falls. Why is this? It is because the young person is *all-in*. Everything that they think, say, and do revolves around this hero.

The same is true about fully investing yourself in *your things*. When you are doing well, and what you have surpasses everything that your friends, family, and associates have, then you feel special and you are on a high point of your good fortune. However, when someone exceeds your status, then in your own eyes *you* have fallen, even though your own circumstances have not changed at all. When this happens, the person who exceeded you is the subject and the target of your jealousy. Such jealousy often causes condemnation of the one who surpassed you.

Are You Jealous of Perceived Prestige?

Another, and perhaps the most prominent, place you will see jealousy rear its head is in the spotlight of prestige, most notably in education. Because so many people have been taught all of their lives by family, friends, and teachers that they are failures if they do not attend college, we have, for this reason, adopted into our hot water the lie that education-status is *what* you are. Our thinking fits an attitude of—after all, if this isn't so, then why all of the emphasis on higher education?—which has become a sort of self-fulfilling prophecy for us.

Because so much emphasis is placed on prestige, prestige becomes more sought after; and because it becomes more sought after, it gets more emphasis. This has gotten to the point where it is now difficult to get a job without the prestige of a degree. Sadly, this façade has caused many of the wrong people who have prestigious degrees to get jobs that would be better done by more brilliant, but less "educated" people. This, in turn, is forcing others to have to bow to the world's view of acceptability. Is there an escape from this? Not likely! Barring an all-out world economic collapse, societally we have trapped ourselves in the act of not appreciating and nurturing the true and natural talents we each have. Socially, worldwide, we will be unlikely to solve this problem. However, we can very easily solve it in each our own selves, and, through that, we can change the world.

Because these prestigious degrees are now usually required in order to get a good paying job (which is typically measured by both money and the social perception of the particular occupation) it has become far more than a degree. For too many it has become their status, and this status has become their perceived identity. While this feels empty for many people, it does satisfy the basic desire to *perceive* ourselves as loved or accepted.

People go to college and party, study, and then graduate. Then they seek a job, get it, and suddenly are propelled into the world of a good-paying career, often, far from home and their loved ones. With all of this emphasis on money and occupational prestige, it has come to be more about your *job-title* than your *pay-scale*. While pay is important to many, the position's *title* seems to be far more important to many of those who hold the coveted degrees. Some people will even spend many extra years going to college so that they can improve their status with a higher degree even though they will likely never utilize the additional education. There's nothing wrong with doing this when it is done for true interest in the subjects being studied, but when it is done to falsely prop up our hot water, then we are deceiving ourselves by believing that we're better because we have degree initials to put with our name.

It's similar with jobs. How many times have we seen someone take the promotion only to make less money per hour than they did before? Salary always sounds so good, until we find that we are often working much longer hours. Sure, the pay is steady, but the hours are often long and arduous. But, when all is said and done, the person who got the promotion is, prestigiously, now "VP" of something.

The newly gained prestige is often flaunted to coworkers and friends, which amounts to bragging rights. The added responsibility, and being in charge of more people, all adds up to status! It's common for a person's newly acquired status to be the point of contention for the friends or coworkers who just got knocked off of their top status position in relation to the person's new promotion. If the friend or co-worker's position status is important to them, then it becomes the point of contention in their relationship, and is often the cause of jealousy.

Why Jealous People Do Not Want You to Be Happy

As is often the case, this type of jealousy can also head in the reverse direction. Let's say that the promoted person is very proud of their new-found status and they share this news with the others. The others will usually respond in the anticipated manner. They will typically respond in a kind but envious manner, thus showing the promoted person that his or her new status is a worthy prize to be had.

But what about the other person who is not much fazed by the promotion? This type of person has either simply given up and cares about nothing, *or* they have a very sound foundation and are happy with whom they themselves are, just as they are. When approached with the news of someone's promotion, they offer a simple "congratulations" and are happy for the person, and then continue with their day, without being envious about the news. No raving review or envy is shown by them; just a heartfelt, "Congratulations!" The promoted jealous person will detect this lack of *awe* and will usually be displeased deep down inside due to their own hot water.

When this sort of behavior persists, then the person sharing each additional piece of glorious news begins to wonder why the other person remains unfazed and is not affected by news of their new status. This part is important to keep in mind as you read: If the unaffected person is a happy, loving, and kind person, which is often the case in these situations, the promoted person will begin to be very frustrated by his or her inability to awe the happy-go-lucky coworker. He or she will wonder how the coworker, who has so little prestige, can be so happy. Left long enough, this will gnaw away at the heart and mind of the promoted person, and then jealousy, and often bitterness, are the result. This, of course, will depend upon the level of love held by the promoted person. If this is allowed to fester for some time, the promoted person will typically begin to demean the happy-go-lucky person in an attempt to diminish them so that the promoted person can feel superior and have their time in the spotlight of the happy-go-lucky person's heart.

It's difficult to feel superior to someone who is always joyful, which will bother a person who seeks *prestige* for their own gratification; this is often the reason why they typically beat other people down in life. If you're a loving person you will be happy and content, but those who are not content, and are unhappy, will often try to take you down a few notches on the happy-scale because they are jealous of your joy and they want what you have. Sadly, this is something they will never achieve with their current state of mind and way of thinking. This type person will often make it their mission to try to destroy the credibility of a genuinely joyful person.

The function in this last scenario is a common dynamic of relationships. Misplaced jealously that is aimed at content people is used on many levels. This scenario is only one of those levels. This also happens in homes between siblings, and in schools between classmates; and it all can start at a very young age.

Are You Jealous of Other People's Joy?

Happiness and joy appear to go hand in hand, and in fact they do; but people usually think of them as one-and-the-same thing, but they are not. Happiness is a *result* of joy, but people can experience happiness from almost any good thing that is not also joy. When a person is in a joyful state they generally are happy. Happy means that something went your way. You could be happy because you acquired a bunch of new customers, but other than the business competition aspects, you don't feel joy because the reason the customers now come to you is because your competitor died and you liked the person.

Joy is to welcome and to be glad. Joy is a higher state of being and will certainly bring happiness, but happiness does not necessarily bring joy. *Things* and *prestige* do not, and cannot, bring joy, but they can bring happiness.

Happiness can be competed with. Where with joy, it cannot be competed with. When something falls into your favor, you will be happy, and when you share this news with others who have a similar but lesser thing or position, then the person will sense your new fortune as a threat to and will typically proceed to try to out-do you or pull you down a notch or two. This is usually done by them, without their full realization, in order for them to feel above you in *their* own eyes.

Happiness is confused with joy because joy will *always* result in happiness, but this is not true for the reverse. When you are joyful you will appear to be happy, and then when someone who felt as if they are above you sees your happiness, then they understand it as—*something that you have is good*—and they want to know what it is. They want to have that "*something*", and they want it better or more of it than you have. The fact that you have acquired fewer things than they have doesn't matter. This will frustrate them if they have the jealous nature in their hot water, which is because they understand this as—someone having something better than them in the tangible and semi-tangible realm. *They* want to be the *most* loved, and they want to be happier than you are.

This connection to *things* runs deep, and these *things* dominate our lives, yet we do not feel joy in them. For some of us, it's our car or our home; for others, it's who we know; and for some, it is what we have done or how we have been educated. This is taught to most of us from a very young age, basically from birth on, and in the beginning it seems okay, but when love and understanding are lacking in our lives, then love and understanding are replaced by a wrong belief that *things*, such as people's status, attire, and money, are what makes us acceptable. (This includes status, jobs, education, body markings, clothing, cars, religious and political beliefs, etc...). This happens with behavioral issues in early childhood, and it is reinforced by those who the child respects or is told to respect.

Often, children are taught by parents, teachers, elders, friends, and society that it is what you have, what you wear, your education, and your job, etc. that makes you acceptable. Parents want their children to have a "better life," and so they send them to college and tell them, or rather *teach* them, that if they do not go to school, then they will fail. This is readily translated into—"You are a failure" by the children. This type situation happens *during* all ages and *through* all stages of our lives.

The only way for anyone to be truly accepted is through Truth and Love, and love is a part of truth. Without truth, true love cannot exist. True love is joyful and honest, and it is eternal!

When we get caught up in the mindset of setting up our identity in things (which most of us do), we become trapped and have a difficult time distancing ourselves from our things. Then we become frustrated, then angry, then bitter, and finally—jealous. One major underlying factor is fear. Fear of what? Fear of being rejected, or rather, fear of not being accepted.

Bullies, Terrorists, and You

Bullies get validation by rejecting others. People do not like to be rejected. We can walk by a thousand people and not be noticed and we will not be or feel rejected. Those people are simply passers-by, and we are as indifferent to them as they are to us. But, when we get rejected by someone close to us we have a difficult time understanding why someone would reject us or why they do not like us. And, if we are not being boastful or mean, the root reason is almost always jealousy or envy.

A bully will *reject*, and by doing so they achieve acceptance because the rejected person will typically make an effort to be accepted by the bully. Attempts to gain acceptance are done by trying to please the bully. In turn, this causes the *bully* to feel accepted, and it empowers the bully.

Bullies also gain strength by humiliating or mocking others. Because most people's deep-down worst fear is rejection, people who are witnessing the bully's rejection of another person will seek to accommodate the bully so that they themselves do not become the target of the bully's tightly-aimed rejection techniques, as is commonly seen in politics.

When people accommodate a bully, they freely hand their power over to the bully; and, by doing so, they strengthen the bully. Additionally, the bullying type will seek attention or acceptance by tearing others down. The person who they tear down will typically be someone who excels and who people are be envious of. Or, it could be a person who had the job of disciplining people, such as a teacher, policeman, or some other authority figure.

When an authority figure reprimands or corrects a person, then the person who has been reprimanded will feel ashamed because people do not like being or feeling rejected. This causes feelings of anger, humiliation, and even jealousy. When this is the case, people typically do nothing and will only complain to their friends about the authority person who they feel had hurt them. These authority figures are prime targets for bullies. A bully will seek validation through attacking the authority figures, or other people who the bully's minions may have a reason to feel jealous of.

When the bully provokes the authority, or person of good standing, it brings those who have felt jealous or hurt by that authority, to the bully's side as supporters of the bully. Bullies detect this and thrive on it. People will cheer them on as they tear into and tear down the authority or person who the people are jealous of or angry with. What happens is that the bully taps into the fear and jealousy that the people have, and uses that to increase him- or her- self. This is usually done unwittingly by the bully, and they simply do this for acceptance as a natural behavior. This behavior starts at very early ages and is reinforced by friends, relatives, siblings, parents, and even bystanders.

Do You Allow People to Use You so that You Feel Loved?

The bottom line for all of us is that this is all done by the bully as an effort to feel loved in a distorted way. A *need* to feel loved is natural in *all* of us, and it is the single most important force in our existence. It is when we misunderstand what love truly is that our problems arise. When our hot water is tainted by misinterpreted love, then we have difficulty recognizing true love, and so we substitute true love with empty praise from others. We feel it, but we don't understand what is wrong in our life and relationships.

This false love is shown by others who offer their praises to us solely based upon what we have, or upon our status—essentially, they use us. We want to believe that we're not being used by people because they ask nothing of us in these scenarios. While it is true that they may ask nothing of you, they can still be using you as bragging rights of knowing *you*. After all, they know the person who has this-and-that, or who is the leader or president of something, or some other position of prestige.

The association that is drawn to—who the person of prestige is—uses that person, but, in general, it is harmless to them. When we draw these associations, then we feel special or loved when others are awed at *our* association with a person of prestige.

The *false love* that people of prestige receive from others is what many of us crave, but no matter what we do or how many people love us in this way, we still can't seem to find fulfillment or satisfaction in our own lives when this is what we thrive on. For those who are in this position, our hot water lacked joy while growing up, or we got on the wrong path at some point during our life. If our hot water is of a very good nature and we do not understand these principles, then we can still step into the wrong path, which includes adopting an affinity for this type of false love.

This can easily happen because when people give us the gratifying attention, the false love feels good and has an outward *appearance* the same as when a person gives true love. Their gratifying feeling is the outcome or the way it is manifested, but this sort of gratifying love can be given without true love being in the scenario at all. This is much like flattery, where you compliment someone even if you do not truly mean what you say. And because the outward signs are the same, it can be difficult to detect the difference, especially when you're not specifically looking for it. This is even more so when your hot water is founded on this and is contaminated in this way.

To better illustrate true love versus false love, picture two lightbulbs: one hooked to a battery, and one to the electrical outlet—the battery being false love, and the electrical outlet being lasting true love. Both sources are connected to a light. The battery will be there and will light up the bulb, but the battery will eventually run out of energy and die when the demand of power lasts too long—it's a fair-weather friend. But the electrical outlet's power will endlessly power the bulb and it will never go out provided that it is always properly connected to the *proper* source. With the battery it's not the same, you can leave the light bulb connected, but the light will *always* eventually go out when the power in the battery is all used up.

Both of the power sources will light the bulb and the result is the same—light. But the level of *commitment* is not the same. The light bulb cannot ask too much of the electrical outlet because the bulb can never consume all that the outlet has to offer, but it *can* ask too much of the battery.

The need for all humans to feel loved is central in our makeup whether or not you subscribe to the God-the-Creator concept.

Although, the central importance of true love is typically more readily accepted if the God-the-Creator concept is your belief.

Your Fear is the Driving Cause of False Love

Because the inescapable human desire to be loved is so strong in all of us, when it fails to happen in our lives, or even when we fail to sense the true love that actually does exist in our lives, then us feeling unloved is the result.

What does it feel like to not be loved? The common term is rejection. Simply put, rejection is the most horrible of experiences for all living beings.

Some people get rejected by a person and it might be of no consequence to them, but when they are rejected by that which they have an affinity for, then they'll feel the deep pain of rejection, with jealousy often being the end product. But jealousy is not really the end product of rejection; rather, it is the end product of the *fear* of rejection.

This goes back to what we discussed in the beginning of this chapter and throughout. When someone's hot water is contaminated with *false* love, then they seek to fill the inherent need for true love with false love, which is done through people paying them tribute in attention and admiration because of their things, position, or prestige. When we see a threat to our false love in this way, we become defensive, and that defensiveness shows up in the form of jealousy.

But *why* are we defensive? The reason is to protect our territory. What territory? Our subjects or our followers, or better stated, those people who see us as great or special because of our *prestige*, *status*, or *things*. Or, it could be our acceptance from someone who we see as prestigious that we offer our adoration to so that they accept us.

If a threat comes along, the underlying motivation to take action will be the fear of losing our status-position that we feel we perceive in the hearts and minds of our followers (those who praise us for our status-position). This type of fear is the most terrible of conditions to us, and we simply do not understand it in this way because it is so thoroughly a part of our hot water.

There's a tremendous danger for us in this because any attempt to try to explain to us what true love is, is also seen as a threat to our way of understanding life. When true love is discussed, it cuts down and reduces the importance of *status* and *things*, and cuts to the core of our lives. If we have nothing except status and things at our core, and if someone makes an attempt at diminishing that core in any way—*even if it's through an explanation with true love*—and we allow it to be spoken to us, then we quickly see that we are void and empty and realize that we do not have the "love" that we thought we once felt, even though nothing actually changed except for our own understanding of *love*.

Some of you who are reading this are likely thinking, "Don't explain true love to people, show them true love by doing it, through truly loving people." This is a good and true thought, but it's not that simple. Those of us who have experienced life in a false-love way simply do not know any better. To us, true love is confusing and we don't understand what it is. Depending upon how well we know someone, if someone is only an acquaintance, we will likely understand their true love the same as we understand false love; this is because we are not be around them long enough to detect that they care about *us* and that they care nothing about our *status* or *things*.

In the event that an acquaintance did immediately express that our status and things were of no importance to them, it is typically seen by us as an attack against us, and the vindictive nature of jealousy in us results. In most cases, an acquaintance will not charge into that sort of controversial discussion for a couple of key reasons: First, it would be rude; and second, it is socially unacceptable and, thus, often brings with it an attack against the bearer of the comment. So, people who have learned to crave false love are generally met with a kind demeanor by acquaintances, which reinforces their misunderstood hot water.

This is different with people who know us well. If we are a person with a jealous nature and our relationship is frequent and close, then the other person will have to compromise their words around us or they will create a great deal of tension between us, themselves, and others around us. Speaking in a frank but kind manner to a jealous person is what is needed, but doing so typically causes some controversy. Because we see a threat to our status, we make every attempt that we can to protect our hot water territory. We fear losing the only form of love that we have come to know, even if it is wrong.

It is nearly impossible to explain this to someone who is in this position because false love imitates true love so well on the surface. If we have never experienced true love or have not allowed true love into our lives, then we simply cannot see the difference—it *is* our hot water.

Do You Provoke Jealousy?

To some extent a large portion of us do provoke jealousy, though, it may be very minimal, and for some it is nearly nonexistent. Even if you have partaken in this form of love, or feeling loved in this way, then you have likely also shown jealousy from fear that someone will surpass you in prestige or things. When this is the hot water of a family, or even of a community, it is very easy to get caught up in it even if it is only occasionally that you desire false love.

Those who have come to know only this type of love show much jealousy when someone outpaces them. If your hot water has this kind of love, but you only partake in it on rare occasion, and you outpace someone who *only* knows this kind of love, then they will take your outpacing them as an attack and you will then be challenged by them. This is where people get drawn into a competition with regard to the prestige of their things. None of it is specifically deliberate, because it is a part of the hot water of both parties. The one who seeks false love the least can get drawn in to competing in this way and can quickly become a fulltime seeker of false love through the competition process. It grows like a disease and eats away at the heart until you turn bitter, which is a *very unhappy* way to be.

In a sort of reverse effect of this type of love, with those who have come to seek false love because of their hot water being so badly contaminated, we often see loving discipline being taken as rejection, when, in truth, it is really true love.

Similar to false love appearing on the surface to emulate true love, so too, does hatred and rejection attempt to emulate true love's discipline. When a person, whose hot water has been contaminated with false love, is disciplined, they typically see it as rejection; the reason for this is because they have not yet come to know true love. And then, when they go to attack someone who they see as a threat to themselves, they are aiming to destroy the other person in effort to bring them down to a position below themselves, if not to crush them entirely. Where with true love there will be stern reprimand, and even punishment if warranted. It is the difference in the underlying goal that decides which is which. True love can take away a privilege to teach a lesson so that the person being disciplined becomes better in the future. Where with rejecting for the sake of jealousy and hatred, the purpose is to steal and destroy and to never have them become more or better.

True love builds up, false love destroys, and the two can be the exact same outward action with different intent. This is why it's so difficult for most of us to discern which is which, and it is also why it is difficult to escape from seeking false love. It is all a part of our hot water; and therefore, we do not perceive that this is going on in our lives at every moment of every day of our lives whether we are doing it to others, or others are doing it to us.

Do You Hunger For Status?

The behavior is all the same. We identify with status or things and we wrongly believe that this is what makes us accepted or acceptable. Sadly, when we believe and behave in this way, we also accept others in this same way. We often believe that money makes the man, when the reality is that it is the man that makes the money. We listen to people boast about their status and how much knowledge they have because of their degrees. But, in truth, they offer little other than their golden credentials. True status need not boast and will offer sound information for open evaluation by others. A person with true status *creates* instead of boasting about what they are qualified to create. There is a big difference between someone actually being able to share their knowledge with others, versus someone who is telling everyone that they have knowledge to share by boasting about their own status. We are never truly satisfied when we live this way, and we are often unhappy and don't want others to be happy. And, consequently, we condemn those who have achieved pure joy in their lives. This common behavior knows no class, status, or income levels. It is a state of mind and a state of being for us *when* we have chosen this way of understanding.

When we have adopted this as our own way to be accepted or acceptable and we meet with resistance to our delusion that what we are is great, then we become frustrated in not being able to convince others that what we have or believe is best, great, or better than what others have. This frustration results in our own jealousy or envy because we do not understand *why* the other person is content without *our* things or status. Further, we then cannot comprehend that the other person is not impressed with our things or status, because we simply do not understand **why** this is so.

Our lack of ability to comprehend those who are not impressed with us, results in our frustration and, in turn, our anger. This anger often manifests itself in the form of envy or jealousy and in the condemnation of the resistor. When the resistor becomes reactant to our taunts and provocation, then we get a type of validation from their reaction, and we can then deceive ourselves into believing that the tables are turned. *We* believe, based upon *their* behavior, that the other person, the resistor, is jealous.

In reality, those who are not impressed by things and status, and go on to show anger in this way, are typically angry at the poor behavior that we show when we set up our identity in *things* and *status*—we mistake their *frustration and anger* at us, for *jealousy*. When we distill this to the very basis or foundation of it, it all comes down to *acceptance*. Status personalities have come to believe that what we *have* or *are* is what makes us acceptable; and, in turn, that's the way *we* view other people when we do this. Believing that the *what*-and-*who* are what make us or others great, amounts to arrogance.

Chapter 10

Perceived Identity and Arrogance

To investigate arrogance within perceived identity, we must first dispel a myth about pride. What is pride? Pride and arrogance are often wrongly interchanged. In much the way that false love and true love are similar in their outward action and appearance, so, too, are pride and arrogance similar in their outward action and appearance. If you investigate the origins and definition of the word *pride* you will find that it essentially means: *knowing* that what you have done is good and being able to properly show that fact. That is to say, you are aware of what you are, and what you are is good—it comes across as confidence.

Do You Know the Difference Between Pride and Arrogance?

Arrogance is different than pride. Arrogant people won't come to you. They want *you* to come to them to prove to themselves that they are wanted. It is a form of control. When we choose the arrogant approach we cannot as easily be rejected, it making us feel safe. We do this because we're afraid. And because we fear, we are rendered insecure. When we lack a proper foundation, we will always feel insecure and fear *rejection*; then, in our arrogance, we demand that others come to us.

Many translators of the Bible have chosen to use the word "pride" where it should really say "arrogance." These two words appear the same because of the way pride is often misused. Arrogance is different than pride, but the end result *appears* to be identical to pride in the eyes of most onlookers; and as a result, pride gets a bad stigma attached to it that it does not deserve. Pride is good, as long as it is actually the "pride" that we're speaking about right now. Because the outward sign of arrogance appears identical to pride, we confuse the two. Remember, *pride* is good.

So what is arrogance? Arrogance is to exaggerate our position, status, or things, or maybe better stated, it overstates a value. A quick example is debt: Debt is typically arrogant. Debt allows us to get something that we have not yet worked for. Arrogance is very common in our world and has been going on since the dawn of mankind. Arrogance in money is especially common when the debt out-paces the monthly pay that we receive. We call this "living beyond our means", which is often done for status positioning. Arrogance does not stop at falsely inflating the value of our money.

Around the time of the end of the twentieth century it was common for people submitting their qualifications for a job, to inflate their abilities on their submitted resume—These inflated abilities amount to lies. This practice came to be expected to a point where those who were going to hire these individuals anticipated this stretching of reality, and they took that into consideration knowing full well that they would need to re-train their new exaggerated workers.

The reason that people falsely inflate their qualifications when submitting their job resume is to make themselves look better in order to increase their chances of getting the job. This deceitful practice was vaguely taught by the schools and by culture. It generally appeared to be harmless because everyone understood that it was occurring. How does this connect?

While many people did this reluctantly, it was still the same as the action of being arrogant. The difference is that some of the people who took part in this are not arrogant and felt badly for "stretching" the truth to what amounts to a lie.

Some people did this reluctantly and only did so because of the pressures from those who taught them to do so. They felt badly about the exaggeration, and so it is not real arrogance in their own heart. True arrogance is when someone goes about boasting about themselves and their value, but what they boast about is overstated. Arrogance is in the heart of the person. If you are forced by someone to behave arrogantly and it bothers you to do so, then you're not arrogant in your heart, but you may be considered foolish.

The fact that arrogance emulates pride is why many women are duped by men who are arrogant. Let me explain: Pride is a good attribute, especially when combined with moderation. If we go out and taut our pride, it will often make those who have fallen short of their own view of success, feel as if they are failures. The reason others feel like failures is because they have not met with what they see as success. They lack a solid internal reality because they have rejected things that are true. When we reject true things, then we are living in a false state of mind—we live a lie.

When a person shows pride they are showing that they succeeded and are celebrating that by sharing their news with others. They can also show their pride by simply carrying themselves tall and strong. With pride this is done **when they have** achieved success and **when they know** that what they accomplished is good. This is an attractive thing, and many people like to associate with people of success because they want to emulate that success and acquire similar success for themselves. Pride *is* desirable because it is the result of self-confidence, and confidence is the result of being honest.

We want to feel good about ourselves and confident in what we do. People who are truly successful *are* this way, which is appealing to the rest of society. This is especially true if it is a confident man who carries himself with true pride. In general, women find confidence to be a very appealing attribute in men because women are typically seeking certainty and direction in a man. If pride is overstated, or if someone has "too much pride," then it is no longer pride, but rather, it is then, technically, *arrogance*.

The problem that many women run into is that they fail to test this in men. The testing can easily be done by simply looking behind the man. When young adults in their late teens and their twenties desire to find a mate, the women are often on the lookout for confident, strong, self-assured men. Men will try to be what the women are looking for by showing off what they know or what they can do—men show-off for women. As a natural instinct, both, the proud men and the arrogant men will display themselves, and because both of these two types of personalities have an end result that appears as confidence, it is difficult for the observing women to detect the difference.

Confidence comes from the word *confide*. To confide is to trust, which in the end means to *know* something. This means that when a person *knows*, and is certain, then they have confidence. When they have confidence, you will see it in them and they will be proud of their understanding. This is simply because they *know* and they are *certain* and have *no* doubt. Typically, their certainty is noticeable.

Arrogance is different in this regard because arrogance is an overstating of what *is true*. When *arrogance* is done well it appears as *confidence* and dupes many women and other people. As explained in the cornerstone book *Red Hot Marriage*, by the time a woman finds out that an arrogant man is a fraud, it's often too late for the woman, and, much to her regret, she has married him.

This does not stop at the man and woman relationship, it includes acquaintances and friends. You don't have to look long to see people repeatedly falling into the arrogance trap. One place where this occurs dependably is in the world of fame. No doubt there are many famous people who have true confidence and are genuinely proud of their accomplishments, but there are also many who are nothing more than arrogant personalities who are forever overstating their life-status. And it doesn't stop there.

If you know a person who is arrogant—a pretender—you will see people clamoring for that person's approval. This connects to the earlier chapters having to do with other people's perception of *your* identity. If people perceive you as confident, but you actually are *not* confident and are only acting as though you are confident by means of your arrogance, then people will be drawn to you. If they have misread what you truly are, then they have duped themselves.

So, what's the difference between the two? Confidence *is knowing*, and arrogance *is pretending you know*. Arrogance is taking a position that does not belong to you because you have not worked to understand or achieve it. Another reason that foolish or erred people come across as confident is that they might truly believe something and yet be incorrect, so they are displaying confidence even though what they speak about is absolutely incorrect.

There is a sad twist in this: People who are proud and truly confident will *never* show themselves above that which they have earned in position. Where, on the other hand, the arrogant person will revel in the opportunity to *pretend* to be of more value than a truly confident person is. The result of this is that, to unsuspecting observers, an arrogant person will appear to be more self-assured than the more accomplished person appears. And, as is often the case, the attention and credit goes to people who have accomplished far less. Additionally, those who have true understanding, and true accomplishments and success, are often overshadowed by the arrogant. This is all a part of the collective hot water of the people involved, as well as each of them individually. This often causes the truly confident person to somewhat withdraw while the arrogant person steals their place in the spotlight.

Arrogance has the effect of having arrogant people act as authoritarians as they believe themselves to be self-important. When we choose this path, then everything is a big deal to us, and we believe that it's a big deal to those around us as well. It is an autocratic way to be, and, in general, it is rejected and not liked by most people even though many of us behave this way to some extent.

Do You Accuse Confident People of Being Arrogant and/or Having "Too Much Pride"

Arrogance is about building ourselves up. Because of our hot water, we have been misled and have learned to seek false and empty love. But when we encounter *true confidence*, then we have seen the source of **true pride**—not *arrogance*. True confidence will be seen as a threat to us if we are the arrogant type.

When we feel a threat, then our defense method is to go on the offensive and attack the other person whose position or status we perceive is posing a threat to us. This is often true even if the person who we see as a threat has done or said nothing to or about us and has in no way acted against us.

If our status in the community is well received and we have chosen the arrogant way, and then another person moves into our community who has accomplished much more than us, but says little, eventually they will draw others from the community to themselves. The community will begin to know this newcomer and may be smitten with their life position. When the attention is drawn away from us we feel our false love from others dissipate. Even if people do show us true love, their attention is now divided and we get less attention. The reduced attention is a threat to us and to our perceived identity. This is just like the child whose parents' attention was divided between the existing child and the new baby.

A confident person will often be attacked by an arrogant person and be accused by the arrogant person of being arrogant and/or having "too much pride."

The word *pride* is largely misunderstood. It is often used in a negative context in such a way as when someone displays utter confidence, an arrogant person will either say that the confident person is arrogant or that they have *too* much pride. In reality, there is no such thing as *too* much pride—Pride is what **IS**— Arrogance is what **IS not**. If someone does have "too much pride" or more than is due to them, then, technically, by definition, they are arrogant, rather than proud.

If you're a person who truly knows what you are doing and you're highly confident in doing so, and you then display this confidence, technically, that is what is called *pride*. But if you attempt to make yourself out to be more than you are, then that is technically called *arrogance*. The sole purpose of arrogance is to build yourself up above others so that you can receive the false love that your hot water has conditioned you to crave. But when you know what you are all about and what you're doing, then you can be confident, and the result is pride. The trouble with pride is that when we *know* something, then it's easy to place ourselves above others, which leads many proud people into a state of arrogance. We must be ever vigilant to **not** allow our minds to overstep our true pride by then stepping into arrogance.

Another thing you will hear an arrogant person say is, "His pride was hurt." It is not really a person's pride that is hurt if it is true pride, but rather it is their heart that is hurt. If someone has truly worked for what they have, and they fully understand their work and are confident in what they do, then arrogant people will often try to tear that person down with insults, derogatory gossip, and a competitive nature. If the confident person feels badly, it is not that their pride was hurt; it is that they were disheartened because they were treated unjustly and falsely accused—they were unjustly violated and rejected. A person of true confidence will not tear others down, and typically only will build them up.

In a reverse situation, a truly confident person may point out an error that an arrogant person has made in order to help them. Even if it is done privately and with dignity and much respect, the arrogant person will still likely take it as a direct attack and will embark on a relentless pursuit of false vindication. It is truly a tragic thing if we point out an error that someone is making and they reject the correction.

Think on that for a moment... "**Correction**" or to "**Correct**." If you correct someone and they reject the correction, then they have *chosen* to proceed in a wrong or **not**-correct manner.

Think of this problem in an example form: Imagine that it is a very dark night and your friend knows the layout of the land better than anyone. You and the friend are walking along when suddenly your friend shouts and urges you to stop immediately. Your friend says, "Stop! Stop immediately! Be careful or you'll fall!" Do you stop immediately and follow their wise counsel, or do you spite your friend and stubbornly and arrogantly continue on your way?

In this example, your friend knows that there is a cliff, and that you are just about to step off of that cliff. They also know that there are only rocks to catch you some two hundred feet below. If you choose to proceed and ignore the "*correction*" you *will* have made a deadly error!

While this example seems to be a no-brainer and the obvious choice is to stop and heed the warning of the friend, it is less obvious in everyday events. It's good for people to make some of their own mistakes because that's one way that we all learn. But it is better if a person can understand *why* something would be a mistake, and then *not* make that mistake to begin with, and, instead, learn from the wise counsel of the friend.

Do You Hate Being Corrected?

Sadly, because we have a tendency to rebel against correction, the reality in our world is much the opposite of embracing *wise* counsel. Please remember that the word *correction*, means to be *corrected*, and if you are *corrected* then you are now **correct**—meaning that you are accurate.

On numerous occasions, I have had people actually say the words to me, "I don't like to be *corrected.*" When a person takes this position, we have a tendency to want to call it prideful, but it is not pride, it is a foolish arrogant position. When we do this, then, in our arrogance, we are wanting to continue in our errors *without* paying for the consequences of these errors. This is a foolish way to conduct life, and it can only lead to self-destruction in the long run.

Here is where confusion can come in for us: When a confident person makes an error, we will see them receive the correction. They might not be happy initially, but they *will* correct their position regardless. If they are not happy being corrected, then it will be with themselves for allowing the oversight in their thinking to begin with. So some frustration at one's self could appear to others as a rejection of wise counsel even though it is not.

The real problem with this comes in when a person truly knows what they are doing, and *knows* that they *know* that they are *correct* and can explain in vivid and accurate detail why they are correct. Then, when another person tells them that they are wrong and persists in this, the confident person is going to persist in rejecting the wrong suggested action that, to them, is wrong for many factually obvious and readily provable reasons. If the person who is offering the incorrect suggestion persists long enough, then the confident person becomes annoyed or angry at the persistence in the matter because the confident person has proof that the suggestion is technically *wrong*.

To the suggester, this will have the same irrational appearance as if you would reject your friend's advice to stop so that you do not walk off of the cliff. I deliberately used the words "irrational *appearance*" because if someone is skilled in some action and they understand *all* of the details of what they are doing, but the observers *do not understand* it in the same way, and then one of the observers makes a suggestion, another similarly experienced observer will likely be in agreement with the erred suggestion. But their suggestion is based on not fully understanding things that are related to what the confident person's work requires. So, if the highly-skilled confident person rejects the suggestion and gets upset at the suggester's persistence, then the highly-skilled confident person will be seen as irrational by those observers, and the observers will see that confident person as not receiving what the observers perceive to be *their own* wise counsel.

Each person's perspective with regard to everything we have discussed so far in this book is completely due to each person's own hot water. If a person has been raised from birth in a situation that had hot water that was accustomed to giving and receiving false love, then the likelihood of the person having similar hot water is extremely high. When a situation occurs like the example that was just given, then they will see that situation similar to the way *they* experienced life, and, in that case, whether they are wrong or right does not matter. They will assume that the skilled person is a fool for not listening to them and that the skilled person is wrong. This is just like they themselves feel when they are being *corrected* in the true sense of the word *corrected*, yet they refuse to listen to the wise counsel of correction.

In their minds they (the observers in our example) were trying to "correct" the skilled person, but the information that they wanted the skilled person to accept was truly *not* correct, and the skilled person knew it. But in the eyes of the observers, they felt that *they* were correct and that the skilled person was wrong, when in reality the *observers* were **not** correct. This is an arrogant approach because they did not consider the possible reasons for the irritation felt by the highly-skilled confident person.

Here is the secret to differentiating the two types of people, one person with *arrogance*, and another person with *pride*: A person who *truly* knows what they are talking about will generally not get angry, and they will allow discussion and reasoning because they want to be *sure*. But with the arrogant type of person, discussion is typically not well-received and they simply want to do it *their own way*. We also must learn to be able to discern between someone's unwillingness to discuss something for fear of uncertainty, and someone understanding a suggestion and knowing it is *not* a viable option, thus causing them irritation from someone's foolish persistence and insistence to follow what amounts to incorrect counsel and outright error.

How We Became Arrogant

Our identities are an interesting aspect of ourselves and are all too often shaped by the demands of the world around us. From the very beginning of our own lives we are told, in many different ways, that we need to be a certain way in order to be acceptable. This is largely a good thing because this is one way we all learn. Trying to please our parents when we were very young children is probably the most obvious display of this. It's good for children to please their own parents, provided that the parents have a good understanding for what truly is best for the children. When parents have a good grasp on this, they will be great role models for their children. In trying to please their parents the children will learn the necessities of life, and they will also learn joy, provided that the parents have great hot water. But this can have a nasty backlash when the children see the wrong things in the parents' hot water—even if those things are not intended.

Seldom do parents intend to mislead their children, yet this misleading effect has been going on for thousands of years. The parents are only doing what they were taught through example. This example will be taught to their children because children see and learn by example from their parents, and, in turn, this becomes an example to the children of the children and so on from generation to generation. It is difficult to discern these effects, because in many ways we are blind to them because we live in them—these effects *are* our hot water.

Behaviors that are not quite where they belong or what they should be will tend to come to light when outsiders come into the family, usually via marriage. But even in this, it is difficult to detect a problem because young love tends to gravitate towards what it is familiar with. The rare person will search for what they truly desire in a mate, rather than what they are familiar with. These people are blessed if they find that person who can be both what they truly desire and are familiar with.

A tragic aspect of the effects of our hot water is when—those who are the influencers of a person or child behave in a way that is not of truth. When a child sees, from their very first breath, that those around them are living in a contradictory manner, then that child seldom realizes that they have a choice. So they end up following what they have witnessed the whole of their lives up until any current moment because it is all that they know and they don't realize that this is occurring.

We can escape this trap when we make a personal decision to question what we experience and make a running analysis to determine if we are truly living to our fullest and true potential.

When *we choose* the path to escape our arrogant hot water, then what happens is that we learn and improve. When we come upon this realization, we will look back at our own history and wonder how we lived the way we had in the past. This good and true cycle will repeat as we learn, unless, and until, we foolishly choose to stop learning. Eventually, we become accustomed to seeing that we typically fall short; and then it is no longer a surprise to us that we have often fallen short. As we learn, during each new phase of learning we will find self-improvement to be the only true and lasting satisfaction that we have in life.

As you can see, it is difficult for us to escape from our hot water when you consider the fact that the mate we seek will likely have hot water similar to our own. Our children will, in turn, be filled with our own hot water and the hot water of our spouse just as was done with our own parents in regard to us. We each have been raised in our parents' hot water, and if our parents' hot water was of an arrogant nature and we grew up in it, then we typically will unknowingly have those same attributes as our parents had. It is only when we stop long enough and consider these thoughts that we can begin to realize what is actually occurring.

If You are Jealous of People then You are Likely Arrogant

When we are raised with certain feelings, then it's easy for these feelings to increase in subsequent generations. This is not to say that these behaviors *will* increase, but rather that they *can* and often *do* increase.

In previous chapters we discussed our perceived identities and how those identities came to be through our hot water due to the expectations that others place on us because of *their* perception of *our* perception of our own identity. Confused... that's right, they have *perceptions* about our *perceiving* our own identity, and their perception is reflected back to us. Sadly, we unknowingly accommodated this all of our lives.

This is to say that, if *we* get *ourselves wrong*, then they will likely get us wrong as well. When they get us wrong, we receive that and it reinforces our behavior and our wrong perceptions about ourselves.

Those of us who were brought up in hot water that did not include true love, generally won't recognize true love when we see it. This causes a void to remain in our hot water from a *lack* of true love, and then the true love will be substituted with false love to fill that void. False love is afraid and competitive; and because it cannot be satisfied, it is always in want of recognition and acknowledgement. The recognition and acknowledgement are received as acceptance, which is mistaken for true love. Substituting true love with false love, and assuming the false love to be true love will **always** result in emptiness for people who have this as their hot water. Jealousy is born out of this hot water, and arrogance follows closely behind or it leads the charge. The two elements called *jealousy* and *arrogance* go hand in hand. Where you find one you will typically find the other. This is not deliberate—it is our hot water.

As living breathing humans, it is our duty to reduce and remove negatives from ourselves and from our children so that it does not spread like an infectious disease. Whatever you pour into yourself and your family *will* spread. It is your choice as to whether you are infected and filled with misery, or pure and filled with Joy.

Chapter 11

Identity and Your Own Self-worth

When contaminated arrogant hot water has permeated your perceived identity, then your feelings about yourself are in error. Removing this from our own lives is very important in order for us to be able to do so on our own via our own self-realization.

Our Arrogance is a Self-Worth Issue

Arrogance stems from our self-worth. If we have low self-worth we usually stretch reality and pretend to be more than we feel that we actually are. The result is arrogance, but the root is the fear that's *in* your hot water. Many of us lack financial abundance and feel the daily pains of poverty. We often feel that if we only had an education, or if we only had money, **then** we would be happy. This is true for some of us because poverty can be a torturous ordeal, but what about those who seem to already have it all? Why do we feel so depressed, or feel so badly about ourselves? After all, we have a great home that's paid for, we have a great job, we live in a great neighborhood, and we have plenty of extra money to do with as we wish, yet we feel as if we need an escape. Our escape is often alcohol or drugs. And prescription medications are touted to be able to solve all of our mental and emotional ailments.

Truth be told, little or none of these are needed. It is seldom that we need any reinforcement of a mind-altering nature or even physically-altering nature. It's interesting to observe people when they drink alcohol and see how much they change. The level of change seen is a telltale sign of the perceived identity confusion that so many of us struggle with. This is only one small way that our self-worth is made evident. In fact, we often find people to be "more fun" when they drink because some people are more themselves, and we get to see *them* and we like what we see, while what is revealed when drinking in others is their pain.

Does Your Identity Affect Your Self-Worth?

Self-worth is closely associated with your perceived identity. Self-worth becomes the value that you place on your perceived identity. When your perceived identity has been formed by much negative hot water, then it is likely that you perceive the people who surround you from a somewhat negative perspective.

How you *want* to feel about others is often a good way to gauge your own self-worth. Depending upon your nature, it will be one of two general ways: First, if you want to see others fail, then that is likely the way *you* see yourself—as a failure, which results in your self-worth being valued accordingly. Additionally, if you see everyone as better than you, that is also an indicator that you have low self-worth.

The second way of evaluating your self-worth is gauging if you want to see others succeed and prosper and are willing to help them do so and you feel joy for them when they succeed. This is a good indicator that your self-worth is high, which is where it is best to have it.

A perceived identity that is improper or misguided will *always* have low self-worth; this is an unavoidable truth. There are reasons for this that we will explore later. Understanding these reasons helps us to get back on track and out of that rut.

How Many Cues of Your Identity have You Received from Others, As Mentioned in Chapter 4?

Consider taking a few moments right now to evaluate your life and your perceived identity, and, in doing so, think about the ways that you respond to people. Do you respond the same to all people? If you do then you are a *rare* individual. There are likely some people in your world who you will behave differently around. The differences in your outward behavior can be small, and can be more about the differences in the feelings you have or hold inside.

Does a certain person make you feel angry? Does another make you feel safe? Is there, maybe, another who makes you feel inspired? Certainly, some people don't even know we exist, but *we* can still have these feelings about those people. However, for the people who you do actually interact with, what feelings do you have about them?

Once you have named your feelings about a person or people, ask yourself why you feel that way about each person who you've considered. Much of your feelings, and often your reactions as well, will have much to do with their unspoken expectations of you and with the way that they perceive your identity.

Regardless of what you have accomplished, or what you have done right or wrong in your life, a confident person is likely going to have a much better perception of your identity than does someone whose life was filled with trouble and heartache.

Both of these people will reflect back to you what they see you as, in the form of their expectations of you that they received from your perception of yourself. The difference is that a

confident person will *know* that you are capable. And even
though they see that you are having a hard time, they will still
believe in you because that is what their hot water is like. That
type of person will likely make you feel very good when you're
around them *if* you can handle correction, love, and support.

On the other hand, someone who has had a lot of troubles in
life, and has very difficult hot water, will tend to see you as a
"loser" if you have a lowly perceived identity and the resulting
low self-worth. They will reflect this back to you and it will
make you feel even worse about yourself. This is why people
often suggest that we try to be around upbeat people. But
sometimes an upbeat person might not want to be with people
with low self-worth because it tends to make the upbeat person
feel down.

If your hot water and self-worth are very low and a confident
person believes in you, it is possible that it will make you feel
like a failure because *they* have expectations of you that *they*
know you can do. But *you* do not believe in yourself enough,
which can make you feel as if you are falling short of their
expectations. This, in turn, makes you feel as if your self-worth is
even lower.

Here is a good rule-of-thumb for when encountering people
with low self-worth: If you cannot bring someone up and make
them feel better, then don't let them bring you down. Depart
from that person and let them in their misery that *they* have
chosen; but if they feel enlightened when they are with you, then
bring them up to a better place along with you, and be a guide to
a better way for them. If they stop moving forward, then do not
let them drag you down! Depart from them because they have
made a choice to believe that they are of little value. People will
not be dependent on your good disposition when they
understand true joy.

All of this is relative because someone can have an extremely
great identity while another can have an extremely poor

perceived identity, and yet another can be anywhere in between the two extremes. To the person with a robust and full identity, both of the other people will be seen to have low self-worth. The person that is in between will find the person with the healthy identity to be upbeat and exciting and the person with the poor perceived identity to have low self-worth. The person with the poor perceived identity will see both of them as having higher self-worth than his or her own self-worth.

The result for the person with a poor perceived identity is usually that of jealousy, and often arrogance by wanting to bring the others low, especially the person with a healthy identity who is often the one they seek to bring low. Their state of mind relative to each other is all a part of each their own hot water and the hot water of the three combined.

If you take a few moments to think of the cues you have gotten from others with regard to their expectations of your perceived identity, then wither good or bad you will likely find that you do behave differently around some people because of the attitudes they have about you and show towards you.

The Danger of You Identifying with Things

Another aspect that was touched on earlier with regard to self-worth is *things* (the tangible), and position or *status* (the less-tangible). Please take note of the subtle important differences in this section from what was discussed earlier. This section is about *how* you feel, rather than the competing factor of trying to tear someone down only to make yourself look better and then, through that, believing that you have built yourself up.

When we have *things* and we allow those things as a part of our perceived identity, then our happiness is dependent upon those things. As an example, consider a woman who has a career that has become a part of her perceived identity. Her career allows her the luxury of buying a beautiful home in a safe neighborhood alongside many other luxury homes, and she can also buy the car and many other things that she wants. All of this becomes a part of her hot water and her perceived identity. All of her success brings much recognition and many friends to her. And assuming that all of her friends are relatively kind, she will be content. This sounds like a great life!

As time passes, the business climate changes and her life-long career is no longer needed by the industry. Suddenly she is out of a job, but she is still many years from retirement. The way she will handle this situation greatly depends upon her perceived identity, upon her hot water, and upon whether her perceived identity includes *things*—both tangible and intangible. All *perceived* identities *do* include *things* and are largely dependent on these *things* and on the *status* that accompanies them.

When the woman's perceived identity is based upon things, then a very large void will be left when her world crumbles and all of the status and things have been stripped from her. A common scenario is for a person in this type of situation to fall into depression or even drugs and alcohol in order to fill the void left by the things and status she once had.

If she is a tenacious person she may be able to pick herself up and begin again, but will likely be suspicious and untrusting, which is to say *cynical*. After much striving she will again have *things* as a major part of her hot water, unless she can overcome her incorrectly perceived identity.

This type situation can become a turning point for people, because, as our world crumbles around us, we realize that we have placed a great deal of importance on *things*. The reason that we can suddenly see the difference, when we're stripped of our things and status, is because there's a deep understanding buried inside all of us that realizes our happiness should *not* depend on things and status.

For many of us, *things* have always played a big part in our happiness throughout our lives, our hot water indicated that things matter, and we accepted that indication from birth onward. These things have become our perceived identity, and when *they* fail—*we* fail. After we are forced to struggle, we then have a sharp contrast to use as our index between being *with* things, and being *without* things. This helps us to begin to see how dependent we were on *things* for our self-worth. For many of us this will be a turning point of realization where we can begin to discover the *true* happiness that can only be found in true joy.

Here is why is this so Important for You to Understand

We are so thoroughly comfortable in our hot water that we simply *cannot* see what is happening in our own lives. We often go to the brink of destruction where a defining contrast will occur, and then we finally begin to see that something is not quite the way it ought to be in our lives. It changes the temperature of our hot water and suddenly makes it cooler. That's when we notice the temperature difference in ourselves.

If we have low self-worth, we can be successful and wealthy and never even realize the level of our self-worth, our success, or our wealth, until our world crumbles around us. When we are *all-invested* with regard to *things* being a part of our perceived identity, we have a very big risk of falling fast and hard. **You are not things,** and **things are not you**! Getting a grasp on this is difficult for most of us, especially men, because so many of us have inappropriately learned, and have as a large part of our hot water, that *things* and *status* are actually important, when ultimately they are not important.

Our misguided understanding has likely become confused into our hot water because status and prestige are often the result of the respect that we sometimes observe enjoyed by our elders. A person who has taken the time to understand, and has worked for and earned the respect of those around them, will often obtain riches and honor as the end result of *true* prestige and status. If someone has a great career where they can *assume* a position of status and prestige, then they will likely get a type of hot water respect from others, especially from those who focus on *things*. The outward appearance of both earned prestige and assumed prestige are the same, it is the recognition of status and prestige of each person's *visibly perceivable* position. This outward sign of recognition is taken as acceptance, and thus seems to validate the person's perceived identity and assumed prestige. In truth, it is the person who has a healthy identity and has *worked* for their position and *earned* their prestige through kindness and good efforts, who actually deserves the prestige and recognition.

A perceived identity that focuses on things and status is false and backwards. These two status points, *things* and *prestige*, are a **result** of a proper identity, rather than the **cause** of your perceived identity. Many people have a backwards approach, where they feel that if they get *things* or a grand job they will be respected and therefore loved. While they may indeed get the recognition that they desire, it is still *false* recognition; but to them it's the only thing that they ever knew, and it is likely the only type of acceptance they have ever experienced.

In the late twentieth century and early twenty-first century, going into debt to obtain status-prestige was very common, but many people suffered the consequences of being heavily in debt. Even after their struggles, many people still never came to understand the difference between *bought* prestige and *earned* prestige. Throughout history this has always occurred, and it always will occur in the future as long as we believe that our things and status make us. Due to an increasing and vast credit network in the late twentieth century, going into debt to increase prestige became a very popular thing to do and is now heavily emphasized, but it is seldom recognized as being done for this reason.

Social Media puts You at Risk

At the turn of the twentieth century, a new means of communication had developed referred to as "online communications" or "networking." By the end of the first decade of the twenty-first century, it came to be known as "social-networking." For some people this helped them to get to know more people, while others ended up with far less actual human interaction. The personal effect of social-networking was dependent upon each person's hot water. If they had poor hot water, then this method of communication could potentially be bad and serve to further contaminate their hot water.

In the same way that all of what we have discussed so far is a part of interacting with others, it was also the same with the new form of social media. Jealousy was also an factor when communicating via social-networking—with arrogance being right alongside of it.

The danger of feeding their hot water even more, often tormented people with low self-worth and poor perceived identity through this form of communication. This effect was especially bad, because with early social media, it was only done with typing and reading, which made it easier to misinterpret the intended attitude through those forms of social media interaction. A person who has a poor perceived identity will more easily misinterpret the meaning of a statement that someone typed. This is because they will interpret the other person's imaginary voice inflection in the way that their own hot water is accustomed to. If they have jealous hot water then a typed statement that is not intended to be a jealous statement can easily be mistaken as a jealous statement. If their hot water is accustomed to jealousy, then they logically see it that way.

When people feel badly about themselves and adopt this sort of false perceived identity, then they often self-destruct in the long run. Additionally, if there is a person with a poor perceived identity who seems to be showing humility and has not gone down the path of arrogance, an arrogant type person will typically belittle the person who thrives on such false humility, serving to drive them deeper into their lowly state of self-perception. It is the expectancy of their lowly perception that is thrown back at them by the arrogant person.

In the early years of social media, this became an even worse problem for some people because they would often misinterpret statements in the way just described. Additionally, people were occasionally singled out by someone who was arrogant and who was trying to bring them even lower. The arrogant offender would begin a campaign to slander the person in an effort to tear them down to destroy them. At that time, this horrible behavior was referred to as "cyber-bullying."

Withdrawing from society is seldom a good idea unless you are doing it as a sort of retreat to rethink your life and revive yourself. People are meant and designed to communicate with each other—in person. If we were not, then it is unlikely that we would have eyes and ears and mouths and an ability to feel the warmth of touch from another human being. A smile would have no purpose, nor would crying, anger, laughing, or any other outward action that can be physically detected while in the presence of another human being.

People who tend to go off into seclusion and who are doing it for reasons of poor perceived identity and low self-worth, will not be served by withdrawing from society or hiding behind social media. Hiding is *not* the answer to finding true happiness—but being your *true* self is!

What Kind of Tree are You?
(The Separateness of Perceived Identity and Self-Worth, and the Connection of Them)

Perceived identity and *self-worth* are very connected. Perceived identity is separate in that it is not your self-worth.

Perceived identity is the *way* in which you have become as you are from a lifetime of good and/or bad hot water.

Your hot water formed you, and your perceived identity is the way you are seeing what was formed. In turn, the way you perceive your identity affects your hot water, and the two reciprocally increase one another.

Self-worth is an entirely different issue; while connected, the two are separate, and self-worth (much like prestige) can be faked. In fact, when someone does purchase prestige via *things*, then that prestige is fake and it is not earned. When we do this, we believe we have a feeling of higher self-worth, but it actually is not real. Self-worth is the value that you place on your perceived identity. True high self-worth is only seen with a truly healthy identity; and while others might attempt to devalue that, True self-worth can never be truly defeated.

We have discussed a great amount of detail showing in various and deeper ways: what is real—**IS**, and how what is *fake* tries to emulate what is real. This is the same in each of the aspects of our lives discussed so far.

Whether it is your perceived identity, jealousy, arrogance, or your self-worth, all of them will follow the same line. On one side you have what is true, and on the other you have what is trying to copy what is true and make it look the same on the surface.

Not understanding that hot water exist, or that you have hot water, and not realizing that you can have true joy in your life, is what causes the desire to copy what is real. The problem with this is trying to get others to understand that the roots of the tree also exist, instead of them only looking at the leaves on the tree.

In fact, that's a perfect analogy. A person with a healthy identity is like a tree with roots deep into the ground reaching deep into the boundless pure, cool, crystal clear water beneath the tree. A person with a poor perceived identity is like someone who has bought a tree cut off at the trunk and stood it in their yard—It will look good for a while, but eventually the tree will dry up and whither and will no longer cast shade and comfort for those who stood under it while it was green.

The tree with its roots deep into the ground, drawing from the abundant, pure water beneath it, will give shade for a very long time. Anyone will be able to come under the shade of that tree for rest, joy, and protection from the scorching sun. However, that tree may only have so much room under it for shading the people from the scorching sun. Those who chose to sit beneath the tree that has no roots will not be able to be shaded by the well-rooted tree because others came there first and filled the space beneath it.

You need to decide what type of tree you will be: Will you be a tree bought and cut at the trunk with no roots? Or will you be a planted tree that can be a refuge for many people because its roots are tapping deep into the ground into the abundant, pure, clean water that will never go dry? *You* also need to decide what type of tree *you* want to sit beneath (that is to say who your friends are or who you will choose to be around). Will you be a tree cut off at the trunk, or a robust willow with its roots tapped deep into the waters of truth?

The type of tree you will be is a choice only *you* can make. You cannot properly make this choice unless you understand that, both, your hot water exists, and that *you* can do something about it. Understand the roots and what they are for, and then you can begin to understand why a boughten tree that is cut off and has no roots has little chance of survival even though it may be a bigger tree and initially appears far stronger and more robust.

Chapter 12

Have You Placed Your Trust in Your Perceived Identity?

You have been Relying on Your Perceived Identity

Understanding our hot water is important for us if we want to get control of our lives, emotions, and circumstances. Many of us place our trust in our perceived identity. From birth to the point at which each of us are at in our lives at this moment, we have been in our own hot water and in the hot water of our families. Because of these various hot waters, *we have learned from* the hot water and *we have taught* the hot water throughout that entire time. Our perceived identity was formed from the hot water that each of us has in us, and then more hot water was added to us by our perceived identity.

With this seemingly inescapable cyclical hot water trap, many of us have succumbed to the power of our own hot water; thus, we have perceived our identity as our hot water is, and all that we do is being built upon our own perception of this hot water. This is an obvious outcome, and when thinking about this it seems that it is unavoidable, which in fact is true. We cannot help but to be what we perceive our identity to be. This unavoidable truth guides our steps in everything that we do; and we will trust in our perceived identity for everything that we do by relying on our abilities that our hot water helped us obtain. Things like our chosen job, our hobbies, and our possessions are a reflection of the perceived identity that we put our trust in.

Similar to how we might trust a friend, we do the same with our perceived identity—we trust it. Depending upon how easily you trust people, you will have varying degrees of how much and how quickly you trust any particular person; but the reason that we generally begin to trust people is because they seem familiar to us. But, it's more than just becoming familiar through getting to know them. Sadly, trust is typically given more for the reason that we are familiar with someone's type of hot water than it is for any other reason. When we meet a person, we quickly sense the likenesses or differences between *their* hot water and *our* hot water. When it is familiar to us we generally take a quick liking to the person and begin a relationship of trust. This trust in each other will be there even if the two are not fully dependable for each other.

All relationships are built around trust: Whether it is completely trusting, or completely lacking trust, or anywhere in between, *all* relationships have their foundation based upon the relationship's trust *level*. In a good relationship, the people trust one another and share feelings and personal stories based on the relationship's level of trust. We have a tendency to believe that people have to earn our trust, and sometimes this is the case; but typically it is our comfort level with them that allows us to trust them.

Comfort is found in familiarity, which can be thought of much like traveling: When you get into a new city that you have never before visited, you feel somewhat uncomfortable, but as you become familiar with the layout of the city you become accustomed to it. Because you have become accustomed to the city, you become comfortable in the city. Conversely, in a city that is much like your home town, you might enter the city and immediately feel at home because of the many similarities.

Relationships are much the same: Comfort equals trust for many people whether or not they realize this is so.

It's the same with our perceived identity: We trust it because it's familiar, which is sort of an obvious observation. Of course, our own perceived identity is going to be familiar because it's ours and it is based upon our own hot water; but I'm referring to the trust that we have *in* our perceived identity. We trust our perceptions and we choose our job, mate, home, and just about anything else you can think of, and we do so based upon the trust we have *in* our perceived identity. This can be either a good thing or a bad thing.

With this in mind, now is a good time to reflect on everything in your life and all that your life encounters—as in asking yourself: "How much of my life is bringing me real true joy?" For many of us, the answer is that very little of our lives brings any *true joy* to us.

What would You do Without all of Your Things?

Many people are unhappy, depressed, or confused, and are led to believe that medication is the *only* solution. If medication were the solution, then people would be cured by the millions and would no longer need the medication, but this is not the case. The hot water of societal culture tries to put the blame on anything but what the actual root cause of a problem truly is. Hot water has an effect as if it has a mind of its own, always trying to pin the blame on something other than itself. In reality, our hot water is the only thing that is ever responsible for the ills in our lives.

Let's take *goods* for instance: We've already discussed how our *things* are not our identity, but we did not discuss whether we do or do not trust *in* those things. Consider smaller insignificant items like your kitchen stove: How would you cook without it? For many people, they simply do not know what they would do. Some of us would choose to eat out every night for supper. That's a fair enough conclusion, but then you are trusting in your money by doing so. This is not to say that there is something wrong with money or using it to purchase food. In fact, I would prefer that everyone had enough money so that finances were never an issue for anyone. What we are referring to here is the fact that most of us would be in a panic if suddenly our money was completely gone and there was no more money in sight in our foreseeable future.

Going into a restaurant for dinner is not wrong, and even relying on them to service you is not wrong. Having a stove is not wrong, and preparing delicious home-cooked meals perfectly to your liking on that stove is not wrong. Having a house is not wrong, and all the comforts and shelter that a house provides are good. All of these things should be celebrated!

The problem comes in with our reasons and attitudes behind it all. One person can have *all* of these things and it is good and joyful; and the next person can have the identical items and it will be bad for them. Why is this? Why is it not the same for both people? Why is it that one person is beaming with joy, and the other person is feeling sad and inadequate even though both of their lives are quite similar?

We discussed some of this in earlier chapters, but we didn't address the issue of placing your trust *in things*. When we rely on something to the point where we trust these things to sustain us, then we have made a grave error, and the things will *always* disappoint us in the long run. If this were not the case, then everyone who has *things* would be incredibly joyful—but as is very apparent, we are not. It seems that with each passing year there are more and more unique inventions to help our lives be better and better, but it also seems that with each new invention people become more and more confused, depressed, or unhappy. Why is this?

It's because we have been placing our trust in these things while making the unrealized hot water assumption that if these things suddenly disappear that we will not be able to survive without the things. This includes food. Most of us have heard the news stories of people who took a hiking trip through a large forest and had gotten their direction confused and were lost for a few days without food. Some of the hikers were even overweight. The people who report these events make it sound as if these people are lucky that they did not die of starvation during those few short days.

Other than needing to drink a little bit of liquid, the hikers could potentially have easily survived for many weeks without a stitch of food because the body uses fat and tissue to survive when needed. This notion that we will all immediately fall over dead if we lose the *things* in our lives is much overplayed. We fall into this trap because of the hot water of our society and because of our own hot water. The only circumstances that can prevent or cure this is for us to either become aware, *or* to have everything stripped from us so that we can experience the fact that we will be fine without all of the *things* that we have worked so long and hard for in order to "survive."

While on the surface it seems obvious that we will survive if we are stripped of everything in our lives, the reality is that most of us won't think it through to that point. And we *do*, in fact, place our trust in the *things* that we have in our lives; but, seldom do we stop and realize that we will survive regardless.

Relying on Your Abilities for Sustenance

The identity problem does not stop at the *things* in our life. The problem carries over to, and includes, our abilities. It's better to trust in your abilities rather than trusting in your things, because it is typically your abilities that did the job that earned the money that bought the things to begin with.

It seems like a reasonable thought to place your trust in your abilities. And I would agree that trusting in your abilities, rather than trusting in the things you obtained *with* your abilities, is better to do; but, I do have to point out one problem with your abilities: What would you do if you became fully paralyzed and could no longer use your body to do the abilities that you had previously done?

You would quickly learn that your abilities no longer have any value. If you are a skilled craftsman and it was *your* hands doing the work that brought the beauty to what you had built, then simply *telling* someone how to do those things, while they are being your hands for you, will not necessarily display the same skilled end result that you desire and were previously capable of accomplishing by yourself.

You could argue, "Okay, but what about a person who gets paid to think, and then shares those thoughts. You know... the typical *idea* person?" Accidents can occur to take even that base ability away, and even if the person was not at all paralyzed, they could still lose the ability to organize words in the way that they were previously able to. They would no longer be able to share their ideas with any efficient clarity as they did in the past.

Again, I must point out that there is nothing wrong with utilizing the abilities that you have in order to earn a living. Nor is there a problem in simply sharing your abilities with others. In fact, that's what this book is about. But what happens to many of us is that our perceived identity and the hot water that formed those abilities have both been dictating the direction of our lives—*all* during our lives. Our hot water chose our occupation.

The case for most of us is that our hot water chooses our direction. This is especially true if our hot water did not have a good start. Yet, even so, we tend to press through it all, and most of us become very proficient at doing our occupation regardless. Your hot water will always form your perceived identity and that truth cannot be escaped from. Another inescapable truth is that your perceived identity will always be forming your hot water and your occupation. And the things that you buy because the wage you earn from your occupation will be determined by your perceived identity; this is yet another inescapable truth. So what do we do about all of this?

First, understand that what was discussed in this book so far is not telling you *how* to fix your problem. So far we are describing, in great detail, most of the ways that it works and **why** it works this way. It's kind of like describing *light* or *air* where the description does nothing to change those things. Light and air are the way they are even if we see or specifically know *how* they work. So far, we have only been describing *how* it all works and the fact that *how* it works is unchangeable. Knowing how it all works can be thought of in these terms: Even if we understand something as simple as how a hammer works, it won't affect the hammer's design—but we *can* change the way we use the hammer. We get to choose whether we will use it for good *or* for bad. It would certainly be sad to lose any of your abilities, but if your heart and mind are right and you understand the principle in this book you could still be a productive person even without your current abilities and still be very joyful.

Do You Trust in the Wrong Things?

Most who read this book will likely have bought it to assist in making some changes in life, but are not really sure how to do it, where to begin, or who to go to. Many of us feel that something is "off" in our lives, but we can't quite seem to put our finger on what is wrong or what is causing our pain. That's because of the hot water effect in our lives and in our perceived identities.

If you have been trying to tap into understanding how to make the needed changes in your life in order to feel better, and even to feel great, then you need to accept and understand that you have been trusting in the wrong things.

Up until now, you have likely heard many self-help teachers, and you have probably felt uplifted by them, but as soon as you get back to work, you quickly slip right back to into your comfortable hot water. Or maybe it's a preacher who has pointed out some great passages in the Bible and you have connected with those passages, but on Monday morning you have to go back to work with the same people, and you slip right back into your comfortable and familiar hot water. Maybe it was a friend or something you read that gave you encouragement to try to become or obtain what you feel is missing in you. When you are with these people, or when you hear or read what they have to say, you feel better. You might even have gone for years feeling better about yourself and life in general because you connected with the messages that any of them may have delivered. But over time your feelings typically faded and you slowly slipped back into your own comfortable hot water. Why does this so commonly happen to so many of us?

Something that once made you feel so good, now no longer has the same appeal to you. Sure, you still agree with the message, but your life still feels as if it lacks something. The reason for this is that when these teachers come along and show you something new and exciting, then you want to feel the way that they say you can feel. Does this make their message wrong? No, while some of them are wrong, most of the messages are good and accurate.

The problem is often either with their delivery, or with *your understanding* of their delivery. This is like selling someone an airplane by telling them how wonderful it will be because they can fly anywhere and that they will never run into stop lights or heavy traffic. And, if they buy a plane with floats they can even land on the water.

These are very compelling reasons to buy an airplane, but there is one glaring issue with this: Most people do not know how to *fly* an airplane. First, we need to *understand* the basics of *how* the airplane works and *how* to fly it. When we have learned the technical basics of flying, then we will better know the kind of airplane we want or need. We also will know how to fly it, and what to do and what not to do when taking off and landing. Without the information about the details of flying an airplane we will likely experience much disappointment in our life's airplane adventures. And trying to fly an airplane without understanding the basics of how it works will likely result in a serious crash that would claim our lives.

Trusting in the wrong things has this same effect: Buying a message without understanding it might hold a promise of joy, but in the long run it often disappoints and damages— sometimes the damage is worse than before you heard the message. The same is true when you trust in your things or in your abilities. This doesn't mean that the uplifting messages you have heard are incorrect, nor it is wrong or bad to own a home or have abundant amounts of money. Most of those *can-do* messages are between the lines of this book, and are ultimately good messages.

Believing What You Are Not

The purpose of this book is to show you *what to do* with those messages and how to implement them for lasting joy. So how do we do this?

It starts by understanding that your hot water *exists*, and that your hot water formed your perceived identity, and that your perceived identity is what drives *all* of your choices and actions. This is simply the way things work. Knowing and understanding this is important for you in order to break the spiraling downward cycle that too many of us have in our lives. *You* are the one who will change this cycle in your life and in your family.

The truth is that this is *all in **your** control* and *your* control only. No one else can make the decisions you make, but they can affect your hot water *anytime you allow* them to.

If you have chosen to read this book because you want to feel better, then it can be assumed that it's likely that you're hurting because of your hot water and that you want life to change immediately. I can also safely assume that you have been somewhat *believing* that you *are* some "***thing***"—which, in truth, you are not.

This is the turning point of this book where we are transitioning from *understanding **why*** to <u>knowing</u> ***how*** !

The first thought that you need to accept is that you have been trying to be what you are not.

Your *perceived* identity has been formed by your hot water, and, up until this point in your life, you were mostly unaware of this. But you were not fully unaware, or you would not be reading this book or hearing these words right now.

The discontent that you feel is evidence that, deep down inside, you really *do* know that something is not right in your own life. If that is the case, then it means that you are partly aware of your hot water or have been becoming aware of your hot water. Often, people stop at the point of becoming aware and will not question it any further because they feel that they will be seen as whiney or a downer because they're always talking about their problems. Or maybe you have no one who is willing to talk it out with you in order to help you get to the deepest root of the discontent that you feel in your own life.

The whole point of this book is to get you to think it through *in your own mind* and see the truth about your own life. It's true that one can dwell on the wrong aspects of the subject too long, which often serves to make matters worse. And depending upon *who* you choose to listen to or speak to about wanting to feel better, it can actually have a negative effect and drive you deeper into feeling low about yourself.

Even many experts do not grasp this aspect of why people often feel confused, down, or depressed. The advice that the experts have is usually solid; in fact, it is often as sound as the advice of a very good self-help teacher or a very good preacher. The same thing is true with counselors, their information is typically good, but they may have delivered it poorly, or, possibly, the information was understood incorrectly by you. In either case, your hot water—and maybe their hot water—is the cause of the blindness of the circumstance.

There is an additional danger in all of the "you can do it!" messages; where, when we hear these messages and implement them into our lives they will work for a short time, but then later we feel the same way as we previously did. This makes many of us feel like we failed, which usually results in labeling ourselves as failures even though we don't think of it in those terms. When we receive good and helpful messages from upbeat people, we feel good, but when those people are no longer around us, then we often lose the emotional high and come crashing down. Why is this?

It's because we have conditioned ourselves to believe something that we are not, and we try to work backwards by trying to create happiness and then hoping the end result will be a good foundation.

*You Expect **You** to be Able to Make **You** Happy with Your Perceived Identity*

Happiness can be bought, but Joy cannot! Our perceived identity is the inevitable result of our hot water. We expect to be happy, and to ensure this happiness we often will try to improve our lives. This is a good thing. But sadly, the way that we try to improve our lives is lacking. Because our perceived identity is the basis of our actions, we expect that if we have *things*, then having those *things* will bring joy and happiness to us. Often our things do bring happiness, but that kind of happiness is fleeting. *Things* simply will not bring *pure joy*.

The same is true for your abilities and money. These things make you feel happy for a time, but they in themselves will not bring true joy. The words *joy* and *happiness* are often used interchangeably, but this is not an accurate thing to do. When we improperly use words that are specifically important to a discussion, then we lose the ability to accurately communicate our complete message. This will leave the hearer incapable of fully understanding the message as it is intended to be conveyed. It might seem petty, but it is an extremely important point.

The word *happiness* has the same root as the word "*happen*" and it means to occur from *chance*. The word *happy* is an association of your demeanor when something good *happens* to you. I suppose we could have called it **happeny**, but in the end, the root word is still "*hap*." It is important to spend time discussing this now because using *joy* and *happy* interchangeably is wrong, and doing so gives the wrong impression. There is a difference, and it is important to understand that the difference exists. When someone is joyful then they appear happy, and it seems that good things are happening to the person. True joy **is not** found in *things*, but with happiness alone it is **only** found in *things*. Keep in mind that "*things*" includes your tangible items, your skills, *and* your beliefs, even people.

There are people who have joy in their lives by *chance* of good hot water and by *chance* of good perceived identity, but those people are at the same risk as those with a poor perceived identity. They might truly be in a state of joy, but that can be quickly brought low with them ending in being filled with poor hot water.

It's when you *deliberately* find joy that gives *you* the control of your life. Understanding the differences in several of the end results that we discussed is of very great importance to your success in obtaining full, robust, and lasting joy. When you achieve lasting joy it does not mean that you will never ever have a bad day, but it does mean that *when* you have a bad day it will be of little concern to you. You will quickly know what to do to make the best decisions in order to make your day the best it can be, and, at a very minimum, you will be able to stop it from getting worse. And most importantly, you will be free of its negative draw the following day!

Understanding that *joy* and *happiness* are not the same, will help you to better understand that when you rely on your perceived identity to provide you with happiness, you in turn achieve it for a time, but that time and the happiness will be fleeting. The things that you buy to comfort yourself, such as food, home, car, clothing, etc. will make you happy at first, but later those things lose their strong appeal and become items of little value even though they all brought you substantial recognition and comfort. The let-down experienced after the happiness is gone leaves you feeling empty and wanting to once again fill that emptiness with more *things*. Getting more things will, in turn, do the same all over again. Many of us accumulate things to the point where we cannot possibly use them all, but we don't want to part with our *things* because we associate them with our fleeting happiness, even though the temporary and fleeting happiness that those things brought us is long gone. After we accumulate these things, we place them in a storage area and shut the door only to clean the storage area out years later and find it all to be meaningless junk.

Does this mean that you should not buy things? No, quite the contrary, it's okay to have things. These *things* help people have jobs and help make our lives more comfortable *when* we're judicious in buying what we truly need to begin with. Our perceived identity has a tendency to gravitate toward the feeling of happiness that buying things appears to bring. The reason for this is that we truly desire the same type of "happiness" that is obtained when we have true joy. "*Things*", like our job, religion, politics, physical decor, and even people, are included in these "*things*" that we have been referring to.

We all need to stop expecting our perceived identity to bring us lasting happiness because there is no such thing as *lasting* happiness when joy is not present. With happiness, once the event or thing has become too familiar to us we become complacent towards it and are no longer smitten with its appeal.

The happiness fades just as quickly, and is then added to our hot water. This all becomes an addiction for us.

An addiction will never be truly broken unless the principle discussed is in this book is understood. In an effort to prevent ourselves from the temptation of falling back into our addictions, we often have a go-to person that we contact when we're feeling weak. It's good to have a go-to person and it's certainly better than bending to the will of a bad hot water addiction. But when we understand *why* an addiction exists to begin with, then we can crush the addiction and it will no longer be known as an addiction because it will no longer be a part of our hot water in that way.

Someone who has a problem with strong drinks or drugs is *no* more of an addict than someone who buys things to satisfy themselves. The only difference between them is that someone who drinks will often hurt others or themselves due to anger or lack of physical coordination, and when a person is harmed it can immediately be felt emotionally, or seen physically, where addictions seem to be far less noticeable when someone buys *things* to fill the same need.

Be of good courage and *understand*, and then all of your woes will vanish.

Chapter 13

What Truly is an Identity?

The rest of this book will not be of much use if you have not grasped the basic message in the previous chapters. The importance of *understanding the root* of the problem cannot be understated. **Make sure** you understand how your hot water works and where it comes from.

When we think of our perceived identity, we typically think of it as *who* we are, which is by and large true. You might want to take it a step further and add to it the word *individual.* Often when we hear the word *individual* or *individuality* we think of the uniqueness of a person or the things that makes them different.

Identity Defined

Since your hot water and its accompanying perceived identity are the core of why you are reading this book, let's examine things a bit further and look into the words *identity* and *individual.* Without even bothering to look them up in the dictionary we can quickly see that *identity* is similar to *identical*, and *individual* is similar to *divide*, but in this case *individual* has the prefix "*in-*" meaning *un* or *not*. We typically think of our *individuality* as our separateness, and our *identity* as our uniqueness.

But, much to our surprise, these words do not truly mean what we imagine them to mean. Instead of meaning *different* and *separate*, they mean *identical* and *inseparable*. In examining our current perception of these two words, as we typically know them today, and then comparing them to the original purpose of these two concepts, it becomes quite clear that being labeled as such does *not* match up properly with what the words truly mean.

Words are symbols or representations of *things* and/or our *thoughts*. It's common in any era that is contemporary at any moment to alter the true essence of the original concept being conveyed in a word. Sadly, in our modern times of abundant printed word we tend to quickly modify the meanings of words to fit with the dominant popular usages and perceptions of the words, only to further obscure the words' true essence even further inhibiting our ability to understand.

Let's first focus on our contemporary view of the words *identity* and *individual*. Dictionary definitions aside, the words *identity* and *individual* are typically felt to mean: *how unique you are* and *who you are*.

How can we make our own woes vanish? We can start by understanding what an identity truly is. Up until this point in this book I have specifically chose to refer to your *identity* as your "**_Perceived_** Identity", because what you have been seeing yourself as all of your life, up until now, was only your *perception*—but it was not necessarily true. Most of us have an incorrect perception of ourselves.

It is Important for You to Understand what Identity Is Not

A point that you should have well understood by now, from reading, is that your perceived identity is formed from your hot water, but that *does not* make your perception accurate. That's why I have been calling it your **perceived** identity. All of your life, your hot water has been a place of familiarity for you. And because of the feeling of familiarity, it is an area that feels safe to you even if it's not so great. Additionally, many of the people around you have had a perception of you from your very early age. By utilizing your own temperament and other people's expectations of you, they, and you, placed a *perception* of yourself upon *you*.

We cannot help but to be as we perceive our identity. If you're lured into believing you are as you act, and that you are as others perceive you, then you have been caught in a hot water trap that is nearly inescapable, **unless** you come to understand what we are discussing here.

Your identity is what truly defines you. If you believe something that's not true and place that in your hot water, then you will have a "*perceived*" identity, and that *perceived* identity *will* be based on something that is **not** true. Your core goal in all of this is to understand what an **identity** truly is.

But first, we will see what an identity is not: While we discussed what a *perceived* identity is throughout the entire book up to this point, we did not discuss what an **identity** is not. Your identity has nothing to do with anything or anyone; not money, goods, or abilities. All of the attitudes that we discussed that are a result of your *perceived* identity are *not* part of your **true** *identity*. Your identity is not jealousy, arrogance, deception, confusion, depression, unhappiness, cruelty, or doubt. *None* of the results of a poor *perceived* identity have *anything* to do with your **actual** true identity.

I used the term *poor perceived identity* to point out that you can have a healthy or wealthy *perceived* identity. Both a poor perceived identity and a healthy perceived identity are **perceived** identities nonetheless, and they are formed from your hot water. And, given enough time, while the healthy perceived identity is generally better, it's also more dangerous, and is more likely to become an inescapable trap. A healthy perceived identity has hot water, as does a poor perceived identity, but a healthy perceived identity lives a more fulfilled life, and on the surface appears much closer to a true identity.

The problem with a healthy *perceived* identity is that, when the poor perceived identity attributes creep in, then the level of self-justification is nearly impossible to escape from for that person. When someone is living rightly and has a healthy perceived identity, then there is no cause for *anyone* to question the person's underlying motives. Then, when the quality of our hot water very slowly changes over time, there are no sudden changes for us to easily compare our previous state of being. When our status overshadows our inner condition, it cloaks the slow continuous contamination of our water. This is why many people look back and compare their lives and wonder "How did it ever come to this?" Slow incremental changes in our water temperature are mostly undetectable to us from one day to the next.

Healthy **perceived** identities are commonly seen in the arrogance of some church leaders, preachers, pastors, and priests. There are certainly many good people in those positions, but there are also many who have the same hot water obstacle to overcome that the rest of humanity has.

So we need to separate out and become aware of the difference between poor perceived identity, complacency, and healthy perceived identity, all versus **true** identity. In truth, the first three: *poor perceived identity, complacency*, and *healthy perceived identity* are all the same with differing hot water. Some are immediately more harmful and some less harmful, but they are all *perceived* identities, and a perceived identity is from your hot water.

Your hot water is *yours* and that is unavoidable. You will be shaped by your hot water and that is also unavoidable. Your perceived identity can shape your hot water and that, too, is unavoidable. But the wrong outcome **is** avoidable **when** you understand that *your hot water exists.*

If you don't realize that your hot water exists, then you are blind to it all and you *will not* be able to see it. Without understanding that your hot water is there, it will make deliberately changing it an impossible task.

Beginning to change your hot water can seem like a monumental task. If we don't notice our hot water because we are too accustomed to it, then where is the hope to become aware of it? The good news is that you are most of the way there *right now.*

Discomfort, discontentedness, depression, unhappiness, confusion, fear, and doubt are all signs that bring people to a point where they begin to know that something is not proper in their lives. Use these indicators to your advantage to more readily recognize your hot water's unhealthy condition.

Knowing that your hot water exists will surely turn the lights on within you. You will begin to notice things that have been unfairly placed into your hot water in the past, and that are now still being placed into your hot water *without* your permission! This is occurring on a daily basis. It is the awareness of this that will allow you the ability to make the needed changes to your hot water in order to stop this abuse from continuing.

I suspect, by this point in reading, that you will have already seen many things in your own life that can now be recalled as being unfairly placed on you that you truly did not want there. Because you were so accustomed to receiving those expectations from others, and from yourself, you never noticed those things enough to single them out—**until now**. You have felt it, and you have felt "off" about it, but you didn't really notice it. (Reading the notes you wrote earlier will be of interest to you now with your newer perspective. Study them and contemplate them. Are they truly valid?)

You can expect to see many more instances of your awareness of unwanted perceptions being placed on you. You will notice this, both, in recalling moments of your past, and in experiencing future moments. Don't get angry about missing all of this in the past. Just as others did it to you, so, too, you likely have done it to others, and it may have been worse than what was done to you.

The end goal is not to be upset about all of this, but, instead, to change this in your future and reflect on past events, and then to change your perspective on those past events as well. This is the only method with which you can ever get to go back in time and do it over. You cannot push back the Sun to yesterday, but you can change your conclusion about yesterday, and *that* is far more powerful and far more accurate than turning back time.

A Brief, but Important, Recap of Chapter 8

Recapping Chapter 8—*You are Not Your Job or Property*: Just because we see ourselves as some *thing* or a job does not mean that we *are* that thing, nor are we our hot water. Our hot water is simply our environment and the environment of our thoughts. It is these thoughts that we allow to create our perceived identity.

A **True Identity** is not a **perceived** identity. The word "*perceive*" implies an understanding of that which you see, but I used the term *perceive* where there is actually a misunderstanding for most of us. This is an intentional usage, and in the context in which it is used here it is very accurate.

Your *perceived* identity is an understanding. That is to say, it is *your* understanding of what or who you are, which was based upon the information that you have had the opportunity to see, or have been allowed to see during your life.

It is as if you are on trial, and you are both Judge and Jury of yourself. You will go into court and produce all of the evidence that you can find about your hot water, and then you will proceed to present your brilliant case to the Jury of *you* for the case that will be judged by the Honorable "Judge *You.*"

Now this all sounds great because *you* get to choose your own verdict and everything falls into your favor. Yet, this is the situation for everyone when it comes to our hot water, but when all is said and done, most of us misjudge the case. Why is this, after all, *we* are judging *ourselves*?

The reason the verdict is often wrong is because the evidence presented is your very own hot water, and you will make your judgments based upon *that* evidence. Just before the jury is sent out to make their deliberations, Judge You asks if there is any further evidence in the case, to which you happily reply "No, Your Honor!" Then the Jury who is made up of *you* will render their conclusion, and then the Honorable "Judge *You*" hands down the sentence. The sentence is your *perceived* identity. You will be stuck with your sentence until you find the *true* evidence about you to prove to the Jury and the Judge that you are not guilty. You will need to call for a retrial and prove that there is far more to you than this little bit of hot water that has been blinding *you* (that is to say, blinding the Judge and the Jury) from seeing what you are truly all about, and then judge with true jurisprudence.

Without **ALL** of the true evidence, an accurate verdict is nearly impossible and is left only to chance. This is because you have been led to believe that your life *is* your hot water, and up until today you have not known to look any further for the truth about your own case. So, it comes down to the fact that you have been a pretty bad representative for your own case—*up until now.*

Up until now, the only evidence that you have presented to the Court was your own hot water. And your hot water had every indication that the *things* in your life are what you were all about. This includes your prestige or reputation, your money, and your job. The Jury of *You* had no other possible choice than to conclude that *you* are your job, prestige, money, and things because that is what you, the lawyer, presented to the Jury. The verdict has then been passed down and your perceived identity has been deemed to be superficially meaningless arrogance and guilty.

No item, job, prestige, or money will make you truly respectable, but it will get you admiration from fair-weathered friends. And in the long run, it will leave you feeling empty when the guilty verdict has been declared in the trial in your own mind. If you doubt any of this about fair-weathered friends, then simply consider sports teams or famous people who are down on their luck. They are usually banished by society—that is to say us.

Besides your own misguided evidence that you presented to the Jury, the public's opinion about your case has also drawn conclusions about your evidence. This is because the public has been seeing the presented evidence for *your* entire lifetime, and the public has been telling you and the Jury of You and the Honorable *Judge* **You** that the evidence that you presented is all there is to know about this person who was on trial. How do you overcome this?

The key to overcoming is *proper understanding* and an awareness that there is more to your hot water than meets the eye. The longer you have grown accustomed to your hot water, then the more difficult it **seems** to be to see it for what it is and then make the proper changes. But this is not true. It only **seems** that way, when in reality it's very simple. Properly understanding one simple small key word will quickly change your entire life.

You Need to Realize and Accept
the Difference Between People and Animals

Being able to discern the meaning of this simple word that we will discuss shortly is the key to ending the lack of joy and the emptiness in your life. But most people cannot discern the word because they have not understood that they have a *perceived* identity. Even if someone *did* realize some sort of a perceived identity, they still likely *do not* understand where it came from or that it can be changed. This is the big difference between humans and animals.

Ever since the notion of human evolution has been injected into the minds of humanity, people have been finding it more and more difficult to explain the differences between animals and humans. Before the thought of evolving came along it was inaccurately assumed that the difference between humans and animals was that people can talk and articulate. But, as discussed in the book series *The Science Of God*, ever since the evolution concept was introduced, many glaringly obvious evidences have been presented that show that animals also can talk or communicate to some extent in their own way.

Due to our hot water, many have foolishly assumed that animals are stupid. And we made the same foolish assumption for people who looked different than us. We also make the same assumption for young children and babies, and sometimes even for ourselves. All creatures are far more brilliant than we give them credit for, and this includes ourselves.

Researchers who study the body and our behavior have looked at what chemically makes up people and animals, and they have found that we are generally made out of much the same elements and arranged quite similarly as well. But there has been a glaring oversight in all of this, and because of our civilization's hot water it has been missed. The difference is our ability to readily grasp the meaning of but one small word, and then *choose* what we will do about it.

Animals are amazing creatures, and at a minimum they deserve respect because of the complexity that they embody in order to function, run, live, and breathe. Many pet owners will confirm that they feel their pet can smile, be happy, sad, afraid, or angry. This is likely true for reasons too obvious to discuss here. The things a pet does or feels can be referred to as animal nature. Pets even seem to have a limited capacity to reason.

What pets don't have is a human ability. Humans have everything that animals have with regard to being in existence, but animals *do not* have everything that humans have. Humans are uniquely different than animals, but because of our hot water we have a difficult time explaining or describing the difference. In many ways, when we adopt a perceived identity, we are just like animals, and this results in us fighting in order to lead; or it results in us competing for a mate or for food. What's the difference? What is lacking in animals, or what do humans have that is extra? This is a question that has been around long before the theory of man and animals evolving from the same source has been around. This question cannot be answered by many people now or anytime in the past for a very key reason— Rejection.

For centuries, humans have sought to know their origins, and it seems that nearly every culture and generation fights the same battle to answer this question. So why, in thousands of years, have we not been able to come to a unanimous conclusion with the collective research of several millennia of generations?

The answer is *our hot water*. Going back a few chapters we discussed jealousy, arrogance, and fear. When we get off track in our lives and adopt a *perceived* identity that includes any one of *jealousy, arrogance,* or *fear,* then it is likely that the other two of these three will also enter in and become a part of our hot water. When they do enter in, then arrogance becomes a trap and will not allow the perceived identity to admit that it is going in the wrong direction.

Now *you* have the opportunity to make a decision that so many before you have failed to do. This is not a test—it is a **decision**. A decision that only *you* can make, and it is *yours* and *yours* alone to make! Many people have failed, and continue to fail to make this freewill choice, where with animals they do not have the option to make this decision in the same way that we humans do.

You Understanding What is Truth is very Important

The decision is—**Truth**. One small simple key word, it is your key and it is an entity in itself; but to use it safely you must understand how it works. This might seem uneventful after all of the discussion. But it is not uneventful and I will explain why. Many of us have gotten so far off track because of our hot water that we can't even tell the difference between what is truth and what is **not** truth. We are not discussing what is true or not true here; rather, we are discussing what *true* or *truth* is.

Based upon present day life and ancient writings about prior eras that I have read, it appears to be common for humans to have a misguided attitude and understanding of the idea of **truth**. The misguided attitude about truth is that we all have our own truth and that we can make our own truth. This misguided attitude also often includes that we are gods and can do what we want, and that we can *will* what we want to happen, and then it will eventually occur. This has an element of the appearance of truth, but that does *not* make it truth.

When we imagine to "make our own truth" we are really making our own circumstances or changing and manipulating our own circumstance for our own benefit. Calling our circumstances truth does not make them truth, and doing so confuses the essence of "truth" in our minds. It may be true that we did a certain thing, but that has little to do with the essence of truth.

Whatever *is*—**IS**—and whatever is not—is **not**. Calling a hammer a plow does not make it a plow. A plow will always be a plow and a hammer will always be a hammer, and nothing will ever change that truth about those designs. You could melt the plow and make it into a hammer, but then the truth is that it was once a plow and you modified it and converted it into a hammer. An additional truth is that, at some point before the materials were made into the hammer and the plow, the materials used were in the ground or were a part of a tree. But it is *not* a truth that the hammer *is* a plow. A hammer's intended purpose is to pound or strike things even though you can use its claws to scratch through the soil in effort to plow the soil. However, while it has the form of a hammer it is still a hammer, and using it for something other than its intended purpose is an abuse of its intended purpose and is typically highly inefficient.

When a person's hot water has been contaminated to the point where a person believes that they can make their own truth, then the truth is that they do not understand the *pure* meaning of *Truth* and they have chosen to be something that they are not.

It's true that someone *can* alter their own *circumstances* by changing their thinking and subsequent actions, but they *cannot* alter truth! Deep down we all truly do understand the concept of what truth is, but we typically do not properly associate the right word with the concept. This results in causing confusion within our minds. This distortion of truth has been in our civilization's hot water since the very beginning of mankind.

Without truth, our hot water has a self-destructive nature. Recalling back several chapters, we discussed how jealousy and arrogance seep into our hot water. We also discussed how our hot water blinds us because we are too accustomed to it to a point that it causes us to be blind to the fact that we have hot water. This means that we will often reject new information, new circumstances, and new beliefs in order to keep them from getting into our familiar and deceptively comfortable hot water. When we do this, opening up our thinking to any new water becomes a nearly impossible task for those of us whose hot water does not include openness. This is the trap that most of us are caught in, and we are caught in it because nobody showed us otherwise.

Our perceived identity has control over us *when* we allow it to. In Biblical terms, we could call it an evil nature. Whether or not you subscribe to the Biblical accounts of man there is a basic truth in what we are discussing here. These circumstances are undeniable and have been written about and printed on scrolls, stone, and paper for our consideration for many thousands of years.

Arrogance, by definition, will cause the arrogant to place themselves above others. Why is this? Because of jealousy! Jealousy is a result of *the fear of rejection.* Arrogance, jealousy, and fear feed each other in a reciprocal manner.

Self-realization seems to be the only escape from this inevitable trap of mankind's free will. Some have managed to avoid this because they had hot water that was clean and free of arrogance, jealousy, and fear while growing up, but even some of those who have avoided this trap are still susceptible to its draw if they are left unaware. Please recall that it is possible to have a perceived identity with very clean hot water and still *not* be self-aware.

The only way to become truly self-aware is to understand **truth**. In the context of this book, the term *self-aware* is referring to the understanding that you have hot water, and that it can be in *your* control **when** you so choose.

It is this self-awareness that brings truth in to your life. Arrogance, jealousy, and fear all bring with them the denial of what *is*. Arrogance will puff up or **inflate** to make something appear to be something that it is not. Jealousy will cut down and **destroy** others to make itself appear worthy, and fear will **hide** to avoid confrontation and avoid dealing with life—*Inflate, destroy,* and *hide.*

If you were to trace the root of the word "hell" in the dictionary you will find that its root is to *hide* or *conceal*. With that understanding, it is fair to say that it is *hell* for those who have hot water with the evil nature of committing yourself to your perceived identity. When we do so, we are submitting ourselves to something that we are not. When we allow this evil nature in our hot water we become trapped by our own deceptions and actions.

When we reject arrogance, jealousy, and fear we can then see the light of truth begin to shine in our own hot water.

The part that is difficult for us to overcome is that, without the understanding that—*we* can each control *our own* hot water—many of us will fall back into our former nature of contaminated hot water when we begin to allow truth into our hot water. This happens because hot water with truth in it will not allow arrogance, jealousy, or fear of truth. When this happens, it feels like a threat to our *perceived* identity which we have become dependent upon. And this often causes people to reject truth that they seek.

Truth is self-convicting and self-correcting. When you *freely* allow truth into your hot water, then arrogance, jealousy, and fear will depart from you and you will quickly see all of your past errors. Seeing our past is frightening for most of us, and when we see those errors we try to hide them, which gives our old hot water even more power over us.

But if you love truth, then you will embrace it and lock arrogance, jealousy, and fear out of your life and out of your hot water. Doing so will keep arrogance, jealousy, and fear far away from you. These three evils—*arrogance, covetous-jealousy,* and *fear*—create hatred, and hatred creates these three evils.

The only thing we should hate is hate itself, which is the only way to destroy hatred. When hatred is defeated, then along with it will go *arrogance, covetous-jealousy,* and *fear.*

If you think about these contaminators to your hot water for a few moments, you will quickly realize that they are the source of *all* pain, and without them you *will* experience joy.

The insatiable feeling of arrogance will always leave you wanting. Fear is the reason that arrogance exists, and as long as you doubt, you will *always* be trapped in fear. But what is it that is truly being feared? The answer to this is the key, which is that one simple word, and that word is **Truth**!

When we have fallen short, we often choose to live in the fear of the truth about the error of our ways. The only escape from this trap is to embrace truth. In order to embrace truth we must *humble* ourselves and *admit* our errors.

Without this simple admission and acceptance of our own errors there is *no* possibility that we can *ever* hope to be able to correct our errors. This is because without admission of error we are in denial and will continue in this denial in order to protect our perceived identity, and thus, to protect our arrogance. If you are in denial of the truth about your life, then you do not have truth, and in your denial of truth you have rendered yourself incapable of repentance of your own errors.

It is because we have identified with the wrong things and because we fear humility. The word *humility* has the root of the word *humble*. And *humble* has the root of the word *humus* or *earth*. It is the same root as the root of the word *human*, and in this case its understanding is meant to be that of being low. From a Biblical perspective, Man, who was made from *earth*, was brought low from their error and put back in their proper place.

We don't need to be Biblical to be humble, because being humble is an act of admission of error and/or accepting your actual position in existence. When we humble ourselves by admission of our error, it is something that cannot be done without truth. This is simply because truth *is* what *IS*—**It is only when we realize our errors <u>on our own</u> that we can begin to embrace truth.**

This is why when people are devastated by extreme loss it's often the turning point for them to begin to understand that their hot water has been misguided. It's when everything that matters to our *perceived* identity is destroyed and/or stripped away from us that we can begin to feel the nakedness of our *true identity*. Until we begin to understand and can admit the truth of our actions, we *do not* have the ability to repent of our errors. Repenting is technically impossible when we refuse to realize our errors.

This can be illustrated in terms of *forcing* two rivaling children to apologize to one another when they have not yet truly resolved their differences within each their own hearts. Forcing them to apologize will not change their real underlying feelings towards one another, and, in some cases, it will serve to deepen their ill feelings towards each another. The same is true with international tensions in our world. When the nations of power try to force peace talks and peace agreements between less-powerful nations it is often heralded as a wonderful thing. Indeed, to not have people killing each other is good, but forcing someone to be at peace cannot be done without *their* permission or their freewill realization and internal admission of error on the part of both warring parties. Is there a solution to international strife?

Only *truth* will solve that problem for us on any level. And as you can see, unless, we start with ourselves, we will *never* be able to change the world.

— *Truth IS* —

Anything that is not true, simply is not; it does not exist and this includes your perceived identity. If your identity is not founded on what is true, then even if it is correct, it is still *perceived* from your hot water. And if your hot water is not of truth, then you cannot have truth.

Hot water can be correct, and thus, your *perceived* identity can fall in alignment with what is true, but this does not mean that you have accepted truth. This is because even a bad *perceived* identity can be *right* or *correct* about *some* things, but still be unwilling to admit to errors when something changes and truth is finally revealed about the other things. Refusing to admit error is denying what is true; where on the other hand, truth *never* stops checking yourself for accuracy. When you are in truth, you will *always* welcome correction and always be willing to make the needed corrections to your thinking and attitude in effort to adjust to what *is*. This is because when you embrace truth, then your deepest desire will be to seek accuracy regardless of how it makes your past erred choices appear—**Truth IS**.

The Difference Between Believing and Knowing

The phrase "Truth Is" is best understood by understanding the difference between *Believing* and *Knowing*. To "*Believe*" is the ability to accept something as true whether or not it actually is true. Where, to *Know* is a certainty that something **IS**. When we *know* something, then we *know* for specific reasons rather than only because we *believe* it. But even though evidence is overwhelming, it is possible to *know* something and not really believe it due to our relentless ability to doubt. This would be like our human inclination to believe that there must be some sort of Supreme Being that somehow put everything that we see together, but we doubt this because of our societal conventional wisdom—we know it from the overwhelming tangible evidence, but we choose to *not* believe it due to societal doubt and social intimidation.

The distinction between *knowing* and *believing* is a vitally important point to understand. Many of us are led to believe things that are not true, and we feel that we "know" these things when truly we do not *know*. If you were led to believe that a box contained a great deal of treasure and you firmly placed this into your hot water, then you would likely go about your life convinced that the box is full of treasure. But the truth about the box, in this example, is that it **does not** contain anything *at all*, and if you have chosen to *believe* that it does contain treasure, *then you will have a belief that is **wrong***. The belief that you have acquired is due to what you have been told, or is due to what you believe you have seen and subsequently assumed about the box that you believe contained treasure. Since the box is empty, then you did not **know** what was actually in the box, but rather, you only *believed* that you *knew*.

Believing is what religion is largely based upon. We are told to have *blind* faith and follow what the preachers and priests tell us. Our blind faith in following what they say is also very dangerous hot water, even though what they say is most often correct. Blind faith is often the kind of hot water that is justified because it might just so happen to be correct. The problem with having *blind-faith Hot Water* is that it is based upon *belief*, and therefore the possibility exists that the *belief* may, in fact, be *incorrect*. This means that *your belief may be **wrong***.

The belief of doubt is also an interesting perspective. When we are chronic doubters, then our perceived identity sees truth as doubtful and negative. This anomaly occurs because when someone understands truth, and stands by it, that truth shatters the perceived identities of others. You could say that it *doubts* their perceived identities. Truth does not see those perceived identities as real.

Truth will appear as doubtful towards our current way of life when we have a doubting perceived identity. So, when we doubt truth, then that is a part of our hot water, and because of this we see truth as doubtful when people who stand by truth assess us. Our negativity affects us when we doubt truth. It's interesting how often we "doubt it" and how seldom we "hope it." In the Bible it explains that miracles could not be worked when there was too much doubt present.

The difference between *Knowing* and *Believing* in your identity is very simple: Believing will often stick with what it believes. Where knowing will **always** investigate to make sure that it is **not** in error. You **cannot** know something without truth! And technically, you *cannot* **know** something that is false.

The one place where *belief* is most recognized is in the realm of religion. It can be any religion, including non-God religions. *Any* belief is a religion as we perceive the word "religion." Whether the religion is a belief of the Earth, of gods, of darker forces, of environmentalism, of science, of evolution, or of the religions that reference the Bible, these are all based upon *beliefs* rather than truth.

Being a "religion" does not necessarily make the *belief* wrong, but the *belief* can make the religion dangerous. When a religious belief is founded on our civilizations' hot water and when our own personal hot water contains *arrogance, covetous-jealousy*, and *fear*, then the believers of that religion will never back down to find the truth—this is how *all* wars begin.

Truth will always prevail in the long run, as it always has prevailed in the past. You can look at any ancient civilization and you will see that it was crushed at some point. While the reason the civilizations were crushed can be debated, the fact that they were crushed or dispersed cannot. The point of contention would be: what actually was it that crushed them?

Akin to happiness versus joy, *Believing* has the ability to look as if it is *Knowing*, because if a believer is arrogant, it gives the impression of confidence. This makes them look as if they actually *know* something when, in reality, they are basing their attitude on their false belief, which is based only on the information that was available to them at the time they formed their initial belief that they are refusing to adjust for accuracy. This means that *they are wrong* just like in our treasure chest example.

Dual-Example "You will get what you deserve."

To illustrate how we can each see things differently and come to different beliefs, we will use a dual example: Consider a dual example showing true inner personal feeling when the statement "You will get what you deserve" is told to different people. Those who have been helpful and caring and have sacrificed much while always caring for others, loving others, always lending a hand, and trying to accommodate others; for this type person this statement will be seen as a reward and compliment. They will be excited for the day that they will "get what they deserve."

Now consider the other group who has been mean and cynical, always condemning and being filled with hate and selfishness, and always taking care of themselves first, while never truly helping others. They always try to make others look bad so that they feel that they themselves will look better than those they condemn. This type of person will see the statement "You will get what you deserve" as a threat and as an insult. Seldom will this type person mistake the statement and feel that it is meant as a reward of their good merit and be expecting to be showered with good things. This is the primary reason why many of us often refuse to believe in the concept of a hell—it is our fear.

Conversely, the other type person, who is always helpful, will seldom or never mistake "You will get what you deserve" to mean that bad things will come their way. Examining your own feelings about this phrase is a good initial way to test yourself to know if you've been in truth about your life.

We know our own truth and we condemn ourselves in this. Because of your hot water, the way in which you see the world is often the way that you are. This will generally be the case unless you are the kind of person who is always trying to better understand the world and yourself. If you are the type who is always trying to understand, then the way in which you see the world will be ever-changing and you will be ever-improving. I must add this important point: There will be some of us who have been so mentally abused that we will believe that we deserve punishment when we actually do not, and some of those who have experienced this might, instead, even actually deserve reward for their kindness, love, and truth towards others, even though they have wrongly been taught otherwise.

Finding Yourself

When we begin to seek to *know*, rather than merely to *believe*, then we begin to truly understand ourselves. When we understand ourselves, then we often refer to it as "finding ourselves."

Around the middle of the twentieth century it was common for young adults around the age of twenty to travel to seek understanding. They often did not understand what it was that they were looking for, but they felt that something was missing in their lives. People would often comment about them, that they were going out trying to "find themselves." While this was often meant as a bit of jesting or making fun of them, it was likely very true.

When we notice something is missing in our lives, it goes far beyond traveling abroad. In the beginning of the book it was discussed that people often feel that something is "off" in their lives. But it might be better to state it as something is *missing* in their lives. When we are brought low and begin to find that our life has no meaning, then that's often when we begin to seek these answers. This *seeking* is the same function as trying to *find yourself* by traveling abroad. Whether we travel abroad or simply do some serious self-reflection in our own homes, it does *not* guarantee a fulfilling joy-filled life.

If we go about the task of finding ourselves with *arrogance*, *covetous-jealousy*, *fear*, and *doubt* at our side, we will likely fall into the same kind of trap, and it is usually an even stronger trap than our previous trap. This is because if we try to find ourselves in this way, and we have not put off *arrogance, covetous-jealousy, fear,* and *doubt,* then those attributes will overtake us. This is especially true if the newly found *perceived* identity that we found for ourselves happens to be accurate or at least close to accurate to our actions and thoughts.

The worst is when we are the pacifist who is willing to accept all things as they are. The pacifist's approach is saying that whatever you choose to believe is okay. While peace is a good and wonderful thing, a false approach to it will not gain us true peace in the long run and will only end in turmoil, destruction, and death. Having the attitude that everyone should believe what they want to believe is both foolish and dangerous. This does not mean that we should force others to believe what *we* believe, but rather to encourage them and ourselves to seek to—*know*—or better stated, to seek Truth!

You will never be able to feel a robust feeling of fulfillment without truth. If your hot water has been contaminated by bad surroundings, then you will have the sensation of being fulfilled; and as long as your surroundings do not change you'll continue to feel as though you are fulfilled. This false sensation will go on until that time comes when things change and suddenly you no longer feel fulfilled. Truth is different in this way, because when you grab a hold of truth and don't let go, then you will *always* feel fulfilled no matter what because *you **have** "found yourself."*

Your Four Cornerstones of Life

When we understand *ourselves* then we begin to be able find many good things in life, and we will find that life is far simpler than we once believed it to be. "Ourself" is *our own self,* this book, *Hot Water,* explains about *our own self,* but it does not explain some other critically important factors in our lives that greatly affect us all. There are four cornerstones in the lives of people. Listed in the order best understood, they are: *ourself, our marriage or relationships, our family,* and *our prayers.* If we are missing any one of these four cornerstones then our life will typically be fragmented, difficult, and often lonely. While this book, *Hot Water*, addresses our own self, we are still likely to be married and will be dealing with a spouse and the typically accompanying children. Then when circumstances become difficult we often turn to prayer, with little success. Why do our prayers so often lack success?

This happens because of our hot water and the hot water of those around us. Each of these cornerstones is a topic in itself and each needs scrutiny for us to cut through the lies and darkness that has blinded the world from Truth for so long.

You deserve a great and joyous life, but if you cannot produce that joy *on command*, then you are caught in the same trap that much of the rest of the world appears to be caught in. Because so many people suffer a great deal in all four cornerstone areas, each of the cornerstones is specifically addressed in its own separate book. I placed the book names in this section so everyone has the opportunity to know that there are answers available to you. If your marriage is great and your children are perfect and your prayers are always answered, then this might appear to not have much significance to you. But, if you are like the rest of us, you can choose to read one or more of the other three very helpful books to work through those persistent troubles.

Besides the cornerstone of *self*, which this book *Hot Water* addresses, there are also three other cornerstones of our lives. The second cornerstone is marriage. The marriage cornerstone book is called *Red Hot Marriage* and it deals with the problems and tensions that so many of us suffer within our marriages. You will quickly learn how damaging the small-things that we do to each other are. *Red Hot Marriage* explains, in detail, what you can do to eliminate these nuisances that silently torment too many couples and unnecessarily destroy many marriages.

The third cornerstone is family. The family cornerstone book is called *Strong Family*, and it attacks the things that attack our families and exposes those things in plain view. You can easily learn how to defeat those problems so that your children can grow up the way you imagine them to. *Strong Family* also addresses how to deal with older children who have gotten off the path that you were trying to create and lay down before them as they navigated life.

The fourth cornerstone is prayer. The ability to fully understand prayer is held by very few people. *Understanding Prayer—Why Our Prayers Don't Work – The Prayer How-To Manual* goes in-depth about what you need to do to make your prayers effectively work so that they can get answered. It exposes all of the wrong information that we have been led to believe about prayer. You will find out a great deal about the truth and promises that reside within our prayers *when* they are approached *correctly*.

If you do not have each of the four cornerstones well placed in the foundation of your own life, then you can expect more of the same troubles that you have always seen within your life in those areas.

By placing any of these cornerstones in the incorrect position, or if you are missing any one or more of them, you will not be able to reliably create the joy throughout your life that you and all the rest of us deserve and want to have in our lives—It is *joy* that we were Created for. As you move forward in life, take your control back by embracing Truth! While we have discussed what the concept of truth is, we have *not* yet discussed Truth's origin.

Chapter 14

Your Identity and God

We must fully understand the word *identity* in order to get a grasp on our own identity. What is it? *Identity* and *identical* have the same root-meaning, and that root is—*same*. This means that the term "our identity" means that we are the *same* as something or someone.

We could say that we are the same as our parents, especially when considering our hot water. And while there is an element of accuracy to this, it is actually our *perceived* identity that is identical to our hot water, rather than our hot water being identical to us. Are you pleased with your *perceived* identity? Have you been happy? Do you know what true joy is?

You Are Identical to God

Since you are reading this book it is likely that you desire joy in your life in the same way that most people desire it. You likely have been unable to find it because of the overbearing pressure of the hot water that you drank in all of your life. Because of that, you may feel confused, down, afraid, depressed, and not in control of your life.

Throughout this book the freedom to believe that you can achieve joy without knowing your Creator was left unaddressed until now. The truth is that you cannot. If you do not already know and believe that you were Created, then you will need to decide whether you will accept the truth of a Creator, *or* will you ignore the information and choose to believe as you have been believing and continue living with internal toil and strife and doubt? This is all inclusive and is not referring to believing in a Creator versus being an evolutionist. Even many people who attend church on a weekly basis do not really **know** that the Creator exists, but instead they only **believe** that this is so. Continuing to believe the way you have been believing will only get you more of the often unpleasant and lackluster life that you have lived so far. Only *you* can make this choice—*no one* can make it for you. It is *your* choice and *yours* alone! If you seek answers about the existence of God, you might find some of the answers that you're looking for in the book set *The Science of God.*

Having read this book up until this point has you tangled in an inescapable truth. It is your choice to embrace or deny something that is true. You can no longer deny without conviction because now you will need to face your denial if you choose to continue in your old hot water. Accepting that you have a Creator is not a mandatory action, but rather it is a result of understanding the truth of your identity.

What is the truth of your identity? As promised in Chapter 3 we'll briefly discuss the reason for not calling your perceived identity the "essence" of you. The root or base meaning of *essence* is to **BE**, or **IS**. It basically means what you **ARE**. So to call your "perceived identity" your *essence* is false and simply incorrect because you **are not** your "perceived" identity—you *are* *the* Identity.

The truth of your identity is that you are identical to something. But what are you identical to, or *who* are you identical to? I will not directly quote the Bible here, but I will discuss some basics: The account of Creation in the Bible makes a statement that Man was Created in the *image* of the Creator. This is to say that we are Created *identical* to our Creator. If your hot water has taught you things that are not of truth about our Creator, then you might have some reservation in your desire to be *Created* "in the image of" the Creator. This is understandable in the common scenario of when your hot water denied the Creator, but was inaccurate in its account of the Creator.

So, how then does one come to know their Creator properly? First, we must understand that we are of Truth and when we accept things that are not of Truth we go against our Created nature and true identity. Our Creator will only Create what *is*, and we are Created in the image of the Creator. This means that we have the ability to discern truth and an ability to *choose* right from wrong, and it also means that we have the ability to articulate that truth to others.

When we allow our *perceived* identity to adopt contaminated hot water into our *true* identity, then we have chosen to deny Truth. It is the denial of Truth that destroys people. Arrogance, covetous-jealousy, and fear-of-truth are all destroyers of man. In the Bible this is called sin.

Regardless of what the Bible says about all of this, the truth of this effect is so even without the Bible's words being recalled. Sin is the Bible's description of what we have been discussing in this book, and what we have been discussing is our error in going against what **IS** true.

When we fail to embrace Truth then we have caught ourselves in a life built upon lies and incorrect information, and, in so doing, we *have chosen to be* **wrong**.

Our **True Identity** is our *Essence* when, and only when, we have embraced Truth.

Are You Stiff-necked?

People choose to *not* want to change, and their unwillingness to change is the same disease that those who are arrogant and those who are lazy have. It is *stiff-necked* and *hard-hearted*. We often stand by our stiff-necked way until death; but this can be good or bad. It is good *if* you stand for *Order*, *Truth*, *Love*, and *Light*, but if you choose to ignore facts to suit a selfish unwillingness to change, then *you* are the problem and *you* are the maker of your own destruction. Changing doesn't come easy for us when we live in fear and doubt. Fear tends to manifest itself as arrogance, covetousness, laziness, and false-humility or cowering.

It is not the purpose of this book to discuss religious philosophy or an afterlife because those are entirely different topics from what we are discussing here. But reading this book in its entirety will facilitate a more rich and robust understanding of those topics when you choose to explore them further as you begin to see—*things* and *people*—for what they truly are.

When we have begun to understand Truth, then we become *fearless* of non-truths, and we will no longer feel any need to deny what is true. When we no longer deny what is true, then our fear of admitting our own errors will vanish. Our lives become strong, healthy, robust, and joyful! This does not mean that bad things will not come our way. In fact, when you embrace Truth you will have people who will try even harder to draw you back into your old hot water. When you refuse to go back, then they typically become agitated and angry because they feel attacked, insulted, intimidated, and judged by you and the Truth that you now work to live your life by. You become a threat to them, causing them to be afraid of you, and they will lash out at you to hide their fear, and, at the same time, they will try to draw you back. Usually attempts at intimidation, mockery, blaming you, and making you a point of contention are tactics used to lure and guilt you back into your old ways. Resist going back because there is only darkness and lack of joy there. Instead, become and remain a beacon of hope for them.

When you have understood and accepted that these attacks will likely occur, then you will find Truth far more exciting to pursue. You will be able to fulfill your purpose and fulfill the reason that you were Created. You will be able to avoid the downward spiral caused by others, and you will no longer remain trapped when you realize that *they* have no power over you.

Why Were You Created to Begin With?

This brings us to the question: If we were Created, then what exactly was the purpose of Creating us? Here it may be best to consult a Bible and read it all for yourself with open eyes and an open mind, and then draw *your own* conclusions as to why *you* were Created.

It is clear, in the Bible, that the Creator always was, and before the Creator there was nothing. Now, we can get all cosmic and start to say that the Creator is some weird energy, or was from a distant place, but that would be an anomaly and a denial of what **IS**. The Creator is not some energy field, or from a distant place. The Creator *Created* those things and spoke those things into existence. For the purpose of this book, we are going to accept that, and then look at the reasoning, or the *why*. *Why* did our Creator Create us?

Since the Creator Created us in the image of the Creator, it is a fairly safe assumption that the Creator wanted to have someone similar to the Creator itself for companionship. There are more detailed accounts of Creation and physics in the book *Bending The Ruler—Time Travel, The Speed of Light, Gravity, and The Big Bang*, and in the book set *The Science of God*.

According to the Bible there were other Created entities besides Man. These other entities could conceive thoughts and even rebel as described in the accounts in the Bible about the fallen angel and the angel's followers. But there was something uniquely special about *Man* who was Created in the *image* of the Creator. What is this nature or image that we were Created after?

Often, the past and present religions of our world make certain assumptions that become "beliefs," but these beliefs *may* or *may not* be true. Many of the religions believe that *they* are *the* chosen people. While this may or may not be true, the Bible speaks nothing about them being the *only* people.

They might have been chosen, but they were chosen *for* something. This does not mean that all other peoples are meaningless. No, it is quite the contrary. *All* people are Created in the image of the Creator, and none have a lock on the Creator.

There's this misguided belief, that is not directly stated as such, but most of the religions have a tendency to act as if they own the Creator and that the Creator is on *their* side. Nothing could be further from truth. This feeling is built upon utter arrogance! The Creator is not on our side, **we** are on the side of the Creator. In other words, *we* must choose to live within the *infinite* bounds of the Creator.

What is even worse is when people attempt to hijack the Creator from others. We act as if we are the creator and that the Creator is subject to us, but this is not the case; we cannot control the Creator. Mankind was Created for a reason, and more specifically, *you* were Created for a reason. When your perceived identity controls your choices and thinking, then you have lost the ability to *understand* and *know* things, and, therefore, you cannot obtain truth.

You were created of Truth and when you turn from that Truth, you deny *who* you truly are. This is a corruption of your design.

This can appear speculative to some who read these pages, but if you open your thinking to this possibility and observe it, then, on your own, you will find that these are simple truths that cannot be denied. Choosing to *not* take serious contemplation of these things is to be deliberately ignorant and foolish. If you refuse to *consider* these things, then you are deliberately and knowingly deciding to ignore information that you might find to be accurate and true. What you choose to believe *after* careful consideration of these thoughts is an entirely different subject. What you later choose to believe based upon your analysis of the information you gather will prove your own worth. You make this choice yourself of *your* own free will—We all judge ourselves with the choices we make.

The goal of this book is not to get you to *believe*, but rather to have you receive the method of *Truth*, and then by that method, *know* from your own observations that these things that we are discussing *are true*.

To deny them will only keep you where you have been wanting to escape from. You were Created of Truth and for the joy of, and companionship to, the Creator. It is that simple! If you don't like this thought, then you should consider and ask yourself why you would ever choose to have a mate and offspring, or friends for that matter. You are Created in the image of the Creator, and you desire companionship just as your Creator did when your Creator Created the rest of Mankind and you.

Black-Room Discovery

To better understand your hot water in regard to Truth, imagine yourself in an all-black and all-dark completely empty area with absolutely no light. If you were in such a place, you would not be able to discern anything because everything would be of the same darkness, and therefore you would not be able to notice any shadow or variance in light. Additionally, the area is completely empty so there is nothing to see to begin with.

Our hot water is much like this darkness. It is the beauty of the difference of light and dark that allows us to actually detect that something is in front of us with regard to our eyes and our vision.

Imagine yourself in that all dark area. You are all alone with no one else around. Now try to imagine that you have never seen another human. All that you know is that you are conscious and aware, and you can detect nothing other than your awareness.

You could begin to imagine many things in your own mind and you could follow those imaginings as a *belief* and you could build a whole philosophy based upon this belief. This hot water that you have created for yourself is the only thing that you know so far, and it is what you believe.

If you were in this dark state and even the smallest tiny light would appear, then you would almost instantly notice that something had changed in your darkness. You could deny that this light is there, **or** you could go to it and investigate its origin. This light might even allow you to see that another being was later created who is just like you, and then you could discover things about that other being. Investigating this other being would begin to reveal truths to you that you cannot see about your own self because it is difficult to see yourself without a mirror.

This light is Truth. If you choose, you can turn away from what you see and pretend that what you have previously thought in your own mind is all that there is, but that would clearly be ignoring what you now *know* exists. Truth is like Light—it is the light of our understanding and deeds! Denying the revealing light is like trying to fill a pot with water *after* someone tells you there is a hole in the pot, yet *you* decide to ignore the information and continue to attempt to fill the pot. No matter how long you try to fill the pot, it will never stay full. You can dump water in very quickly, but the moment you stop filling it, the pot soon becomes empty and you will need to work to put more water back in it to try to fill it again. You will repeat this until you come to the realization that your water vessel has a flaw that is causing the good fresh water to leak out through the hole. Trying to fill a pot that has a hole in it is like a consuming fire that can never be satisfied, which is much like your *perceived* identity.

Just like in our example of the dark area, all things that are dark can be illuminated with only the smallest amount of light. If you choose to cover or to extinguish the true light, then you will be denying the true things that you see. And while it is your hot water that causes you to act in this way, it is still your own responsibility to *allow* or to *deny* truth within you. *No one* can do this for you, and, in the end, no one else but *you* yourself will be to blame for your denial.

Earlier I mentioned that I have had people say to me that they don't like to be *corrected.* Not wanting to be corrected is like placing a bucket over the light gleaming in the darkness mentioned in the example just given.

What possible reason can we have to *not* want to be *corrected*? **Corrected**! This is an anomaly in our thinking. The very reason that we don't want to be *corrected* is because we desire to be *correct*, but to be *correct* we *must* know truth. However, we cannot know Truth if we deny Truth. To reject *correction* is placing a bucket over the light of Truth that presents itself to you. If we can cover the light in our mind by pretending that it does not exist, then in our mind we pretend we are correct. But this is *not* true. So what is this light... this *Truth* we speak of?

Allowing your Creator in You

Light of Truth is the result of the Creation that was Created by the Creator. We are a part of this Creation. When we allow the Creator into our hot water we are accepting that truth. Truth is not what you see in the Bible, or what your preacher says it is. Those things may be true, yet they in themselves are not Truth.

Truth is a method of—*being* or *existing*—where you will **always** be open to changing your thinking to accommodate what **IS** when it is revealed to your open mind. You must understand, though, that being open to changing your thinking means that you will **not** choose to accept information that lacks the credibility of Truth. Truth is a method of discerning that you can know more, and that everything around might *not* be as it appears to be because you could be missing some information. Truth is also void of fear, jealousy, and arrogance. When you allow Truth into your hot water, then your hot water is allowing truth into your heart and soul, thus you are allowing Truth into your very being! Since Truth is of the Creator, this means that you are allowing the Creator into your heart when you embrace Truth in this way.

You don't need to follow the doctrines of some church to do this, you simply *need* to embrace the Truth with all of your heart, soul, and mind.

When you have done this, then arrogance, covetous-jealousy, and fear of Truth will quickly flee from you. When this happens, Truth will be in you and will live within you. You will, in fact, be allowing the Creator into you, which is why you were Created to begin with.

Allowing Truth into your life will renew your strength. When you have Truth you are no longer misguided by the incorrect information that is often offered by others. You will hear and receive the information, but you will quickly be able to discern its truthfulness or lack thereof. You will *know* that you are valued no matter what anyone says about you. You will be able to immediately *know* when to disregard or when to question information that is inaccurate.

If you find yourself being puffed up from having this power in you, then you do not truly have it, and you have fallen right back into your previous trap of darkness and contaminated hot water.

Truth will convict you and guide you to a new place in life. Truth is an unshakable foundation that *cannot* be broken.

If you truly have found truth, then arrogance, jealousy, and fear of truth will be nowhere near you. Arrogance, jealousy, and fear will try to fight Truth, but they cannot prevail without *your* permission. The *Truth of Order* will always prevail in the long run and *cannot* be defeated in us unless *we* allow it to be. Arrogance, covetous-jealousy, and fear will battle with the Truth in you, and, if you allow them to, they will destroy you and bring you low by creating confusion, depression, destitution, and feeling worthless when you do not play their way. But when you *fully* accept Truth into you, and replace your old contaminated hot water with Truth, then arrogance, covetous-jealousy, and fear no longer have power over you—you will have become victorious! Empty yourself of arrogance, covetous-jealousy, and fear, and only allow the water of Truth to pour into you, and always remain vigilant about keeping contaminated water out of you.

Allowing Truth into your hot water is the same as allowing the Creator into your heart. It is not *like* it—**it *is* it**. The Creator and Truth are inseparable; so to accept Truth into your heart is to accept the Creator into your heart. This is where your true identity is derived from. Do not be deceived by false preachers. It doesn't matter how much someone talks about God, because if they are wrong, then they are wrong. Even if they believe something with all of their heart, and with all of their mind, and with all of their soul, they are still wrong if they are *wrong*, and that makes them a *false* preacher.

Accepting Your Creator Identity

Your true identity is that of the Creator. This is not to say that you *are* the Creator, but rather that you are an image of the Creator. You are *identical* to the Creator.

If you conceive in your mind that you are the Creator, then you have stepped into arrogance and are trying to build yourself up to be something that you are not! When *you* can make everything from nothing and Create all that is, then that may be proof of being the Creator. But for obvious reasons this is not likely to happen—ever.

Being made in the image of the Creator is a very privileged position. When you deny Truth you have chosen to **not** be made in the image of the Creator, and you have placed your *perceived* identity into you in free exchange for your original and authentic Truth; and, in doing so, you have rejected your Creator. You have made yourself subservient to your hot water and its resulting perceived identity, causing you to have lost **all** of your **true** power, causing you to frequently be wrong.

You are individual with your infinite Creator when you embrace and love Truth! This means that you **cannot** be separate, but rather you are a part of the Creator because you are Created in the image of the Creator.

There is a lot of speculation in the various religions about "punishment" from the Creator, and it also appears that the Bible indicates that the Creator *punishes*. The root of the word *punish* is to cause *pain* and the root of *pain* comes from *revenge* or *avenge* which means to lay *claim* to, or *reclaim* what is yours. When the Creator *punishes*, it is to rightfully lay claim to something. What is that something?

When you consider that arrogance, covetous-jealousy, and fear often are manifest through destroying or taking, then to *punish* or to lay *claim* to something makes perfect sense. *Why* would the Creator *not* take back what an arrogant person has, without permission, stolen? And *why* would the Creator *not* pay back an unfair and jealously-covetous attack on a person? Is any person's life so special that *they* should be able to harm others without cost to themselves? This is not logical and does not hold up in any realm except for the foolish realm of our own contaminated minds.

The notion that Truth should stand down and not take its rightful and proper place is very distorted thinking; and that line of thinking can only be done outside of the presence of Truth. When someone tries to steal away our freedom of Truth by means of giving us incorrect information, it should be of great concern to us. If we fail to be concerned and fail to take mental action to protect the Truth that lay within us, then we have forfeited ourselves to lies.

When Truth is absent from us, then the replacement for that missing Truth will be fear; and fear will bring with it arrogance and covetous-jealousy. Truth does not need to fight. Truth will *always* stand on its own, but *you* can cast Truth out of you, and then the void, from the now absent Truth, will be filled with more bad and contaminated hot water—better described as *fear*. If you choose fear, then Truth will depart because the fear of truth is a chaotic corruption and will always try to distort what **IS**. Fear is a choice, and choosing it is a perversion of Truth. Truth will depart from you if *you* accept fear, because Truth cannot be perverted, but **we** can.

Fear of Truth is a destroyer, and when you allow fear into your heart you are rejecting your Creator and corrupting yourself, and you will ultimately end in destruction. All of this is *your own* choice.

There is a tendency to blame everything on the Creator, but it's interesting to note that when we do so we typically will not accept the fact that *we* are living wrongly. Denying our ways *will not* change the truth about our ways.

An additional point that we tend to ignore having much to do with our hot water is that we have a tendency to blame the Creator for being a bully and punishing us for our errors. But I would beg you to consider that many of the things written in the Bible are *warnings*. Taking part in those behaviors that people are warned against will result in a certain outcome. In other words, the Creator is not punishing you—*you* are doing it to *yourself*. This is like the example from earlier in the book, where one person warned their friend to stop immediately or risk falling off of the cliff onto the rocks some two hundred feet below the cliff. Does this make the man who warned his friend the punisher of his friend if his friend chooses to continue over the edge? The answer is clear—it would be the friend who punished himself because he would not heed the wise warning of the other person who understood the peril that lay two hundred feet below. There are many events in the Bible that fall into this category. We should not see the "laws" in the Bible as rules, but rather as warnings of impending danger for our own destructive and foolish actions. If we don't want to abide by that, then we are subject to the ramifications of ignoring the warnings, and it is done of each *our own choice* and freewill.

Assuming that an all-knowing and all-powerful Creator does exist, then, do we dare to imagine that the Creator should have to put up with us rejecting and attempting to pervert Truth in the way that we do? Should the Creator accept our denial of Truth and be overjoyed at our arrogance when the Creator *knows* that we are living outside of what **IS**?

If you are not accepting Truth then you have denied Truth., there is *not* a middle ground on this point. If you have not accepted Truth, then you have rejected Truth; and instead, you have accepted arrogance, covetous-jealousy, and fear. Inviting Truth into your hot water changes your identity back into the manner it was Created as and as it was intended to be—in the *image* of the Creator.

Are We the Creator Then?

So does this mean that we are the Creator? No it does not! But we are certainly a part of the Creator. Many of us fail or fall short throughout our lives, and we struggle unnecessarily because we will *not* embrace Truth. We have been told that we must go to college and become a certain occupation, and that if we do not, then we are of little value—this is not of Truth! You are of great value when you fully accept Truth into your life no matter what good occupation you have. Rejecting Truth devalues your *true* identity and renders it worthless. We all feel this because it's built into us. We can detect it, which is why we never feel satisfied by the *things* of this world. It's okay to have things, but it is not okay to identify with them in such a way that the *things* become your *perceived* identity.

You are *of* the Creator and *of* Truth, and accepting anything less than that Truth: is **not**, it is **un**, it is **void**, it is **without**, it is **empty**, it is **blank**, it is **dark**! When we accept Truth, then we are *like* the Creator, but *we* are not the Creator. The Truth lives in us when we accept it, and Truth will thrive in us causing us to have joy when we accept this Truth and receive it fully into ourselves.

You can throw out the concept of a Creator if you choose, but the fact remains that Truth works in the way just explained regardless, and that is irrefutable Truth. Having Truth either **is** or **is not**, it is either **yes** or **no**. If it is *yes* then Truth is in you, if it is *not yes* then Truth is *not* in *you*. It is a simple *yes* or *no* choice that only *you* can make for yourself. Will you be true or will you deceive?

You can deny that the Creator exists, but then the Truth will not be yours and you have then chosen—of your own free will—to live in the darkness of arrogance, covetous-jealousy, and fear, causing you to be incorrect and wrong in many aspects of your life. This fear of Truth will result in you being enslaved to your former fear and darkness.

You are of Truth, and Truth is of the Creator. You are a part of the Creator, and the Creator is a part of you. When you deny this, then you have chosen to live in fear, and you have chosen to hide from Truth and have corrupted your true purpose. When you deny Truth you have chosen sin.

Chapter 15

Starting Over

Truth is its own powerful entity, and it is best to think of Truth and treat it somewhat like a person that can stand without us, yet we can allow Truth to become a part of us. Understanding what Truth is can be a difficult task for many of us because we have lived without it for so long that we do not recognize it as Truth. Our hot water has done this to us, but Truth is the easiest thing to grasp when you allow it in your hot water. When we allow ourselves to understand this one simple key, then we can change our past mistakes and make them *all* worthwhile!

Truth is not what is true—it is what **IS**. Truth is a way of looking at things in an honest way, and it includes a willingness to take the needed action in your thoughts to assure that you are in understanding and alignment with what **IS**.

Truth is not having things your way, and Truth is not in agreement with you—*you* are in agreement with Truth, **or** you are not in Truth and therefore you are *wrong* and are in sin. ("Sin" is Spanish for "Without." Sin is to be without Truth.)

Truth is such a base concept that it is difficult to explain to someone who is missing its meaning, because there is no deeper or more basic level to use in effort to explain it. When we allow ourselves to be duped by contaminated hot water, then we lose our ability to grasp Truth.

In the simplest form, in our example of the dark area, if two people were in pitch dark room they should be in agreement that it's dark in the room. If a light then appears, they will both be able to see the light. If one of them mistakenly says that the light is not there and then refuses to admit that the light is there, then *that* person is not correcting their error, and in doing so they are not in Truth and are being arrogant in attempt to *appear* "correct." Through the method of *denial*, that person is trying to make it appear as if they were accurate in their erred quick answer. It's easy to detect the error of the person who, after the light has appeared, claims that there is no light. But in life, things are not always as readily visible as light. The fact that life's all-too-common darkness is hard for us to detect, causes us to be better able to hide the many errors of our ways. But for those who dwell in truth and who allow truth to dwell in them, they can easily detect such darkness.

No matter how hard we might try to make our wrong ways appear right—the Truth is the Truth—and *nothing* can or will ever change that. Generations of people have made attempts to distort Truth, but they did not succeed and they never will. Truth is a word we use to relate to what **IS**. "Bending the truth" cannot be done. But, our hot water can be influenced and mislead due to either our ignorance and/or our arrogance.

In the Bible it says, "My people perish for lack of knowledge." In our context, this is a very meaningful and a very power-filled statement. As indicated earlier, if the people are without Truth they eventually will destroy themselves because they lack the knowledge of Truth. It is this knowledge of Truth that is being referred to in the "lack of knowledge" statement from the Bible.

How to Erase Your Past

Truth is *all* inclusive. You will know when you have Truth because you *will* welcome correction, and you *will* seek to see what **IS**. You will reject inaccurate information, and you will turn away from and resist anything that is not accurate and just.

When we *reject* Truth, then we have trapped ourselves in our own errors and those errors will follow us the rest of our lives. Where when we *accept* Truth, we can go back in time and erase our ill past by means of admission of our errors and by changing our ways. Admitting our own errors uses our past experiences to make our lives better in our own future, all *while* we are learning from the activity of reviewing and analyzing our own mistakes.

This does not mean that you must confess to the world every error that you have ever made, but you must confess *all* your errors to yourself and to Truth. You cannot pick and choose which errors you will confess and admit to Truth. You must do this with *all* errors. Every time an error comes into your memory you must freely admit that error to yourself and to Truth, and then change and do it *no* more.

The only time you need to confess to other people is when that confession will free *them* from **your** non-truth and other violations that you committed against them. If you have done anything to bring anyone low or to harm others, then make it right as best you can and as soon as you can. With the exception of yourself and Truth, it does not do anyone any good for everyone to know every error you have ever made, and it can actually harm or unnecessarily and unfairly burden others.

As your past errors come to your mind, you cannot be in Truth without your full admission of those errors to yourself. If you refuse to face and admit your errors to yourself, and you refuse to allow Truth to reveal your errors, then you are still corrupted. Until you freely confess and admit to your errors of your own free will and choice, you will remain corrupted and the past errors you have made will continue to weigh you down in the abyss of your contaminated hot water.

Regretting making wrong choices is a natural state of Truth. If you do not feel badly about your past errors then you are only sorry that you got caught, rather than actually regretting doing what you got caught for. Being sorry for getting caught is similar to forcing two arguing people to apologize to one another when they do not want to apologize and are actually *not* sorry.

Make your error-filled past count for something and embrace Truth, and then you will quickly see your past become useful to your future. While you will not be proud of your errors, you will be able to use those errors to make *your* future world a better place! There's a reverse type of occurrence of this, and that is when your hot water was contaminated *but you did things rightly* regardless, and then others, who made many errors, forcefully told you that *you* were wrong about your thoughts, opinions, and beliefs. Had you been in a better environment of hot water you may have had a wonderful robust life because you would have seen the Truth that surrounds us all for what it truly is, but is often hidden by our own and other people's lies. Because of the high level of contamination of your hot water, you were told, and subsequently believed, that you were wrong. You *believed* that you had made errors because that is what *they* told you. The negative hot water that surrounded you is badly contaminated in this case, even though you may have been correct.

Remove negative people from your life if you are not strong enough to overcome their negativity.

Here is a good way to determine what to do about the negative influences of people. If you are not strong enough to overcome their negative influence, then depart from them. Protect yourself from this negativity and non-truth. Husbands especially should protect their own wives and children from this negativity and non-truth.

If you are able to help others rise out of their negativity then do so. But do not sacrifice yourself or your family for people who **choose** to be un-teachable.

If a person does not like to be, or rejects being corrected, it is a very clear sign that they have rendered themselves un-teachable and they are not in Truth. Depart from people who have chosen this way of life, and keep your strength up and assist those who seek to know Truth. You can go back to help the others who rejected Truth when their time is right and when you are strong enough to withstand this challenge.

Associating with people because of their *status* is of little value if they do not accept Truth. The appearance of arrogant people is not true, and it has only the **appearance** of those who have received the confidence of Truth. Being around this type of arrogant person will serve no purpose for those who want true joy in their lives. Arrogant people are negative and will typically try to bring *you* low so that they can feel better about themselves.

A very important point to remember is that just because someone is arrogant does not mean that they have any sort of high status. In fact, the opposite is more common: There are more arrogant people of low status than there are arrogant people of high status and prestige. Those of high status are more noticed because they are usually in more prominent positions, and therefore more people are aware of them. Additionally, people are often jealous of high status and will incorrectly label them as arrogant. Statistically, those of lower status are often either more jealous or more arrogant than those with higher status. In most cases, the lower status people will exhibit both jealousy and arrogance, which is the majority of those who do not accept and embrace Truth, which is the reason our status is low.

Do what you can do to show others Truth. And the best way to show others Truth is by your personal example of integrity for Truth! If they see you being *of* Truth, then they will typically either reject you, or they will be intrigued by your example. If you intrigue them, then you will have the opportunity to reveal the simple mystery of Truth to them through your example.

It's good to gather with like-minded people, but, when we do so, our Truth often dies within the group. Groups are good to regain strength, and it is good to be with like-minded people who embrace Truth, but to go no further and only be with those people is selfish and will only serve you and them. This doesn't mean that you must go out and preach Truth all around the world, but it does mean that your example will shine bright for others to see when you have *deliberately* replaced your hot water with the pure oil of Truth.

You will be a wonderful example of the good of Truth and it will spread because others will want to be like you. There will be those who will reject your Truth and find it to be a threat to them. But when you truly embrace Truth with all of your heart and all of your soul, then these people who feel threatened by your Truth will not faze you while they are trying to attack you. If someone, such as a manager or boss, has been given power over you, then when you accept only Truth, your new status could cause them to cast you out, thus, leaving you with nothing to fear. If the worst they can do is fire you for being truthful, then it is an *honor* to be fired for that.

In circumstances where you can depart from those who refuse Truth, you should do so. An old friend who brings you down and causes you to err is a good place to start. Sadly, it is often our siblings, parents, and close relatives who cause us the most grief. If this is the case, it is better to keep a distance from them and see them less often—until they choose to embrace Truth.

The situation becomes more difficult when it is your own husband or wife who tries to bring you low with covetous-jealousy, arrogance, and fear of Truth. The cornerstone book *Red Hot Marriage* discusses what to do when departing from them is not an option, this is especially true when children are involved as described in the cornerstone book *Strong Family*. The best solution is to live a life of Truth and be uncompromising and loving in Truth. Teach your children the simple mystery of Truth and it will eventually spread to your spouse. With a spouse, you must remember that they probably have had very contaminated hot water, and, after you married, it is likely that *you* contributed to that hot water through your expectation of your spouse's behavior, even if your own internal hot water was fairly pure.

How Negative People Try to Turn the Tables on You

Whether it is a spouse or someone more remote, a common tactic typically used when we deny Truth is to try to turn the tables on Truth and call it wrong.

Often the louder and more passionately people shout, the more others tend to be bullied into believing that what is being shouted is correct. The person being attacked and bullied will also often fall prey to these brash tactics.

When you have Truth in you and you speak, then you will be intimidating to others who are not of Truth. This is what the arrogant are trying to emulate when they attack—they are trying to be intimidating. Sadly, because so many, who want Truth, have such badly damaged hot water, they have been duped into believing that those who act passionately are correct when they are actually *not* correct in this case. Behaving in a passionate manner when you do not have Truth is nothing more than fear and arrogance. Such passionate outbursts amount to being a bully.

False accusation is the method of operation that we use when we lack Truth. What happens is that the person with Truth will make a statement of a true nature. Then the person to whom the statement was directed, and who is denying Truth, will feel attacked and often falsely accuse the person who made the true statement.

A classic example would be when a person, who chose *not* to follow Truth, makes an inaccurate statement, and then the person who embraces Truth will comment that the statement is not accurate. The person who denied Truth will then proceed to attempt to defend themselves, but they cannot do so because something that is not true has no defense, thus they will go on the offensive in attempt to discredit the person of Truth. This is usually done by distorting what the true person did or said, and also by falsely and belligerently accusing the true person of making *errors*. This is the very thing that they themselves did that created the situation to begin with—they made *errors*.

We often see this happen in our court system where the defense attorney will try to discredit a witness and accuse them of not being reliable so that there is no "credible" evidence against the accused. When we are able to discredit the eyewitness testimony in our tangible world that we live in, then there is nothing left to accuse us with. Our judicial culture is based upon having *people* bear witness to ill deeds, and it also uses *evidence* to bear witness of the wrong doing. When the evidence or witnesses are discredited, then there no longer remains credible testimony with which to make an accurate judgment.

Falsely Accusing the true and innocent is the primary tactic used by us when we reject Truth. When we choose arrogance we will accuse the innocent, and then the false accusation *appears*, to our own minds, to be a "correction" of the innocent. I have seen correct brilliant people tell others what is true, and then I watched the others utterly reject the obvious and true information while at the same time proceeding to attack the correct person and accuse them of not telling the truth all while the attacker invents their false answers—a common political tactic.

Because our societies are so accustomed to rejecting Truth, once doubt is placed in the minds of the Jury and the Judge, then it is often difficult to redeem the credibility of the unfairly discredited witness ("Do not bear false witness".) The biggest reason for the lack of credibility of a witness is that most of us have lived with hot water that has been badly contaminated, and while we may be telling the truth in court about the account of a crime, our other past deeds that were not of Truth have power over us and can discredit us.

This seems almost depressing, knowing that our past errors can harm us. It is important to embrace Truth *as soon as possible*, so that you make no more errors in that way. When you are not trying to hide, then you are far more credible. But if you have changed, and embraced Truth with all of your heart, and then you are asked about a former error and you try to hide the Truth about the fact that the error happened, then you are likely to lose some credibility. You don't need to tell *all* of the details of your errors. But to be able to admit to those who you offended, that you made a mistake and were in error, will regain you much of the credibility you lost with them due to your errors.

A heinous tactic that the arrogant use to make those who embrace Truth stumble, is to *repeatedly* ask someone a question that was already answered, as if it was not answered. We see this occur in all types of news media. When they want to discredit someone, they ask them a question in such a way that there is no possible acceptable answer as perceived by the listeners or viewers. And the interviewer will keep repeating the question until the person succumbs to their questioning and then stumbles by trying to answer the unreasonable question.

Sometimes life's circumstances are unpleasant, causing wrong actions to be taken by people because they feel that they were forced to pick one of two bad options. Then, later when the people who report the news push this person for an answer, they frame their question in a way that it cannot ever be truthfully or properly answered to the viewers' satisfaction. This makes the person look like they are not being truthful. This tactic is prominent in political election advertising and interviews. If you went into a store and did not do anything wrong, and then upon leaving the store you were asked "Did you steal the red jacket or the black jacket?", how would you answer if they kept repeating the question even though you did not steal anything? These tactics are common anywhere arrogance, covetous-jealousy, and fear of Truth exist. Arrogance, covetous-jealousy, and fear of Truth exist wherever Truth does not exist. If you lack Truth then you *will* be arrogant, jealously-covetous, and you will fear Truth.

Are You a Negative Person?

The negative people who use these tactics are *us*—almost all of us! We have all fallen short of embracing Truth, at some point in our lives, and when we have not embraced this Truth then we behave poorly by rejecting what **IS**. When you reject what **IS**, then you are accepting what *is not*. This is a negative behavior.

Everything in our world and existence operates on the same *yes* or *no* principle, it either *is* or it *is not*. We refer to this as *positive* or *negative*, and *yes* or *no*. **Truth** and **not truth** are the same way—*Truth* is positive and *not truth* is negative.

If you have ever encountered an intensely negative person, then you will quickly find that they *do not* believe that anything can be done. Through their discouragement they will lend their doubts to the conversation and, because they believe it cannot be done, they will often try to stop others from doing great things, all while the others believe something *can* be done.

When people who believe that something *can* be done, actually try doing something, they often succeed and it is then no longer a belief they held because it has become *knowledge* of the truth that the thing can be accomplished. Even after witnessing this evidence of success, some negative people will continue in their disbelief and be amazed that the thing was done, but they will often assign it to an error, luck, or a fluke. When we think this way, it is our fear that paralyzes our belief; the reason for this is that we have not come to *know* anything because we only have *beliefs*, and we lack *Truth* because we have refused to embrace Truth.

Another aspect of negativity is the jealous aspect. Jealous people might not appear as negative as the fearful people do. *Most* fearful people are jealous, but deep down inside *all* covetous-jealous people are fearful; however, some fearful people are nothing more than lazy. Jealous people *fear*, which is why they are jealously-covetous.

When we fear, then we're afraid to act on something. We are often even afraid to act on a thought, and because we will not act on this thought, we feel less valuable. When we refuse to act, we think that we are not taking a risk and therefore we believe that we *cannot* fail. While there is an element of technical accuracy in that thought, we need to re-consider what "*failure*" really is.

When we fear and we're jealous, the reason that we are jealous is that we seek the level of confidence that a person who follows Truth shows; it is their confidence that we are jealous of. But when we are filled with covetous-jealousy it is technically impossible to obtain the same level of confidence that someone who embraces Truth has. This sort of negativity is somewhat harder to detect than it is in those who are only afraid and display little jealousy, because when we are arrogant, our negativity is mostly veiled by the arrogance that we display. Fear of failure is the fear of Truth. This means that through your hot water you have come to the false belief that you cannot measure up to Truth. You, therefore, run from Truth because of your fear of failure.

When fear is cloaked by jealousy, then arrogance typically follows and imitates that which it is afraid of. It imitates the true confidence that accompanies Truth. The negativity of arrogance will make an attempt to discredit Truth and then dominate Truth. When we allow the arrogant to dominate us, then we have submitted ourselves to non-truth.

When Truth does not exist in a person then they will be, largely, negative and will draw joy from others while offering little or nothing in return. But those who have Truth will contribute to the Truth in others and build them up.

It is not Wrong to Change Your Environment, But there is Something More Important

Now that you *know* what you *know* about Truth and negative people, it's time to make the decision to change *your* environment. While changing your workplace or living quarters can be an effective method to remove yourself from such negativity, changing your environment goes far beyond those changes. Changing your environment includes changing what you watch and listen to *and* changing what you think. Be sure that you are embracing Truth with your whole heart and soul when making any changes.

When we are arrogant and jealous, we are trying to build ourselves up or trying to make ourselves look better than others even though we haven't truly earned the position. When we do this, then we are thieves and have stolen what is *not* rightfully ours. We want all of the credit without any of the effort. Changing your environment can have the same effect. You can look around you and find negative people all around who are arrogant, jealously-covetous, and who fear Truth, but your biggest enemy in this regard can be seen right in your very own mirror. If you only change your circumstances by changing occupation and removing toxic people or departing from them, then you are trying to get the result without doing the act of embracing Truth, which means that you have once again stepped into arrogance, covetous-jealousy, and fear.

The first change needs to be in your thinking and in your heart. Embracing Truth is the easiest thing that anyone can do in their life, and it can be done *instantly* and fully. Embracing Truth is *far less* work than it is to remove people from your life or to change your job. It's okay to change those things, but without changing your thinking first, you have gained nothing and are the same as you were before changing your job, and you will eventually end in a repeat situation of what you just tried to escape from. In fact, when you change your job for the purpose of working with people who are more agreeable with you, then you are at an even greater risk of falling deeply into the trap of arrogance; this is because you have chosen to only have people who are agreeable with you, near you. Doing so will allow your hot water to go unchecked anytime you have not fully embraced Truth.

This is often seen when people "find religion" and begin to change their ways. I have watched many people change religions only to see them lose interest in the new religion, or to become arrogantly self-righteous by having only people who agree with them around them. If they have not embraced Truth, then they will typically force their religion on others and try dominate their friends in this way. We often see this with religious zealots who suddenly change their beliefs. When you are in Truth you will not try to set yourself above others. When you have not embraced Truth, then any changes you make are *not* of Truth, and while your changes can make you feel better, and it might be better for your well-being, you still cannot obtain true joy without Truth.

When we want the glory without the effort, it is our fear that paralyzes our ability to embrace Truth. In effort to "prove" ourselves to the world, we go through much work trying to impress people who are making the same empty attempts at impressing people as we do, and it then, to us, becomes a competition. When we tangle ourselves in this trap, we end up doing so much more work than was needed, and, in the end, what we are left with is actually a counterfeit.

Truth is free and it is a choice that only *you* can make, and it is very easy to obtain. It is instant, and it gives instant gratification!

Fully embracing Truth with all of your heart, mind, and soul and with every fiber of your being will, in the blink of an eye, give you what arrogance, covetous-jealousy, and fear cannot offer in an eternity.

While changing your physical environment is okay, and is often a good thing, those changes should be a *result* of your thinking. If you make those types of changes without fully embracing Truth, then you have stolen something that does not truly belong to you. And doing so will lead to more unhappiness and feelings of inadequacy for you because you have not earned it.

But when you fully embrace Truth, the outward actions will be an automatic result of your freewill choice to embrace Truth. When you fully embrace Truth you will find it difficult to be around arrogance. And arrogance will find it difficult to be around *you*. Now that you have begun to grasp what truth really is, you are likely to experience a feeling of humiliation when you embrace Truth, because there is an admission being made by you that *you* have often been wrong and erred in your past. These feelings are normal and will go away once you forgive yourself and no longer deny Truth.

How to Forgive Yourself and Bad People

I need to point out again that there are two types of jealousy. The one we have been discussing is a covetous-jealousy, which is where you want something that is not yours. The other jealousy is the reverse because it is when someone is trying to take what **is** yours, and it is actually the opposite side of covetous-jealousy. Think of it in terms of someone trying to steal your spouse away from you, being jealous in this situation is a *proper* jealousy. In fact, to not be jealous in the case of a spouse being pursued by someone else would be quite insulting to that spouse, because it essentially says, "I don't care about you."

The word jealous has its root in the word *zealous* or *zeal*, which means: To do something with great interest or care. So, as you can see, it is proper for us to act in a jealous manner when it is our *right* and *duty* to do so.

But when it is *not* our right and we are *taking*, then the term jealousy, by definition, can still be considered accurate, but it is better described as *covetousness*. Our zeal for the *thing* or *position* is not valid, because when we are trying to take what is *not* ours—*we are stealing!*

When we admit the errors of our former ways, then we will be freed of arrogance, jealousy, and fear of Truth. The feeling of humiliation is natural, and the term humiliation is not a *thing*, it is a description of being brought low to where you belong—where before, you had puffed yourself up to a place that was not truly yours.

Remember: we can think of the word *humiliate* as **human-iliate**. We are being human, and that is to be like Adam who was also brought low to his proper place. There is a reason that Adam is called a *human*. And the connection to *humus* (earth or dirt) has to do with what we discussed in a previous chapter about the origin of the word *human*. *Humus* and *human* and *humiliate* are all of the same root origin, and since Adam was made of the dirt of the ground it would make sense that the ground and his kind share definition-origin. Thus, when we are put in our *proper* place by Truth we are *humiliated*, which is to be where we truly belong—as we were Created, vessels of the pure water of Truth.

If you fight this feeling of humiliation and refuse to accept your proper position that you have worked for by your former rejection of Truth, then you have again chosen to reject Truth. To some of us this seems to be an inescapable conflict that we do not want to experience, but the thing that we do not want to experience is actually not the *humiliation*, because that is only the *description* of what is happening and it is our proper place. It is the *fear* of admission that we don't want to experience—it is our covering of *guilt.* Admission of guilt is the first result of embracing Truth, and with it, the forgiveness of yourself along with the forgiveness of others must and will follow.

Forgiveness is perhaps one of the most misunderstood acts we can do for ourselves and others. Admission and forgiveness are parallel, and in the end one will not be without the other. When dealing with others, we often have a problem with properly understanding—*not tolerating people's non-truth*—and we confuse it with *unforgiveness.*

If you're dealing with a person who has hot water that is very jealously-covetous and arrogant, then you might feel that you don't want to forgive them for what they did to you in the past. But when you embrace Truth, then **not** forgiving, is something that is *not* possible for you because forgiveness becomes automatic for you to do, like a reflex. You will automatically forgive their past errors against you, and you will forgive their future errors against you. But this **does not** mean that you must put up with their repeated assaults against you if they continue in their ill ways. You have the option to depart from them, and depending upon your situation, it is probably wise to do so. Departing from them does not mean that you have not forgiven them. Departing from someone who refuses to stop harming you is just good judgment.

Regarding your spouse and children, the situation is a bit different; you should not easily discard your spouse and children. But with other people, including your parents, siblings, and friends, it is okay to distance yourself from them if they are negatively influencing you and/or your family and drawing any of you away from Truth.

If or when people who have been harming your family choose to change, then you can always easily rebuild those relationships *after* they have come fully to Truth. If you tolerate their poor behavior, then they will never have any reason to change the way they behave around you or the way they treat you. When we embrace Truth, we will be excited for the day that those who injure us by means of their arrogance, covetousness, and fear of Truth decide to choose to embrace Truth. We will be pleased for them and pleased with them and we will welcome them when that true change occurs.

An unforgiving person will not be pleased when those who hurt them choose to embrace Truth. If we will not forgive them when they have embraced Truth, then it is apparent that we are still arrogant and are jealous of them, and, in truth, have *not* embraced Truth.

The same is true of ourselves to a point, because when we err we can hurt others, but the error is truly against ourself. When we have embraced Truth we immediately begin to see the contamination of our error when the light of Truth shines through our filthy hot water. And while we will feel our humiliation of being put in the place that we have worked to get to, *we* will need to forgive ourselves in order to fully embrace Truth. If you will not forgive yourself with the act of admitting your errors to yourself and to Truth, then you have bound yourself to an eternity of emptiness that can never be filled, and you will spend all of your days attempting to fulfill yourself with the vanity of things, status, and prestige. And just like the water pot with the holes in it, you will never stay filled with joy, and you will be an eternally consuming fire of tormenting anguish that is never satisfied with anything. It has not worked up until this point in life, and it will not work in the future as has been repeatedly proven by many past generations.

Do You Know Who You Are?

*We **are** Created.* And with regard to our origin, if any evolutionary changes have come to humanity, they have been to *decrease* humanity and not increase us. A Truthful exploration of this quickly reveals the Truth of our Creator. Without acceptance of this eternal Truth, you cannot fully embrace Truth and you will forever bind yourself in a darkness that is absent of all Truth. There is no workaround on this. If we have arrogance, covetousness, and fear of Truth so deep in us that we will not ever admit the existence of our Creator, then we have judged ourselves as eternally unworthy and have departed from the Truth that we were originally Created with. You are offspring of the Creator, and you were Created of Truth. That Truth departed as your hot water became corrupted throughout your life, and the corruption has become your contaminated hot water which has replaced Truth in you.

It is now time for **you** to decide if you are going to embrace Truth, or if you will continue in an unhappy state of being— always wanting, but never being able to satisfy your wants, which can include wanting happiness and joy. You will never achieve full happiness and joy without Truth.

Will you live in depression and hide your pain with alcohol, illegal and prescription drugs, and things such as money, fads, and status? Will you continue to feel like you're not worthy, and then try to hide that fact with your fear, covetousness, and arrogance?

Your time is now! It's not tomorrow or the next day. You can feel better when you complete this book and through it understand that your time is **now** !

You are Created of Truth! You are made of this Light, but through the corruption of doubt, fear, covetous-jealousy, and arrogance, the Light of Truth has departed from you and you have been darkened. Where the innocence of Truth once was within you, there is now foul contaminated hot water placed there by other people, life circumstances, and yourself, that has slowly become this way over all of the years of your life. But, you can throw it out in an instant and embrace Truth—***right here— right now*** at this very moment! When you do so, you will feel convicted on many past things that you have done in your life. This is normal, and it is good to realize your errors, but then you must forgive yourself and go on to live in Truth even more so with each remembrance and forgiveness of another of your own past ill deeds.

When you do this you will be renewed. Your strength of heart will immediately return, and *you* will control your life the way *you* were meant to—through and in Truth! Your hot water will no longer control your thinking or actions, and instead, the Truth from our Creator will fill you and guide your steps. You will have been restored to the innocent state that you where as a child. This is the message that the Man who hung on the cross so long ago wanted us to know and understand. It was *He* who made the way for you to do this through Truth and understanding. But here, people often struggle because they don't have the accurate information about Creation and the Creator that is explained from a scientifically logical perspective in the book *The Science of God*. Nor do many people know about the inaccuracies in science about the big bang and evolution that are discussed in the book *Bending the Ruler*. Believing inaccuracies about our origins causes error in our rationalizing most aspects of life. But, embracing Truth allows you to be able to know things and have true faith.

Chapter 16

Redefining Yourself To Yourself

Forgiveness is the first part of starting over. Understanding what Truth is will deliver you to the initial forgiveness part, but in order to start again you must first forgive *yourself*. Your Creator has always already forgiven you when you embrace Truth. It is you who needs to forgive yourself and start with a clean slate by *understanding* and then no longer denying Truth.

How to Start From a Clean Slate

Just as when *you* fully embrace Truth and you forgive people for *their* past and future errors, but will not tolerate their future violations against you, so it is the same with the Creator. Because Truth is of the Creator, this is the way the Creator *is*: You are already forgiven the moment you accept Truth.

So then it becomes up to *you* to forgive *yourself* and allow your errors to be wiped away when you accept Truth. Admitting your own errors because *you* realized them on *your own*, and then forgiving yourself will give you a new start in life that is fearless and will cause you to find joy almost immediately! There will be uncomfortable situations that you'll have to work through because of your past errors, but when *you* embrace Truth these scars of the past will serve as examples to others and as reminders, to you, to *always* hold fast to Truth. Your scars become a map and a guide for your life as you soar forward in life. You can use your past errors as lessons for the good of your family and for the good of mankind! Your direction in life becomes clearer, your family will be stronger, and as discussed in the cornerstone book *Understanding Prayer,* your prayers are able to work on command.

You have Always Understood what "*IS*"

We all have been born with the ability to *know* Truth, but we have learned to deny that Truth. Now that you have removed the blinding hot water from your perceived identity, remember that you are identical to the Creator and that you are identical to Truth. Also, remember that this is your *True* identity **if** and **when** you choose to embrace Truth—Truth is what **IS**. Denying this is a corruption that will not serve you or anyone around you. Being strong in this is important because it's not only you; but those who are around you will also be watching and wondering why *you* are so joyful now, when before you may have been mean, depressed, and/or arrogant. If you falter, they will be led *by you* to believe that Truth is not what **IS** and *you* will have deceived them. You always *knew* what **IS** and you always *knew* Truth; if you did not know then you would not have felt the way you did nor would you have read this book.

When we feel that something is "off" in our life, then it is a clear sign that we likely have strayed from Truth. And it is the fact that we are not aware of our hot water that causes us to miss these signs. But, this is no longer a problem for you now that you have become aware of your hot water.

Be True to Yourself

There is a special purpose of Truth in each one of us that has been stolen from us by our contaminated hot water. Everyone has been Created with wonderful gifts that come natural to each of us. Your hot water has told you that those gifts are of no value and that you must forget about them. Through covetousness, our contaminated hot water has told us that we want to *be* things that we are not. The sad fact is that because of the corruption in your hot water, you have likely not been doing the Truth that you were Created to do.

As you march forward with your new armor of **Truth**, your *true* purpose will begin to reveal itself to you, and you will recognize it and embrace it. For some it may be as simple as having a desire to be at home to raise your children with Truth and love. For others it will be to lead others to a true new and better way. It could even be to masterfully serve food at the drive-through to your fellow man while you smile with a welcoming smile on your face every day. It will be wherever your Created gift is within you, and when you pursue it you will find your fullness of joy *there*. When you place your *trust* in *Truth* and utilize your natural and Created gifts, then you will fly as if with wings on the air. Only **you** will be able to **know** what those gifts are. It can take some time to become apparent to you as you re-teach yourself to always recognize Truth. But without Truth you cannot see it—*ever*! This is because contaminated hot water *will* blind your ability to see your born-in gifts, but when you live in Truth you will see them and question about them with much intrigue when your gifts begin to show through in your own life.

How You Boldly Move Forward

When your Truth and Gifts begin to show through, you will boldly march forward with the armor and protection of Truth, and then things will slowly line up for you to do what you were designed to do. Many people have great abilities that where taught to them that have *nothing* to do with what the person was designed for. This is much like the plow and hammer example from several chapters back.

If you are designed to be a plow, then *be* a plow and stop trying to pound in nails. You might be able to do it and possibly even do it well, but you will be far more effective plowing because you were created as a plow, and you will enjoy it much more when your accept your design. Do not listen to people who tell you to defy your design, and do not fall into *their* trap of having to become something that you are not. When you be what *you* were designed to be and do what you were created for, then what you do will be natural to you, and only a lack of Truth on your part will be able to stop you—*you will have no competition.*

Much the way water is wet and flowers bloom, Truth just **IS**. Birds just sing and the sun just shines, and none of these things have to try. So also, you are what you are, and no one or nothing can change that! This is in *your* power alone and it is done by choosing Truth to be what *you* were created to be. And what you will be will always be *Just* and *True* and *Moral* and *Good.*

Act Who You Are and Be Who You Are

As you begin to discover your Created purpose, then **BE** as you are, and stay far from arrogance, covetous-jealousy, and the fear of Truth, and then you will have built your house on a rock foundation that *cannot* be shaken. You will have received the eternal promise that cannot be taken from you without your permission. Only *you* can decide whether or not you will reject or receive Truth.

Keep this book near to you to reference when your embrace of Truth gets put to the test, and when that occurs, remember these things:

- Those who won't take the time to understand others are the cause of *all* problems. And the "those" in this statement are *us*.

- *Knowing* where you have been, helps you to *know* where you are now.

- *Knowing* where you are now is your index to where you are going.

- *Knowing* where you are going is your key to life!

- Where you are going is **far** more important than where you have been or where you are now.

What you do today **will** affect your life twenty years from now—and twenty years from now comes a whole lot faster than we would like it to! If you make bad choices today, you will pay for those choices in twenty years (or sooner) and beyond, and "you will get what you deserve." And if you make great choices today, then you will be rewarded in twenty years (or sooner) and beyond. It is *your* decision what you want the rest of your life to be like. Believing wrongly will replace your truth with incorrect perceptions, inaccuracies, and lies. You must remember that the decisions that will affect your life twenty years from now **are made today**—they are **not** made twenty years from now. This is a good application for the old adage: "Don't put off until tomorrow what you can do today." Make only **great** choices from now on! Your efforts should always be to make tomorrow a bit better than yesterday, in doing so your life will always be little bit better today than it was at any time in the past.

It is time for you to **BE** what **IS**—*you* are Created of Truth. Embrace Truth and become a part of Truth and allow this Truth in you, and then your foundation will be unshakable and filled with Joy. You **cannot** be wrong when you have Truth in you— that is a wonderfully unavoidable truth!

With this new understanding, re-read what you wrote earlier about yourself, and see *now* how differently you view life and how differently you see what is truly important in life. Allow these seeds of Truth to grow in you, and water them only with the crystal clear pure water of Truth, then the oil pressed from the fruits of Truth will become an anointing.

You will notice that nearly every day of your life will be better than the last day from the point where you have grasped what Truth **IS** and embraced it with your whole heart, mind, and soul.

You will look back in a year or two and wonder how you ever tolerated the things in your life that you had tolerated in the past.

God does not bring people into our lives so that we can form them to be like us. The Infinite Creator wants everyone to be their own individual selves and to share their gifts of infinite Creator-like Creativity with the world around them. Sadly, people often try to force us to do what *they* want, and to like what *they* like.

When we fail to embrace the infinite differences in us that were placed there by our infinite Creator, then we all become cheap copies of one another, doing what others do just to be perceived as being "cool."

Instead, let's appreciate the positive infinite differences between us all that have been embedded in us by our Creator from our conception! Their *differences* should be respected, and so should yours. Stand strong in who you are and be an individual with Truth and identical to Truth; for *that* is your true *Identity* and *Individuality*.

Your true identity is

TRUTH from the Creator!

Blessings of Truth to Those Who Seek Truth

When You Dream... DREAM THIN™
The Weightloss Repair Manual

Learn How to Lose Weight While Sleeping

How many people do you know who exercise and still can't seem to lose weight? Has that ever happened to you? As a matter of fact, because we don't know the vital secrets that are shared in *Dream Thin*, many of us actually end up *gaining* weight when we exercise.

Do you hit your weight loss goals? And does your weight stay off when you do actually lose some weight? Even many doctors miss the *real* answers to weight loss. If you doubt this, then simply look at the waistlines of many medical doctors and nurses.

Weight loss is easily mastered when you understand a few basic principles. We often go on fad diets or follow the orders of our doctors, only to put the weight back on even faster than we lost it. Many of us suffer from unnecessary disease, and some of us will die too young.

Dream Thin does more than simply share answers to weight loss mysteries. *Dream Thin* explains the important details of *why* and *how* weight loss connects to mind *and* body. The information in *Dream Thin* allows you to make weight loss permanent without having to try so hard. Don't make more of the same empty promises to yourself each New Year's Day. Instead, quickly and easily change things today and make all of your tomorrows better with *Dream Thin* while still enjoying all of the foods you eat today—and yes, even fast foods!

Only you can choose if you want spend your hard-earned money on medical bills and funerals, or if you would rather spend your time and money looking great while being out and about and enjoying life with friends and family as intended!

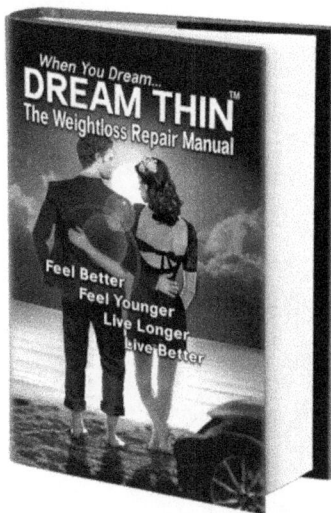

Search: Dream Thin Book
SayItBooks.com

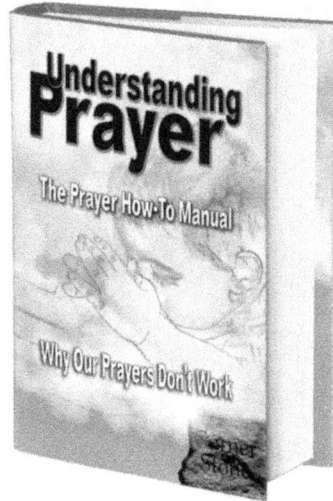

Volume 1 - The First Four Days

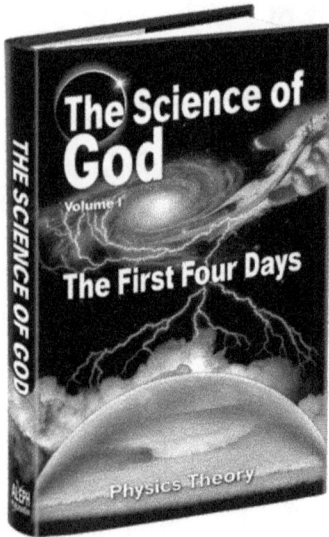

Is there a God? Did we evolve? Did everything start from a big bang? These questions have been plaguing our minds for many years. Only science-minded people and clergy seem to have the answers. But do they really have any true answers?

Is what we are told by science true? Is what we are told by the Church true? Or are there other better explanations for everything? Did we hitch a ride from Mars, or is that all fantasy science? Was everything Created in six twenty-four hour days, or did it all take billions of years to happen? Few people are willing to even fully consider these questions, and even fewer have any coherent answers. *The Science of God* challenges your current beliefs while asking tough questions of science and of the Church.

For years, Christian after Christian has attempted to argue for God and the Bible's Creation only to fail miserably. Why is this, why is it that Christians cannot seem to win this debate? Often Christians think they are winning the debate only to find themselves at a loss to answer the real questions, and then they get mocked for their poor answers.

Whether you are a scientist or an average Christian and want to discuss the Creation debate, *The Science of God* is a mandatory read for you. *The Science of God* takes you through the thought process to enable you to speak intelligibly about Creation, the cosmos, evolution, and astrophysics.

Search: The Science Of God Book
SayItBooks.com

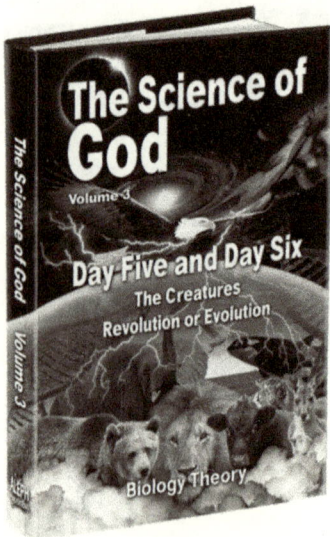

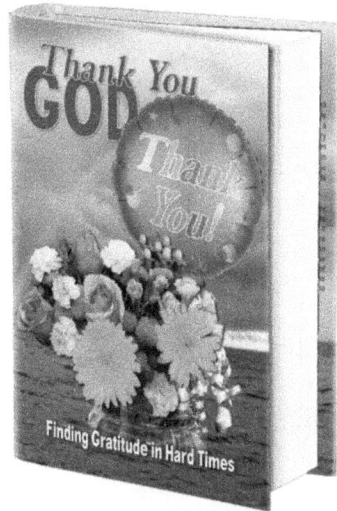

Notes

Notes

www.ingramcontent.com/pod-product-compliance
Lightning Source LLC
Chambersburg PA
CBHW021501090426
42739CB00007B/407